PRAISE FOR KRISHNA DHARMA'S UNABRIDGED VERSION OF *MAHABHARATA*

"Dharma successfully captures the mood and majesty of a rich and ancient epic, and in the process, does full justice to the critical elements of the complex story…. A well-wrought saga that will be appreciated by Western readers and admirably serve to introduce a new generation to the rich spiritual, cultural, and historic legacy of India. Highly recommended."

-The Midwest Book Review, USA

"Dharma's *Mahabharata* is very readable, its tone elevated without being ponderous. Though condensed, it still runs to more than 900 pages and would interest all serious students of Hinduism. Recommended for academic libraries and public libraries with collections on religion."

-James F. DeRoche, *Library Journal*, USA

"Rarely, if ever, has an ancient epic received such modern blockbuster treatment…The narrative moves effortlessly, often as racily as a thriller, without compromising the elevated style and diction. The visual imagery is every bit as impressive as anything achieved in the cinematic editions."

-Mahesh Nair, *India Today*, India

"With its intense love scenes, jeweled palaces, vast battles, superheroes, magical weapons, and warring families, this novelized version resembles a 20th century saga-cum-soap opera, a marriage of Barbara Taylor Bradford and Arthur Hailey."

-James Meek, *The Guardian*, UK

"As we enter the third millennium, the *Mahabharata* is an intriguing, useful, and formidable companion. Its truths are unassailable, its relevance beyond dispute, and its timelessness absolute."

-Joseph Ray, *Atlantis Rising,* USA

"When I dove into the *Mahabharata* I expected something along the lines of a dry Arabian Knights, but what I got was something else! Once I began to read, I just could not tear my mind away from the book. Even as I write this, my mind lingers on the glorious spiritual Indian mythology captured on its pages. If you are looking for a cross between Arthurian legends and cultural epic spiked with romance, and overarching spiritual guidance, *Mahabharata* is for you. Aside from the wonderful magical tales, the novel is an ancient authority on karma, reincarnation, and yoga."

-Rachel Styer, *Magical Blend,* USA

SCHOLARS' ENDORSEMENTS FOR *MAHABHARATA*

"Next to the Vedas, [the *Mahabharata*] is the most valuable product of the entire literature of ancient India, so rich in notable works. Venerable for its very antiquity, it is one of the most inspiring monuments of the world and an inexhaustible mine for the investigation of the religion, mythology, legend, philosophy, law, custom, and political and social institutions of ancient India."

-Vishnu S. Sukthankar, p. iii of the Prolegomena of the
Critical Edition of the Mahabharata, published by
Bandharkar Oriental Research Institute (B.O.R.I.), Pune, India.

"The *Mahabharata* represents a whole literature rather than a single homogeneous work; it constitutes a veritable treasure-house of Indian lore, both secular and religious. No other single work gives such insight into the innermost depths of the soul of the people."
-H. Raychauduri, "The *Mahabharata*: Some Aspects of its Culture,"
in CHI vol. 2, 71ff.

. . . AND COMMENTS FROM OUR READERS

"In a world searching for values, virtue, and role models, one need only turn to the pages of the *Mahabharata*. The examples set by the heroes and heroines of this great epic embody the ethos of Vedic culture and are truly inspirational. This particular retelling, with its flowing and engaging style, is an outstanding, 'can't put down' edition."

-Robert Morrill, California

"It is certainly the best book I have ever read. I can't put it down. I find myself reading it late at night, when I should be asleep. I am almost finished, and it has been the fastest 1000-page book I have ever read. I am almost pained anticipating finishing this *Mahabharata*. Only one solution: I will read it again (and again and again).

"Of course, the subject matter is sublime, but the way Krishna Dharma has crafted the entire book together, it reads so fluidly. Formerly, any edition of *Mahabharata* I read was exciting but clunky. This edition excels in every way...I have never found this enlightened devotional thread so nicely woven through the whole epic as in Krishna Dharma's book. In fact, nothing comes close."

-His Holiness Sridhar Swami, India

"As a teacher, I find Krishna Dharma's rendition of the *Mahabharata* a real godsend. For the first time, I feel safe and at ease using the *Mahabharata* in our school. Unlike others, Krishna Dharma's *Mahabharata* is written in proper English, the way we want the children to learn to write. Furthermore, it is free from questionable philosophical slants that taint other versions I've dealt with over the years. It is a smoothly written text. Putting this altogether, the result is children rapt in attention while reading or hearing the *Mahabharata*. That's a success. Thank you for publishing such an important addition to our library."

-Brian Bloch, Vice-principal,
Bhaktivedanta Swami International Gurukula, India

MAHABHARATA

The Condensed Version of the World's Greatest Epic

MAHABHARATA

The Condensed Version of the World's Greatest Epic

Retold by Krishna Dharma

TORCHLIGHT
PUBLISHING

First Printing 2000

Cover design by Kurma Rupa and Padasevanam
Interior design by Christopher Glenn / Glenn Graphics
Printed in India

Published simultaneously in the United States of America and Canada by
Torchlight Publishing, Inc.

Library of Congress Cataloging-in-Publication Data

      Mahabharata : Selections.
       Mahabharata : The condensed version of the world's greatest epic /
       Krishna Dharma.
          p.   cm.
      ISBN 1-887089-25-X (cloth)
       1. Mahabharata—Abridgments. I. Dharma, Krishna, 1955- II. Title
      BL 1138.22 .E5 2000
      294.5'92304521—dc21   00-037731

Attention Colleges, Universities, Corporations, Associations and Professional Organizations: *Mahabharata* is available at special discounts for bulk purchases for fund-raising or educational use. Special books, booklets, or excerpts can be created to suit your specific needs.

Torchlight Publishing, Inc.
For more information, contact the Publisher.
PO Box 52
Badger CA 93603
Email: torchlight @spiralcomm.net
www.torchlight.com

DEDICATION

To His Divine Grace A.C. Bhaktivedanta Swami Prabhupada,
my constant spiritual inspiration and one of the
greatest exponents ever of the
Mahabharata's divine teachings.

ACKNOWLEDGMENTS

My first thanks are due to Alister Taylor, my publisher and friend, who works tirelessly and without profit to make sublime literatures such as *Mahabharata* available to the reading public. I must also thank my good wife, Chintamani, for her support and encouragement. My heartfelt thanks also go to Kurma Rupa Dasa, Padasevanam Dasa, Christopher Glenn, Maithili Dasi, Sujana Dasi, and Subala Dasa, all of whom contributed significantly toward the production of this book, and to Goloka Vrndavana and Manjari, whose willingness to help out was much appreciated.

TABLE OF CONTENTS

Foreword. 7
Introduction. 9
One: FIVE GODLY BOYS..11
Two: SEEDS OF CONFLICT......................................18
Three: A TRIAL OF ARMS 27
Four: THE BLIND KING 33
Five: ON THE RUN 42
Six: THE FIRE-BORN PRINCESS.................................54
Seven: A KINGDOM DIVIDED....................................65
Eight: THE CELESTIAL HALL 78
Nine: VIRTUE ESTABLISHED 88
Ten: THE GREAT SACRIFICE 95
Eleven: EVERYTHING IS LOST 102
Twelve: EVIL TAKES A HOLD..................................115
Thirteen: THE KURUS SEAL THEIR FATE........................125
Fourteen: HEROES IN EXILE..................................133
Fifteen: MORAL INSTRUCTIONS IN THE FOREST 140
Sixteen: ARJUNA MEETS THE GODS 148
Seventeen: HEAVEN ON EARTH 155
Eighteen: DEMONIC INFLUENCES 163
Nineteen: THE GODS TAKE A HAND 171
Twenty: A LESSON NOT LEARNED 182
Twenty-one: PREPARING FOR WAR 193
Twenty-two: KRISHNA'S PEACE MISSION........................201
Twenty-three: ETERNAL WISDOM ON THE BATTLEFIELD 211
Twenty-four: THE SLAUGHTER BEGINS 220

Twenty-five: THE OLD WARRIOR 228
Twenty-six: TWO GENERALS FALL 237
Twenty-seven: A FITTING END 248
Twenty-eight: POWERFUL EMOTIONS...........................259
Twenty-nine: DELIVERANCE.......................................268
Glossary...279
Author's Note...281

FOREWORD

Mahabharata is originally an immense work of some 100,000 Sanskrit verses. Deeply revered as a sacred text to the people of India, it has formed the basis of their religious and philosophical thought for thousands of years.

For too long this profound work has been unavailable to Western readers—the complex Sanskrit did not lend itself to translation, at least not in easy-to-read English versions. Krishna Dharma has therefore rendered a valuable service, condensing the classic into an enthralling novel-like story, while retaining the authenticity of the original.

Mahabharata deals with just about everything imaginable, from romance and intrigue to politics, astrology, and the martial arts. Its central narration focuses on a fierce conflict between the divinely born Pandava brothers and their cousins the Kauravas. Gods, sages, kings, and heroes are all drawn into the conflict, which culminates in a great war that takes the lives of millions. Everything is ultimately revealed as being a part of Krishna's cosmic plan—it should be pointed out that Krishna, who also plays a central part in the narration, is seen throughout the text as the supreme being. Unlike many translators, Krishna Dharma does not obscure this important point.

Sit back then, and enter into the world of the *Mahabharata*, a world that, in many ways, is not unlike our own, as it draws upon universal truths and feelings. The text holds up a mirror in which we can gaze upon our human frailties and higher aspirations. It illuminates our darker side and brings us into the light of God consciousness. It deals with selfishness, deceit, dishonor, and atheism. But it also shows the way to selflessness, truthfulness, honor, and the essence of theistic bliss. Although we are separated from the characters of the *Mahabharata* in terms of time and culture, what we learn from them is as meaningful today as it was in India 5,000 years ago.

In fact, because of its universal applicability, the *Mahabharata* boasts one of the world's oldest living traditions, one that can reinterpret itself generation after generation, revitalizing itself in the lives of people from any epoch in world history. Hundreds of millions of contemporary Hindus attest to this, as was evidenced by the recent television series of the epic, which virtually brought the country to a halt every time it was shown. It also attracted two million viewers when it was shown by the BBC in the UK.

Perhaps as a further proof that the *Mahabharata* continues to speak to people thousands of years after its initial telling, we need look no further than the success of Peter Brook's stage and film adaptations of the epic in the early '90s. Peter Brook's revisioning of the *Mahabharata* brings us into the modern era. Another example would be the work of Steven Pressfield, who, in 1995, published a novel, *The Legend of Bagger Vance*, in which he brought the essential story of the *Mahabharata* onto a golf course. Or at least he did so with the section that deals with the *Bhagavad-gita*. So popular was this book that it is now being made into a major motion picture, which will probably be released well before you read these words. Krishna Dharma's work is an important contribution to this list of modern-day *Mahabharatas*. His book allows us to look into our own hearts to see if the *Mahabharata* does not indeed play a part in the drama of our own lives.

Steven J. Rosen is the author of *Gita on the Green: The Mystical Tradition Behind Bagger Vance*, as well as fifteen other books on East-Indian spirituality. Currently editor in chief of *The Journal of Vaishnava Studies*, he is also a substance editor and copyeditor for the 18-volume Encyclopedia of Hinduism project (forthcoming, University of South Carolina Press).

INTRODUCTION

MAHABHARATA, A PART of the ancient Vedas of India, is a story quite unlike any other. Few books have survived as long as this five thousand-year-old epic; its enduring popularity is itself testimony to the profound wisdom contained within its pages. This great epic includes the *Bhagavad-gita*—a masterpiece of spiritual knowledge revered by millions world-wide—and is the narration of the factual events leading up to the revelation of that illuminating text.

Mahabharata deals with the activities of Krishna, who spoke the *Bhagavad-gita* and is said by the Vedas to be the Supreme Person. This gives it a unique quality. Although from the external point of view it is an exciting tale of conflict and intrigue among kings, demons, gods, and sages, there is a deeper, spiritual meaning that pervades the entire work. One feels spiritually uplifted by reading the book. It is intended to bring us closer to an understanding of the Divine and awaken within us a transcendental pleasure surpassing all other happiness. *Mahabharata* can be read again and again without becoming stale or boring. In fact, one can discover different layers of meaning with each reading.

Along with its spiritual message and gripping story, *Mahabharata* presents a fascinating overview of life in the ancient world. It has been called a 'cultural encyclopedia of India,' but its scope is even broader than that, embracing basic universal truths common to all men. The range of subjects covered in *Mahabharata* is too numerous to mention, but in one famous verse of the original it is said that whatever is not found in *Mahabharata* will be impossible to find anywhere else.

However, I shall leave it to you to discover for yourself the wonderful treasure house that is the *Mahabharata*. This is an abridged version, and I hope it will stimulate your interest to go on to read more complete texts. I have also written a longer novelization that runs to about a thousand pages. It includes many of the wonderful tales that surround *Mahabharata's* central narrative which, for the sake of brevity, I excluded from this book. If this is your first dip into the delightful *Mahabharata* waters and you find that plunge refreshing and enlivening, I recommend that you dive in even more deeply by reading the full version, also published by Torchlight.

Finally, I must give all credit to Srila Vyasadeva, the immortal sage and original author of this work. May he bless us all that we can perceive the deepest meaning of *Mahabharata*.

KRISHNA DHARMA
JANUARY 2000

AND HE WHO KNOWS THE DEEPER CAUSE
THAT MOVES ME TO THIS MORTAL SPHERE
IS FREED AT ONCE FROM SUFFERING'S SOURCE
AND RAISED TO REALMS BEYOND ALL FEAR.

(*BHAGAVAD-GITA* 4.9)

One

ॐ

FIVE GODLY BOYS

SPRING HAD ARRIVED in the mountains; the atmosphere was delightfully fresh. Pandu strolled through a field of fragrant flowers, admiring the celestial scenery. Cuckoos sang from the nearby champaka trees, and black bees hummed as they swarmed around the bright yellow blossoms. Pandu's young wife, Madri, walked ahead of him, her long silk robe flowing in the gentle breeze. She sang softly to herself as she stooped to gather the flowers. As Pandu approached, she turned and smiled at him. The warm sun shone from behind her. Pandu could see the silhouette of her graceful form through her billowing dress. The Madra princess was indeed beautiful. Bright sunlight shone through her golden hair, framing her perfect features. Pandu felt his heart stirring. It had been more than seven years since he had embraced her. An irresistible urge overpowered him. Placing on the ground the sack of wild vegetables he had gathered for their meal, he took a step toward his wife.

Madri could immediately understand his feelings. Seeing him seized by desire, the princess was fearful. "O king, remember the sage's words!" She spoke urgently, but Pandu seemed not to hear. She put up her hands to stop him, shaking her head. "My lord! Stop! O great hero, control your mind. A deadly danger now threatens you."

But Pandu was oblivious to her warnings. Her attempts to make him desist only fueled his desire. Taking hold of her outstretched arms, he pulled them around his body and took her in a firm embrace. Madri struggled desperately, trying to free herself. Entirely overcome by lust, Pandu laughed. He dropped to the soft grass, dragging Madri down with him. With the princess clasped in his powerful arms, he rolled over. Pinning her to the ground, he sought her lips with his own.

Suddenly Pandu felt a terrible pain gripping his chest. He gasped and his limbs froze. As his horrified wife looked on, he fell from her body. With a stifled cry, he breathed a final choking breath and his lifeless body went limp.

Madri cried out and scrambled toward him, great sobs wracking her frame. It was too late to do anything. The *rishi's* curse had come to pass. Pandu was gone. The princess collapsed on his body and wept uncontrollably. She lamented piteously, addressing her dead husband. "O unconquerable one, how were you conquered by lust? Alas, I blame myself. Why did I come alone with you to these woods? How was I so foolish? O lord, I cannot live without you. I shall surely follow the path you have taken."

Her cries rose up and were carried on the breeze. They echoed through the woods. Not far away, in Pandu's forest ashram, his other wife, Kunti, was preparing a fire to cook their evening meal. Madri's wails reached her and she stood still, trying to ascertain where they were coming from. Madri's two young sons, Nakula and Sahadeva, were with her, and they too heard the cries. "What is it, Mother Kunti?" they asked. "Who is that?"

"I am not sure, but I will go and see. Where are your brothers?"

"They are just returning from the river," Nakula replied.

"Then you two boys should stay here and wait for them. Tell them to follow me when they get here."

Kunti made her way into the woods, going quickly in the direction of the cries. She was sure the voice she had heard belonged to her co-wife, Madri. What could have happened? Could it be that Kindama's curse had come to pass?

As she came out of the woods and entered the field, her worst fears were confirmed. To her horror, she saw the fallen Pandu, his head cradled in Madri's lap. For some moments—moments that felt like hours—she stood staring in shock. Then, her legs leaden, she ran toward them. She dropped to the ground by Pandu's side. Seeing that he was obviously dead, Kunti wailed in uncontrolled sorrow. She looked with streaming eyes at the anguished Madri. "O princess! What happened?"

Kunti's voice was accusatory. How had Madri allowed the king to become allured? She knew well about the curse. "O Madri, I was ever careful in our lord's presence. I would hardly even smile at him. He was always grave and self-controlled, remembering Kindama's words. How did he lose his composure in your presence?"

Kunti's words came between sobs. Her head fell on Pandu's chest. Where had he gone? How could she live without him?

Madri buried her face in her hands, weeping silently. She already felt guilty for having caused Pandu's death. Kunti's words only exacerbated her pain. She took a deep breath. "O noble Kunti, dear sister, with tears in my eyes I tried to stop the king. But I was helpless."

Seeing Madri's piteous expression, Kunti felt compassion. She spoke more softly. "You are surely more fortunate than I, for you saw our lord's face light up with joy as he approached you."

That thought deeply pained Kunti. She fought back her envy as Madri shook her head and replied, "I am utterly undone. It seemed the king was intent on making the *rishi*'s curse come true. There was nothing I could do."

Kunti felt her anger subside. Madri was surely being truthful. Somehow this terrible tragedy must be the Lord's arrangement. What now was her duty? She looked at the face of her husband, serene in death. The virtuous monarch had certainly gone to the higher worlds. Could she follow and serve him there? Doubtlessly, Madri would also wish to follow him, but someone would have to look after the boys. Kunti took hold of Madri's hand. "O sister, I am the senior wife. It is therefore my right to go with our husband to the region of the dead. Do not prevent me. Rise up and rear our children. I shall enter the fire with our husband."

Madri looked up pleadingly. "See how I am still clasping our lord and have not allowed him to go. Let me follow him. He came to me with the desire for intercourse. That desire is not yet satiated. Should I not therefore go to Yamaraja's kingdom in order to gratify him?"

Madri saw that Kunti had stiffened slightly. Sensing that her natural womanly jealousy was being aroused, she changed tack. She reached out to hold Kunti's hand and said, "O revered sister, how could I raise the children as well as you? Unlike you, I will not be able to see them all with an equal eye. Please stay and serve our lord by looking after his sons. Grant me leave to enter the fire and go where he has gone."

Kunti looked at Madri, fallen again onto Pandu's body. It would be hard for her to carry on living with the memory of this moment. Guilt would consume her. And she was right about the boys. One of Pandu's wives had to remain in order to take care of his sons, and Kunti, with the greater number of sons, knew that it was more her duty than Madri's. It would be better to let Madri follow Pandu.

Kunti rose to her feet and said softly, "Let it be as you wish, dear sister."

Getting up slowly, she walked back toward her cottage. The boys would have to be told.

* * *

Not long after Kunti had left the cottage, her three sons returned. They saw the twins, Nakula and Sahadeva, sitting alone. The eldest of the brothers, Yudhishthira, asked them, "Where is Mother Kunti? We heard cries. Was it she?"

The twins shook their heads. Nakula replied, "No. Mother Kunti also heard the cries and has gone into the woods. She said you should follow her."

Yudhishthira looked around at his two brothers, Bhima and Arjuna. "Come on! Let's go quickly. Mother may need us."

He raced off into the woods, followed by all four of his brothers. The cries had stopped and he was not sure which way to go, but he chose the path leading to the fields. That was the way his father usually went to collect vegetables for their meals. Yudhishthira had a feeling that the cries were something to do with him. As he ran, his mother came into view ahead, stumbling toward them, her head in her hands. Obviously, something terrible had happened.

As Kunti approached the brothers she tried to smile, but they could see the tears streaming down her face. As the five boys gathered round her, she said, "Dear sons, our only shelter now is the Lord. Father is no more. He has gone to the higher world of your ancestors."

The boys looked at her in shock. None of them could speak, as Kunti wept softly. Finally Yudhishthira said, "How did it happen? Surely no one could have killed father. Was it an accident?"

Yudhishthira knew his father to be a powerful warrior. He also knew that they were living in a place where practically everyone was an ascetic, devoted to meditation and the practice of religion. Who could have harmed his father?

Struggling to contain her grief, Kunti replied, "Your father has fallen victim to a rishi's curse. He is lying on the other side of these woods. Madri is with him."

The boys ran past their mother and burst out of the woods. Seeing their father lying dead and Madri next to him, they cried out. They dropped to the ground, wailing and rolling about in grief. Madri, feeling more peaceful knowing that she would soon follow her husband, spoke gently to the twins, who had run to her side. "My dear sons, the ways of the Lord are mysterious. You must now serve your mother Kunti with love. She will take care of you. I must follow your father into the next world."

The twins stared at their mother, not knowing what to say. This was only their eighth summer, and they could hardly comprehend what was happening. The situation was completely overwhelming. They ran to Kunti and she held them to her bosom, her tears falling on their heads. Their three brothers continued to vent their grief with loud wails. Hearing the cries, a number of rishis came into the field. Seeing the dead king, they went over to him and immediately began performing his last rites. As the rishis rhythmically chanted the holy mantras, the boys felt soothed and they stood up with folded palms. The distraught Kunti stood by their side, watching as the rishis led Madri away from Pandu. They lifted his body onto a bier and began carrying it out of the woods toward the river, followed by the weeping Madri.

Supported by her two eldest sons, Kunti walked behind Madri. Some of the rishis led the younger boys back to the ashram as Pandu's body was taken to the riverbank, then garlanded with forest flowers and daubed with the sacred Ganges clay. A large pyre was built by the water's edge and the body was placed upon it. With the rishis constantly reciting Vedic mantras, Yudhishthira set fire to the sandalwood pyre. As the flames rose up, Madri suddenly threw herself onto the body, crying out, "My lord!" Within moments, both Pandu's body and she had been reduced to ashes.

Kunti cried terribly. Her sons stood by with tears streaming down their faces. As the flames subsided, the rishis recounted verses of wisdom from the Vedas, describing the eternality of the soul. Pacified by the sages' words, Kunti and the boys slowly returned to their ashram. It seemed empty and lonely. They looked at each other in silence, realizing that they could not stay there without Pandu.

As they sat in sorrow, a leader of the rishis came into the cottage and spoke to Kunti. "Now that your protector has gone, you must return to your family in Hastinapura. Take the boys and have them assume their rightful positions as heirs to the throne."

The boys knew their father had been the king in Hastinapura, the great capital of the world and seat of the powerful Kuru dynasty. He had told them he came to the forest as a result of a *rishi's* curse, but they did not know the full details. It must have been a truly terrible imprecation. What had he done to deserve it? They looked querulously at their mother.

Devastated by the sudden loss of her husband and co-wife, Kunti found it difficult to speak. "I will try to explain as we travel to the city," she said, wiping her face with the end of her sari. "Your father and I had been meaning to tell you."

The sage advised them to leave at once. He and the other rishis would accompany them to the city. Kunti agreed and she began gathering her few belongings together, telling the boys to do the same. Within a short time they were ready to go.

A long line of rishis set out for Hastinapura, with Kunti and her sons in their midst. They were accompanied by a number of Siddhas and Charanas, celestial beings who also dwelt on the mountain where they lived.

As they walked, Kunti tried to gather her senses. She had to tell her sons about the curse—and especially about their births. Bringing the boys around her, she said, "Once when your father was hunting in the forest, he accidentally slew a *rishi* named Kindama who had assumed the form of a deer. To free him from the reaction of that sin, the *rishi* uttered a curse. Your father had shot Kindama when he was just about to beget a child with his wife. The sage therefore told the king that if he ever tried to beget children, he would immediately die. Your father then decided to live a life of asceticism."

Kunti explained that Pandu, thus unable to beget children, had sought some other way of continuing his line. "I told him of a boon I had received from another sage when I was a girl. That sage, named Durvasa, had been pleased by my service. He blessed me that I would be able to summon any god I desired. Thus, your father had me call various great deities. First of all, Dharma, the god of religion."

She looked across at her eldest son, who was listening intently. "Dear Yudhishthira, that powerful god is your seminal father."

Kunti said that Bhima was the son of Vayu, god of the winds. Arjuna was the son of Indra, the king of the gods, and the twins were born of the twin Ashvini gods, the celestial physicians. "Thus were you three eldest boys born of myself, and the twins of Madri, who had begged me that she be allowed to use the mantra. A heavenly voice was heard at each of your births, prophesying great things for all of you. Yudhishthira will be the lord of the earth, Bhima the most powerful man, Arjuna the greatest among archers, and the twins possessed of celestial beauty and energy."

The boys looked at each other. They had never guessed the truth—sons of the gods! Their father had often told them that a great destiny awaited them—that one day they would return to Hastinapura to become rulers. But he had never explained how they had been born.

Kunti smiled a little through her grief. "Your ancestors have long ruled the earth, keeping it firmly on the path of religion. That duty will surely fall to you boys in due course."

In what seemed only a short while, they saw the city ahead of them. They were walking on a broad paved road with great archways over it, carved with numerous representations of the gods. Cultivated fields lay on either side of the road, filled with neat rows of vegetables and patches of golden wheat. Many farmers worked the land, tilling the ground with teams of black oxen. They looked in wonder at the procession of celestials and rishis, saluting them as they walked by, and the sages offered them blessings.

By late afternoon the procession reached the city gates, which were set in the huge granite wall that surrounded the entire city. Messengers went quickly to inform the king of their arrival, and soon a large crowd of citizens came out of the city. They were astonished to see the many rishis and other celestial beings, resembling an assembly of the gods.

When the greetings were complete, a leading *rishi* told the king what had happened. "Steadily adhering to the path of virtue, Pandu has ascended to heaven along with his chaste wife Madri. Here are his five sons, born of the gods."

The *rishi* named each of the deities who had fathered the five boys. After instructing the king to take care of their welfare and studies, he rejoined the other rishis. Then, before the eyes of the amazed citizens, all the sages and celestials disappeared from the spot.

One of the leading Kurus came up to Kunti and greeted her with folded palms. She introduced him to her sons. "This is your grandfather Bhishma." The boys all bowed low in respect. Bhishma then led Kunti and the five boys into the city, arranging for their accommodation in the royal palace.

The last rites ceremony was performed for Pandu and Madri. All the leading Kurus, accompanied by thousands of citizens, entered the Ganges and made offerings for the departed souls. The whole city then observed a twelve-day period of mourning that concluded with a great feast. Large amounts of wealth were given in charity to the brahmins, and everyone in the city was fed sumptuously by the king. Life then returned to normal, and Pandu's sons took their place in the royal family.

Two

ॐ

SEEDS OF CONFLICT

WHEN THEY WERE settled in Hastinapura, Kunti told her sons the Kurus' history. She explained how Pandu, after he was cursed, had handed over the rule of the kingdom to his elder brother, Dhritarashtra. Due to being born blind, Dhritarashtra had been unable to assume the throne before Pandu, but when Pandu left for the forest, it fell to Dhritarashtra to take his place. He was assisted by Bhishma and by Vidura, another brother of Pandu, who was acting as the Prime Minister. Vidura had been born of a maidservant and, therefore, could not become the king himself.

The boys were curious to know why Bhishma, as the seniormost Kuru, was not the ruler. Kunti told them his history:

"Long ago, Hastinapura was ruled by a king called Shantanu. That king fell in love with the goddess Ganga after seeing her one day at the riverside. They married, and their son was named Bhishma, whom she raised and educated among the gods."

Kunti described how Shantanu had later fallen in love with another maiden, this time the daughter of a fisherman who set a condition for her marriage to Shantanu. The fisherman wanted his daughter's son to be next in line for the throne. Shantanu could not agree, as he had already installed the highly qualified Bhishma as Prince Regent. He tried to forget the girl, but when Bhishma learned of his father's disappointment, he went to see the fisherman. He promised that he would never become king, but still the fisherman would not agree, fearful that Bhishma's sons would demand the throne. It was only when Bhishma made a vow that he would never marry that the fisherman finally agreed to the match.

Kunti concluded her story. "Thus Shantanu married the fisherman's daughter, Satyavati. Her son was your grandfather, who unfortunately died before having any children. At that time, the Kurus became fearful that their dynasty would end. They asked the great *rishi* Vyasadeva if he could help. In accordance with scripture, Vyasadeva then fathered three sons in your grandfather's two wives. They were Dhritarashtra, Vidura, and your father."

As the months passed after their arrival in Hastinapura, Pandu's sons, who were known as the Pandavas, became increasingly dear to the Kuru elders. The five brothers exhibited every good quality. Humble and submissive to their elders, they were pious and ever truthful. As they grew to maturity, the Kuru elders saw that they would be worthy successors to the throne. The godly boys pleased the Kurus in every way.

However, the Pandavas were not well liked by everyone in the city. Thanks to a blessing from Vyasadeva, Dhritarashtra had one hundred sons. These princes, who were known as the Kauravas, quickly became envious of Pandu's sons. The eldest of them, Duryodhana, was particularly angered by their presence, perceiving that his claim to the throne was being threatened. He and his brothers had never displayed the kind of virtue shown by the Pandavas. Indeed, there had been widespread concern about Duryodhana becoming king, since his birth had been accompanied by many fearful omens. It was clear to everyone that Yudhishthira would be a far better choice.

Seeing his position diminishing with the Pandavas' presence, Duryodhana fumed, deeply resenting the fact that his assumed right to the throne was now challenged. Apart from their many personal qualifications, it seemed that the Pandavas also had a superior claim to the kingdom. It was their father who had been the king. His own father, Dhritarashtra, had only taken the throne by default.

Duryodhana's pain and humiliation at losing his status in the Kuru house was compounded by the way Bhima treated him and his brothers. The second eldest Pandava had no time for the Kauravas' arrogance. He found the haughty Duryodhana especially unbearable, and a rivalry quickly developed between the two princes. From Bhima's side it was only a boyish source of fun, but for Duryodhana it grew increasingly earnest, and he found Bhima's antics intolerable. The son of Vayu possessed incomparable physical strength. He would laughingly challenge all hundred Kauravas together to a wrestling contest. When they came at him, he would toss them about like so many pieces of straw. He delighted in practical jokes and would frequently embarrass his weaker cousins.

Duryodhana felt he would have to take matters into his own hands. One day, after a particularly humiliating incident where Bhima had shaken him out of a huge fruit tree he had climbed, he felt he could take no more. He took the next eldest Kaurava, Dushasana, aside and said, "This Bhima

is a thorn in our sides. We just cannot get the better of him in anything!
Even at eating he consumes as much as twenty of us together. I tell you,
brother, it is driving me to madness. Something must be done, and indeed,
I have a plan."

Duryodhana had been consulting with his uncle Shakuni, whom he
found to be a sympathetic confidante. Shakuni was Gandhari's brother. He
had been offended that the Kurus had not sought his sister's hand for Pandu
rather than the blind Dhritarashtra and attributed the fault for this to
Bhishma. On behalf of Dhritarashtra, Bhishma had gone to the kingdom of
Gandhara asking for Gandhari as a bride. Her father had agreed, even
though Dhritarashtra was blind, considering an alliance with the mighty
Kuru house desirable under any circumstance. But Shakuni was angered.
Why had his beautiful and qualified sister, who had received a boon from
Shiva that she would have a hundred sons, not been given to Pandu, the
incumbent Kuru king? Shakuni therefore went with Gandhari to
Hastinapura and began looking for ways to get back at Bhishma. He soon
found his chance in Duryodhana. The young Kaurava quickly accepted his
scheming uncle as a mentor. Shakuni had given the Kaurava an idea how to
deal with the Pandavas, whom he knew were dear to Bhishma.

The corners of Duryodhana's mouth lifted in a slight smile. "Listen,
brother. Tomorrow we shall go to the river with the Pandavas. Once there,
we can enjoy a feast with our dear cousins. I shall personally arrange for
some special dishes for the ever-hungry Bhima."

Looking about furtively, Duryodhana showed his brother a stem from
the deadly poisonous datura plant. "I hear this makes a delicious preparation when cooked with various spices. I am sure Bhima will eat a whole pot-
ful."

Speaking softly, the Kaurava described how he and Dushasana should
wait near Bhima till the poison took effect. Then, when everyone else had
gone, they could throw him into the river to drown. "With the powerful
Bhima gone, what can the other Pandavas do? My claim to the throne will
be safe."

Dushasana smiled and nodded eagerly. He had also been suffering at
Bhima's hands. And he only wanted to do whatever was pleasing to
Duryodhana.

Laughing together, the two princes rejoined their brothers and began
walking along the wooded path back to the palace. They looked at Bhima
bounding ahead and laughed all the more.

The next morning Duryodhana suggested that the princes go to the
river for some water sports. It was a hot day and everyone agreed. They

mounted their gleaming gold chariots and set off with loud shouts, sending up clouds of dust as they raced away. Reaching the river, they jumped down from their cars and entered the pleasure house that the king had built for them, an elegant seven-story mansion constructed of white marble. Rows of colorful flags flew from its high roof. Inside were dozens of well-appointed rooms offering every kind of luxury. Royal musicians and dancers entertained the princes, and a force of a hundred armed bodyguards stood ready to protect them.

Duryodhana led the way through the mansion and out into the central gardens. "Come, my brothers, let us take our lunch together and then go for some fun in the river."

The prince knew that Bhima would not easily succumb to the poison. It would likely be some time before it took effect, so he wanted to administer it as soon as possible. He brought the princes to the large lawn, where the food was waiting. Sitting places had been arranged for all of them, with gold plates and cups set out on low tables.

Suspecting nothing, the Pandavas contemplated the beautiful garden, with its large lake filled with lotuses and surrounded by soft grass. The sweet scent of blossoms spread everywhere, and the pleasant sound of a tinkling crystal waterfall could be heard.

Servants showed the boys to their seats and began to serve the food. The expertly prepared dishes were delicious and the boys ate hungrily. Duryodhana went to the kitchen, where a trusted servant had placed the poisoned food meant for Bhima. He personally brought it out and, with a pretense of affection, served Bhima with his own hand. Duryodhana piled Bhima's plate with mixed vegetables, then gave him many cakes, pies, and drinks—everything undetectably laced with poison. The Kaurava prince smiled in glee as the guileless Bhima cheerfully ate the deadly dishes.

After the meal was over and the boys had rested for a while, they went out of the mansion to sport in the river. They raced down the forest path to the grassy riverbank. Throwing off their silken robes, they leapt into the clear waters, where they wrestled and tossed each other about, laughing and splashing around. Bhima, not yet affected by the poison, was his usual energetic self. He picked up and hurled the Kaurava princes way out into the river. Thrashing his mighty arms, he created big waves that threw the princes off their feet.

As the sun headed toward the western horizon, the boys began to tire. They gradually got dressed and made their way back to the mansion to rest for the night. Just then, Bhima began to feel the effects of the poison. His head swam and his eyes felt unbearably heavy. Hauling himself out of the water, he lay down on the riverbank and fell into a deep coma.

Nearby, Duryodhana and Dushasana watched carefully. They got dressed very slowly, telling their brothers to go on ahead. When everyone had gone, they took a long length of hemp from their chariot. They bound Bhima tightly with the rope and then rolled him into the river. As the unconscious prince sank beneath the waters, they turned and ran after their brothers, praising each other for a job well done.

By the gods' arrangement, Bhima did not drown. He was immediately carried by underwater currents, which swept him along a watery path that led deep beneath the earth to the abode of the celestial serpents known as the Nagas. Seeing that a human had mysteriously arrived among them, many Nagas at once bit him. Their virulent poison than acted as an anti-dote to the poison given by Duryodhana. Bhima slowly came to his senses and looked around him. He was lying on a strange riverbank, surrounded by large serpents with their fangs bared. Bhima flexed his muscles, bursting the ropes that bound him. Leaping to his feet, he picked up the snakes with both hands and dashed them to the ground. Some he pressed into the earth with his feet and others he threw to a distance.

When dozens of the snakes had been rendered unconscious by Bhima, the others fled away. They went to their king, Vasuki, and fearfully said, "A very powerful human has come into our midst. We could not overcome him. He is down by the river."

Vasuki knew that no ordinary human could come there. He had to be either a *rishi* or a god. The Naga king assumed a human form and rose from his jeweled throne. He went toward the river, accompanied by another chief Naga named Arka. Many years before, Arka had lived in human society. He was Kunti's ancestor and, by his celestial vision, he recognized Bhima as his great grandson. He introduced himself to the Pandava and embraced him warmly.

Vasuki felt pleased to see the pious Kuru prince. Realizing that the gods must have brought him there for some purpose, he asked Arka, "What good can we do for this boy?"

Arka looked at the strapping youth and smiled. "I think this prince would benefit most from drinking our rasa."

Vasuki agreed at once. "Yes, bring him to the palace and let the rasa be fetched."

The Naga's ambrosial drink was distilled from many heavenly herbs and conferred celestial power upon anyone who drank it. The Nagas watched in amazement as Bhima sat and quaffed eight pots one after another. After finishing the drink, Bhima again felt drowsy. Vasuki showed him to a bed in his palace and he lay down. For eight days he remained in a deep sleep as his body digested the rasa. On the ninth day he awoke, feeling almost unlimitedly powerful. Arka said to him, "You now have the strength of ten thousand elephants. None will be able to defeat you in battle. Come now and eat something. I shall then show you how to return to earth. Your family is anxious about you."

The Nagas offered Bhima varieties of celestial dishes, dressed him in fine silks and gold ornaments, and then took him back to the river. Telling him to close his eyes, Arka entered the water with him, and within moments Bhima found himself standing on the Ganges bank near the mansion. Arka was gone and Bhima immediately began to sprint back to Hastinapura.

In the city, Kunti sat sighing with worry. Where was Bhima? His brothers had been surprised to see that he was not in the city when they returned. After failing to find him anywhere near the river, they assumed he had run on ahead.

Kunti suspected some evildoing. She knew of Duryodhana's disposition toward her sons. Revealing her mind to Vidura, she said, "I fear the Kaurava prince may have killed my son."

Vidura shook his head. "That can never be, O queen. The *rishi* Vyasadeva has prophesied that your sons will live long. The gods also have predicted a great future for Bhima. Those words cannot prove wrong."

But remembering the malefic omens seen at Duryodhana's birth, Vidura nevertheless warned Kunti to be on her guard. "The Kaurava prince might try anything, even against you."

During the eight days of Bhima's absence, Kunti and her other sons were in complete anxiety. Then, soon after sunrise on the ninth day, they saw him running along the road toward the palace, his white silks billowing in the breeze. He went straight to his overjoyed mother and touched her feet. His brothers embraced him with tears in their eyes, eagerly asking him where he had been.

Bhima understood what had happened. When he had seen the cords with which he had been bound, he immediately suspected Duryodhana, and his fears had been confirmed by Vasuki, who could see everything with his divine vision. Bhima told his family about his visit to the celestial world of the Nagas. They all thanked the Lord for his safe return. It seemed that, by the Lord's arrangement, Bhima had been fortunate, despite Duryodhana's efforts to dispose of him.

Yudhishthira was shocked to learn of Duryodhana's antagonism. He considered the situation carefully and discussed it with his mother and brothers. He concluded it would be best to remain silent. If the Kuru elders were informed, there would be open hostility between the two sets of brothers. With Pandu dead, their position as his sons was weak, because now Dhritarashtra was the king and he doted on his own sons. He would be unlikely to go against them in order to protect his nephews.

Vidura was the one person they trusted, and Kunti confided in him. He confirmed Yudhishthira's decision. The brothers therefore said nothing about the incident, but from that day they were vigilant, always expecting some other treachery from Duryodhana.

*　　*　　*

Through their godly behavior, the Pandavas became great favorites of Bhishma and Vidura. Bhishma was especially fond of them, acting just like their father. The brothers also became dear to their martial teacher, Kripa, the virtuous son of a *rishi* named Sharadvan who had taught his son every martial skill.

The Kurus were pleased with Kripa's teachings. Their sons were becoming adept at all forms of weaponry. But Bhishma realized that for their education to receive a final touch, they needed another teacher. There were hundreds of pupils in Kripa's school—kings from many countries had sent their sons to take advantage of the talented brahmin's skills. It was difficult for him to spend time teaching the princes the finer points of the science of arms. Bhishma therefore began wondering where he could find someone who was Kripa's equal and who could concentrate on honing the boys' martial skills to perfection. He had been searching for some time, but without success.

One day some of the boys ran to him. After bowing at his feet, they said excitedly, "O grandfather, we have been sent to you by an unusual brahmin we met outside the city. He said you would know of him."

The boys told Bhishma how they had been playing ball in the woods. Their ball dropped down a deep, unused well. They had been standing around the well wondering what to do when the brahmin had approached them. Laughing, he said, "Just see the great Kuru princes, baffled by the loss of their ball. Where is your prowess in arms?"

The dark-complexioned brahmin told the blushing boys that he would retrieve their ball in exchange for a meal. He took a ring from his finger and threw it in the well, saying, "I shall show you how to bring out even that ring."

Yudhishthira replied, "Esteemed sir, if you can recover the ball and the ring, then be assured you will find a permanent livelihood in Hastinapura."

With a smile the brahmin took up a handful of long grasses. He chanted some mantras and threw a blade into the well, piercing the ball. The other blades of grass were all thrown after the first, in quick succession. They stuck together to form a long chain, which the brahmin pulled out to recover the ball. Then, taking a bow from one of the princes, he concentrated for a moment and shot an arrow into the well. It came straight out again with the ring on its point.

The princes crowded round the brahmin, clamoring to be taught the skills he had just displayed. He told them to go to Bhishma and relate what they had seen. The Kuru chief would know who he was. If Bhishma was agreeable, the brahmin said, he would come to Hastinapura.

Hearing this tale, Bhishma's eyes lit up, for he knew that this brahmin was surely Drona, a disciple of his own martial guru, Parasurama. Drona's fame had spread far and wide. He was the son of Bharadvaja, the great *rishi* who had practiced asceticism for thousands of years. What better instructor could there be for the princes? Bhishma went in person to see him, immediately offering him the post of royal teacher. Drona accepted and went to Hastinapura with Bhishma.

Bhishma had Drona tell the curious princes about himself. Although a brahmin, Drona was inclined to the military arts. He explained how he had learned all the secrets of weaponry from Agnivesha, a powerful brahmin who dwelt in his father's ashram. He had received further training from Parasurama, who was said to be an empowered incarnation of the Supreme Lord.

"However, despite all my learning I am still poverty stricken, with hardly the means to maintain my family," said Drona. "Thus, I came here in search of students who might afford me a little charity in return for my lessons."

Bhishma smiled. "Your search is over, O brahmin. We shall give you everything you need. The Kurus are at your command. Whatever wealth we possess is also yours. Teach our sons your matchless skills. It is our good fortune that you have arrived here."

Drona then took up residence in Hastinapura. He had his wife and son brought to the city to live with him. Opening a school, he accepted both the Kauravas and Pandavas as his students. Kings from many surrounding countries also sent their sons to take training from him, sending great offerings of wealth along with those boys.

Under Drona's tutelage, the princes' skill in martial arts became highly developed. He had them practicing daily from dawn until dusk. Among all the boys, Arjuna excelled. He quickly mastered the use of all weapons and became particularly expert in archery skills. His ability, speed, and perseverance were unmatched. Seeing his humble and respectful attitude, Drona felt increasing affection for Arjuna and he carefully taught him every skill he knew. "None on earth shall equal you in battle," he told Arjuna.

Ever more determined in his study of the martial arts, Arjuna would spend time refining his skills long after the other princes had left the school. Even late at night he would stand with his bow, shooting at invisible targets. With his eyes closed, he could lift and string his great bow, fire an arrow, and strike the target, all in a matter of seconds.

Bhima and Duryodhana, deadly rivals, developed unparalleled skill in mace fighting, and they too would spend long hours at practice, each trying to outdo the other. Among the other princes, Yudhishthira was the most talented with a spear, and the twins developed incomparable skills with the sword.

Three

A Trial of Arms

THE TIME CAME when Drona considered that the Kuru princes had completed their education. All of them were proficient in the martial arts, capable of fighting from chariots, horseback, or on foot. They could wield any weapon and knew the secrets of the mystical missiles presided over by the gods. Drona was confident they could take their place as protectors of the people and stand against any antagonist.

Satisfied that his work was done, Drona went to Dhritarashtra and said, "O king, your sons' training is complete. With your permission, they can now display their prowess; I shall arrange an exhibition."

Thanking Drona, the king replied, "Let it be so. I envy those who will be able to witness my sons' skills. Make preparations. O best of brahmins, I shall attend the display with Vidura, and he will be my eyes."

Drona then selected an appropriate site near the city and had a great stadium constructed. Its tiered seats seemed to rise to the sky, and it could hold hundreds of thousands of people. Rows of golden thrones encrusted with gems were built on the royal platform. From the high walls flew tall flags that fluttered in the breeze.

The stadium was sanctified by brahmins who performed ceremonies to satisfy the gods. Then, on a day marked by favorable stars, the citizens of Hastinapura entered the vast building. When the stadium was full, the king entered, followed by all his ministers. The royal ladies accompanied them, dressed in fine robes, their heads covered by silk veils. As they went up to the royal dais, the senior Kurus with their wives resembled so many gods and goddesses ascending the celestial Mount Meru.

The stadium buzzed with excitement, sounding like the roar of the ocean. Trumpets were blown and drums beaten, and the blast of hundreds of conches resounded everywhere. Brahmins entered the arena to perform auspicious rites. Along with his son, Asvatthama, Drona then made his entrance. Dressed in white robes, with a white garland around his neck, he resembled the rising full moon. The people loudly cheered him, and he raised his hands to silence them.

When the stadium was quiet, the princes entered with Yudhishthira at their head. They strode in like mighty lions, clad in brilliant armor and equipped with all kinds of weapons. At Drona's command they began to display their skills, one by one. Mounting tall chargers, they sped about the arena wielding their weapons. Arrows flew in all directions, striking both moving and stationary targets. Some citizens ducked in fear, while others sat fearless, wide-eyed with wonder. Shouts of 'Well done! First class!' resounded through the stadium.

Drona had Bhima and Duryodhana come together for a mock mace battle. They squared up to each other with fury in their eyes. At Drona's shout, they clashed like two enraged bulls, their heavy iron maces smashing together with showers of sparks. As they thrust and parried, they appeared like expert dancers on a stage. As the crowd gasped, Vidura described the scene to Dhritarashtra. Kunti did the same for Gandhari, who, after learning of her husband's blindness, had decided to always wear a blindfold over her eyes in order not to exceed him in any way.

Everyone became absorbed in the contest, which was becoming more than an exhibition. The crowd's loyalties were divided, with some shouting for Bhima and others for Duryodhana. Drona saw that the fight was becoming too earnest. He told his son to step between them and halt it. Ashvatthama quickly went forward and managed to separate the roaring princes, who stood back, glaring at one another.

Drona then announced that Arjuna would display his talents. "This son of Indra is the finest of all warriors and best protector of the Kurus. Watch now and be dazzled by his skills."

The people all cheered loudly. Dhritarashtra asked Vidura what the noise was about. When Vidura told him, he replied, "Blessed am I to have such boys as Kunti's sons in my care. They shine like so many blazing sacrificial fires."

However, the blind king secretly felt resentment. Why had the people not cheered Duryodhana in the same way? Was he inferior to Arjuna? Dhritarashtra squirmed in his seat. If only he could see for himself what was happening....

As the crowd became quiet, Arjuna began to display his mastery over the celestial weapons. With the Agneya weapon, presided over by the fire-god Agni, he produced blazing fire, which he quickly extinguished with the Varunastra, controlled by the god of the waters. Then the wind-god's weapon was invoked and a great wind rushed through the stadium, which

Arjuna checked by means of the Parvatya weapon, causing a hill to appear in the arena. He demonstrated a number of other mystical weapons before the astonished gaze of the people, then began to display his skill with the bow. Drona had a mechanical boar run swiftly across the arena, and Arjuna released five arrows straight into its mouth, in such complete unison that they seemed as if they were a single shaft. He then shot twenty arrows into the hollow of a cow's horn that swung around a pole on a rope. After this, Arjuna showed his skill and dexterity with both sword and mace.

The crowd cheered and waved their garments. Arjuna bowed and returned to Drona's side. The exhibition was drawing to a close and the musicians began to play gentle music, calming the crowd. Suddenly they heard a man bellowing at the stadium gates, sounding like an infuriated elephant. All heads turned in that direction, and they saw a tall, golden figure striding into the arena. He forcefully slapped his arms, creating a noise like the splitting of rocks. He wore a brilliant coat-of-mail that seemed to be a part of his body, and fire-colored earrings swung back and forth as he walked straight toward Drona.

The people stared silently at this new arrival. He seemed like a moving hill and shone like the sun. His heavy steps shook the earth. Reaching Drona, he offered a half bow, not showing much respect. He did the same to Kripa, then spoke to Drona in a booming voice. "I am Karna. If you permit me, O brahmin, I shall display skills which exceed even those of Arjuna. Prepare to be amazed."

Hearing this bold proclamation, the crowd rose up as if one person. They cheered and shouted encouragement to the unknown warrior. Arjuna felt abashed and angry. He clasped his bow and glowered at Karna.

Drona assented to Karna's request and the powerful youth stepped into the center of the arena. He immediately began his demonstration. Matching every feat shown by Arjuna, he frequently threw him disdainful glances. The crowd roared their approval. When he had finished, Duryodhana went over and embraced him warmly. Here was someone who could match Arjuna. For too long the proud Pandava had been the main attraction. Perhaps that would now change.

In a loud voice Duryodhana said, "Welcome is your appearance here, O hero. You have shown wonderful skills. What can the Kurus do for your pleasure in return?"

Duryodhana smiled at the smoldering Arjuna. Seeing their obvious enmity, Karna replied, "O king, your friendship is all I desire. But grant me one request: I desire single combat with Arjuna."

Arjuna stiffened. He had felt an intense rivalry the moment he set eyes on Karna. The Pandava looked at Drona, seeking his permission to fight. Maybe he would get an immediate chance to curb Karna's arrogance.

Drona nodded and Arjuna turned to face Karna. Duryodhana again embraced Karna and urged him to step forward for combat.

As the two men closed slowly on each other, the sky grew overcast. Flashes of lightning were seen, and Indra's great rainbow appeared over-head. At the same time, brilliant shafts of sunlight shone through the clouds onto Karna, gleaming on his golden armor.

As she witnessed the scene in the arena, Kunti was horrified. She sud-denly fainted and fell to the royal dais. Surprised, Vidura jumped up and sprinkled her face with water. She came round and he asked her what was wrong. Kunti sighed. How could she tell him the truth—the secret she had carefully kept for so many years? "It was just the heat," she replied, taking her seat again. Looking down on the arena, she struggled to conceal her anxiety.

Just as the duel was about to commence, Kripa stepped forward and spoke. He knew all the rules of combat and, in accordance with custom, he asked Karna to announce himself and his lineage. Duels were only to be fought between equals.

Karna looked embarrassed. He said nothing. Clearly he was not from any royal line. Realizing this and seeing Karna's discomfort, Duryodhana said, "Birth is not the only factor which determines nobility. Power and heroism are also to be considered. However, if it is a problem for Arjuna, then I shall here and now confer a kingdom upon Karna."

Duryodhana immediately arranged an installation ceremony for Karna. As everyone looked on in bemusement, he had water fetched and sprinkled it over Karna's head, saying, "You shall be the king of Anga." Brahmins per-formed the rituals, and when they were complete, the people cheered as Karna stood up, his head still wet and his body covered with rice grains thrown during the ritual. He was deeply moved by Duryodhana's gesture of friendship. In a choked voice he said, "O king, I can never repay you."

Duryodhana placed an arm round his shoulder. "I only desire your friendship."

Karna turned to face Arjuna again. The crowd murmured with excite-ment. Surely now the fight would go ahead. But suddenly another man hur-ried into the arena. He was elderly and supporting himself on a staff. He went up to Karna, who at once bowed at his feet. "This is my father, Adhiratha," Karna explained to Duryodhana. "He adopted me as a small child."

Adhiratha had been in the crowd, and when he saw his son crowned as a king, he could not contain his excitement. He came into the arena to congratulate him. By his name and dress he was plainly a charioteer; seeing this, Bhima laughed out loud. "How does this charioteer's son deserve death at Arjuna's hands?" he jeered. "Indeed, he should never be made a king, any more than a dog should be given the sacrificial offerings meant for the gods."

Karna blushed deeply. Duryodhana leapt up in anger and exclaimed, "Bhima, you have no right to speak in this way! Karna's birth may be mysterious, but then so is yours and your brothers'. How can this man be low-born? We have all seen his power. See his natural armor—how he shines like the blazing sun! I take him to be the best of heroes and warriors."

Duryodhana looked around belligerently. "If anyone wishes to take issue with my words, then let him step forward and bend his bow in combat."

Roused by Duryodhana's heroic speech, the crowd cheered. They looked on, expecting a fight of some sort to soon start. But the sun had reached the horizon. Drona called a close to the day's proceedings. The dispute would have to be settled another day. Duryodhana took Karna's hand and led him out of the arena. Drona also went out, followed by the Pandavas. Gradually, the citizens dispersed, talking excitedly together.

Kunti watched as Karna left with Duryodhana. There was no doubt that he was the child she had long ago abandoned. She remembered that painful day only too well. Having just received Durvasa's boon, she had lain on her bed, idly wondering if it would work. Seeing the sun shining into her room, she began chanting the mantra. To her astonishment, she saw the blazing form of the sun god, Surya, appearing within the sun disc. He was brilliantly beautiful and she felt her mind being attracted to him. Suddenly he was standing before her. His deep voice had filled the room. "What shall I do for you, O gentle maiden?"

Kunti's mouth fell open in surprise. "I do not desire anything," she replied in a shaky voice. "I was merely testing the mantra. Please forgive me. O great god, you may return to your abode."

But the sun god had said that he could not leave without giving her something. "You have desired me; therefore, let me bestow upon you a celestial child."

Kunti had been shocked. How could she, as a maiden, accept a man's embrace? Surya had smiled and reassured her that, even though she was conceiving a child by him, she would retain her virginity. And so it had come to pass. Unknown to anyone in the palace except her most trusted servants, Kunti gave birth to a boy. She recalled how she had marveled at his natural bodily armor and glowing earrings—the very ornaments she had seen on Karna as he marched into the arena. She also clearly recalled every detail of the day she had let the child go, too scared to tell her elders what had happened. Praying to the sun god to protect the child, she had placed him in a basket and pushed him out into the swift-flowing Ganges current. The memory of that moment was still vivid in her mind—watching with tear-filled eyes as the basket bobbed away and finally disappeared in the distance. Adhiratha must have later found him and adopted him. Kunti looked over at the tall young man leaving the arena with Duryodhana. It seemed her destiny was interwoven with his. Her heart felt tremulous. Without doubt, Duryodhana would feed Karna's obvious envy of her other sons. Torn by conflicting emotions and praying for strength, she stood up and led Gandhari out of the arena.

Four

THE BLIND KING

THE DAY CAME for the princes to leave Drona's school. It was time for them to give him *dakshina*, the traditional fee a teacher asked of his students. Drona wanted only one thing. "Bring me as a captive King Drupada of Panchala."

The princes knew why Drona had made this request. He had told them how he and Drupada had once been friends, living together in Rishi Agnivesha's ashram. Drupada had promised Drona that when he inherited his father's kingdom, he would give him half. But when many years later that time came and the penniless Drona had reminded his old friend of the promise, he had been insulted. "What use are past friendships?" Drupada had asked, laughingly. "Only equals can be friends. You are now a poor mendicant, and I am a great king. Do not try to revive a long-dead relationship."

Offering him only a little charity, Drupada had sent Drona on his way. Offended and sorry that the king had broken his word, Drona left. Since then he had acquired an unrivalled skill at arms, but he had no desire to wreak vengeance on Drupada by killing him. It would be better to simply curb his pride and make him keep his promise. And the best way to do that would be by forcing him to accept defeat at the hands of the princes, Drona's students.

Duryodhana clasped hold of his bow. "O teacher, consider it done. You will soon see that arrogant king brought here, tightly bound."

Mounting his chariot, he sped away toward Kampilya, followed by his brothers. They rushed into the city with weapons raised, shouting out their war cries. The Pandavas waited outside with Drona. They did not expect the Kauravas' impetuous attack to succeed against the powerful Drupada. "Let us make our attack after theirs is repulsed," Arjuna suggested.

Discovering that his city was under attack, Drupada immediately mounted his war-chariot and sped toward his aggressors. An army quickly

assembled and they met the Kauravas on the city streets. Drupada assailed
them with countless arrows, twirling in his chariot like a dancer on a stage.
His soldiers engaged all the hundred princes from every side. Kampilya's citizens also joined the fray, coming out of their houses to fight the Kauravas
with clubs and sticks.

Fiercely attacked by thousands of soldiers and citizens, the Kauravas
found themselves being driven back. As Drupada's arrows began finding
their mark, the princes howled in pain and turned to flee. They fled out of
the city with the Panchalas in hot pursuit.

The Pandavas laughed. Arjuna said to Yudhishthira, "These brash
princes are all talk. It is time for us to tackle Drupada. Allow me and the
others to fight while you remain here with Drona."

Yudhishthira gave his permission, and his brothers offered their obeisances to Drona, then turned to face the Panchalas. Expecting another
attack, Drupada had arranged a row of great elephants in front of the city
wall. Bhima bounded toward them, whirling his mace. He was followed by
Arjuna on his chariot, flanked by the twins. Arjuna released arrows in such
large number that they appeared like swarms of black bees descending on
the Panchalas. Bhima reached the elephants and began to smite them with
tremendous blows from his mace. The huge beasts screamed and toppled
over. Bhima resembled a tornado as he twirled into the ranks of the
Panchalas. He drove them back as a herdsman drives cattle.

Bursting into the city, the four brothers encountered Drupada surrounded by his troops. Arjuna shouted his battle cry and immediately shot
volleys of arrows at those forces. Shafts left his bow in a straight line and
spread out in all directions as he fearlessly entered the enemy ranks.

The Panchalas fought back with furious energy. Arrows, darts, spears,
and clubs flew at the Pandavas, but the brothers expertly parried the attack,
striking down the missiles with their own weapons. Arjuna then became
enraged and fought with redoubled energy. No one could detect any inter-
val between his taking up his arrows and firing them. They flew from his
bow without cessation. At the same time, Bhima rushed about with his
mace whirling. The two brothers were unapproachable, and the Panchala
soldiers fled in terror.

Only Drupada stood to face them. He was mounted on a great golden
chariot. Praising the Pandavas' prowess, he raised his bow and let go a number of fierce arrows. They struck Arjuna forcefully and glanced off his armor.
Other shafts sped toward Bhima, who struck them down with his mace. In
seconds, Arjuna responded with fifty arrows that broke apart Drupada's

bow, smashed his flagstaff, and slew his steeds. Another wave of arrows sent the Panchala king reeling.

Arjuna threw down his bow and took up a long sword. Leaping down from his chariot, he raced over to the stunned Drupada. He jumped up and seized the king, holding the sword to his throat. The four brothers then went out of the city and presented the captive king to Drona.

Drona smiled. "So, great monarch, it seems your kingdom and riches are now forfeit to me."

Drupada stood with his head bowed. He could not make any reply. Drona put an arm round his shoulder. "Do not fear. I am a brahmin and am bound by duty to always forgive. Indeed, I still feel affection for you and would like our friendship to continue. But how can those who are not equals be friends? I shall therefore give you back half of the Panchala kingdom."

Drupada breathed heavily. He ground his teeth in silent frustration. Drawing on all his patience, he managed a smile and replied, "O Drona, you are truly a noble soul. Let us again be friends, as you wish, each ruling half of the Panchalas."

After brahmins had performed the ceremonies to install him as ruler of the northern Panchalas, Drona had Drupada released. Left with only the southern half of his kingdom, the king went away seething with anger and humiliation. His honor had to be avenged. But how? Who could face Drona in battle? Even his students were invincible, it seemed. The king slowly returned to his palace.

*   *   *

The situation in Hastinapura remained tense for the Pandavas. They were constantly on their guard, expecting Duryodhana to attempt some further treachery at any time. The Kaurava prince was always arrogant and given to licentious behavior. He and his brothers took pleasure in wine and women, and they laughed at the Pandavas, who strictly adhered to virtuous principles. Dhritarashtra was kind toward his nephews, but he over-indulged his own sons, allowing them their excesses and not checking their antagonism toward the Pandavas.

An emissary from nearby Mathura arrived one day to visit Dhritarashtra. Mathura was the capital of the Yadus and Vrishnis, who were friendly with the Kurus. They had a family link through Kunti, who had been born in the Vrishni line. Her brother Vasudeva had a son called Krishna, who was described by the rishis as being the Supreme Lord, descended to earth in human form. Hearing of the tension that his aunt

Kunti and her young sons were experiencing in Hastinapura, Krishna sent his counselor, Akrura, to the city to assess the situation.

After the Kurus had formally received Akrura in friendship, he went to see Kunti. She was overjoyed to see him and began asking about all her family members. Kunti was especially interested to hear about Krishna, whom she accepted as God. In her anxiety for her sons, she was continuously praying to him for protection. "Is my nephew Krishna thinking of me and my sons?" she asked Akrura. "Does he know how I am suffering here amidst so many enemies, like a deer among wolves?"

Kunti was sure that Krishna was fully aware of everything. Nothing could be outside of his knowledge. Akrura's arrival in Hastinapura was proof enough that Krishna was thinking of her. She was simply revealing her feelings to Akrura.

Akrura gently reassured her. Krishna often spoke about her. He had heard of Duryodhana's antagonism and would surely come to see her before long, after he had taken care of important business in Mathura.

Kunti had heard how Krishna had recently killed a vicious king named Kamsa, who had somehow come to rule Mathura. Kamsa had repeatedly tried to have Krishna and his brother, Balarama, killed. The two boys had been raised in a small village called Vrindavan. Hearing a prophecy that Krishna would be the cause of his death, Kamsa sent numerous great demons to destroy him, but all of them were slain by Krishna and Balarama. Finally the divine boys had gone to Mathura and killed Kamsa himself.

Akrura comforted the weeping Kunti. "Your sons are all expansions of the gods. Besides that, they are devotees of the Lord and thus always under His protection. The Kauravas will not be able to harm them."

Akrura remained in Hastinapura for some months, wanting to get a full understanding of the whole situation. When he was finally ready to return to Mathura, he spoke with Dhritarashtra. The intelligent minister from Mathura had seen that everything ultimately depended upon the blind king. Although not openly sinful, as Kamsa had been, Dhritarashtra was nevertheless covertly encouraging his evil-minded sons. It was in his power to prevent conflict by checking Duryodhana, perhaps by sending him off to some distant country.

Dhritarashtra listened in silence as Akrura spoke. "O king, the throne has only become yours by default. It was rightfully Pandu's, and thus, his sons have the first claim, or at least an equal claim, with your own sons. You should therefore deal equally with all the princes. Indeed, a wise man deals equally with all living beings, seeing them all as equal parts of the supreme spirit. Affection for family members arises from illusion. As a great king, it is your duty to rule impartially, always keeping in mind such eternal spiritual truths."

Dhritarashtra made no argument as Akrura offered his advice. The Vrishni minister made it clear that the blind king was courting disaster by opposing morality. If he did not deal virtuously with the virtuous Pandavas, he would, in the end, reap only sorrow.

Dhritarashtra sighed. "I accept all this, O wise Akrura. If only I was able to follow your advice. My attachment for my own sons is too strong. Perhaps I want them to be what I could not."

Dhritarashtra had always cursed his blindness. Born in Kuru's line, he was a powerful warrior but had never been able to prove it. It had been Pandu who had gone out and spread the Kuru glories. And it was Pandu who had won the people's love and admiration. They had not been happy when Pandu went to the forest, leaving the blind Dhritarashtra in his place.

The king continued, "What can I do? I am a mere man, influenced by desire and hate. The Lord has made me what I am. Everything moves under his supreme will. Now he has appeared to remove the earth's burden, and that will surely happen. Who can prevent the course of destiny?"

Dhritarashtra had heard the sages describe how Krishna had appeared to destroy all demonic elements on earth. Maybe Duryodhana and his brothers were in that category. If so, what could be done? And why should anyone worry? Krishna would no doubt rectify the situation—if indeed he actually was the Supreme Lord.

Akrura could see that his advice was falling on deaf ears. Dhritarashtra's blindness was compounded by a refusal to see the facts, or at least to act responsibly. There could only be one outcome, which Dhritarashtra must surely realize. By his intended policy of favoring the Kauravas over the Pandavas, he would cause a conflict that would ultimately destroy the Kuru house. Akrura took his leave from Dhritarashtra and then left for Mathura.

After Akrura's departure, Dhritarashtra felt great anxiety. Perhaps there was more he could do. Pandu's sons certainly had first claim to the throne. As well as it being their rightful inheritance, they were virtuous, powerful, and well loved by the people. Yudhishthira was especially qualified, showing a remarkable understanding of religion and law. The king had to admit that his own sons were inferior. But it was hard to think of them standing aside to let the Pandavas take over the kingdom. And if that happened, of course, it would mean that he himself would need to stand down.

Torn by duality, Dhritarashtra took counsel from Bhishma, Vidura, and the brahmins. All of them were unequivocal: Yudhishthira should be installed as prince regent. Bhishma said, "This is the only virtuous course, O king. Representations of the people have come to us many times asking that the prince be made heir to the throne. He is now fully trained and highly capable. Do not delay in his installation."

Dhritarashtra could not argue. He soon had the ceremony performed. To the people's joy and Duryodhana's horror, Yudhishthira became the heir apparent. The Kaurava prince was astonished. How had his father allowed it? Seeing his anger and dismay, Bhima sneered at him, mocking his miserable expressions. Taking Karna and Dushasana, Duryodhana stormed away to see Shakuni.

When the four of them were alone, Duryodhana exclaimed, "O uncle, I cannot tolerate any more! Bhima is vicious and vile. Yudhishthira is now prince regent, and I have become a nobody in the palace. What can be done?"

As the angry Duryodhana raged on, Shakuni appeared thoughtful. After some moments his face lit up. "I believe the great festival in Varanavata will occur soon. The king always sends a representative to that distant city for their yearly celebrations. Why not let the Pandavas be the ones to go this year?"

Duryodhana looked mystified. Shakuni's mouth twisted in a slight smile. "Fires often start in these hot places. Would it not be a terrible tragedy if the Pandavas were caught in such a conflagration?"

Duryodhana's eyes opened wide and he nodded in understanding. Dushasana laughed and shook Shakuni's hand, but Karna could not agree with them. He jumped to his feet. "I cannot condone any treachery. We are warriors who possess strength of arms. If we have enemies, let us march out onto the battlefield and settle the score in the proper way."

Shakuni went over to him and took his hand. "Dear child, you are doubtlessly heroic. Yet you seem to have forgotten the Pandavas' power. It is never wise to confront those of superior strength. Do you not recall what happened at Kampilya? Have you not seen the easy way that Bhima tosses about the Kaurava princes?"

Karna scowled. He would prefer to forget about Kampilya. They had been caught by surprise. Drupada had been more powerful than expected— and, unlike the Kauravas, the Pandavas had been given the opportunity to see that before they attacked him.

"Say what you will, O Shakuni. I, for one, do not fear Bhima or any of his brothers. I favor open combat and cannot join with any cowardly schemes to attack them covertly."

Karna marched out of the room. Duryodhana tried to stop him, but Shakuni told him not to worry. "Let him be. He is headstrong and impetuous, but he will never leave your side. Doubtlessly you will have cause to use his power and heroism before long."

Shakuni then revealed his idea to Duryodhana. The prince should use his influence with his father to ensure that the Pandavas be sent to Varanavata. The cunning Shakuni had carefully analyzed the situation. He could understand Dhritarashtra's mentality. "If you press him, your father will certainly agree to this proposal, O prince."

Trusting Shakuni's judgement, Duryodhana readily agreed. Sitting alone with his uncle, he carefully worked out the details of their plan, then left to see the king.

*　　*　　*

Dhritarashtra sat alone in his chamber, his chin resting on his hand. After Yudhishthira's installation he had seen how Duryodhana was fuming. The prince had hardly spoken to him since the day of the ceremony. Upset by this, Dhritarashtra had spoken with Shakuni. His brother-in-law had then suggested that he speak with a brahmin called Kanika, who was an expert in statecraft and politics. This brahmin was also a friend of Shakuni and shared his devious mentality. When the king asked for his advice, he told him that he should immediately destroy the Pandavas. "If you view these brothers as your enemies, then you should have no compunction, O king. Do not hesitate. Before they become too strong they must be rooted out. Otherwise, your position will be seriously threatened."

Kanika suggested that the king employ some secret means to dispose of them. Externally he should maintain a friendly disposition toward them, but as soon as an opportunity arose, he should strike. "You will not have the support of your ministers for a direct confrontation. Nor will the people be happy if they see you harm the Pandavas."

Dhritarashtra pondered Kanika's advice. How could he ever hurt Pandu's sons? What sense was there in seeing them as his enemies? What harm had they ever done him?

But when he thought of Duryodhana, the king's mind wavered. His son would never be happy in the Pandavas' presence. Nor would he ever assume the throne. That much was clear. There was no question of the people or indeed the Kuru elders choosing Duryodhana over Yudhishthira, or even any of his brothers. Already he was hearing many reports of what the people were saying. "Let Yudhishthira be given the throne now. Why should we be ruled by the blind Dhritarashtra?"

The king knew he had to decide one way or the other. Either he took Duryodhana in hand, making him accept the fact that Yudhishthira would be the next king, or he would have to follow Kanika's advice. Neither course seemed very attractive.

As the king sat thinking, he heard Duryodhana's heavy steps approaching. As the prince came before him, Dhritarashtra could sense his agitation. He asked what ailed him and Duryodhana replied, "I am hearing worrying reports of the kingdom. It appears the people want Yudhishthira installed as king immediately. They are not happy with you, dear father, and it seems they do not care for me either."

As he spoke, the prince paced back and forth, his many gold ornaments jangling together. "Ignominy will soon be ours. With Yudhishthira as king, our line will be cast into misfortune. How do you think the harsh and inimical Bhima will treat us? We will be the butts of ridicule. Rejected and despised by everyone, we will have to abandon our family home."

Duryodhana then told his father that he had thought of a means of saving the situation. He carefully revealed the plan that he and Shakuni had discussed, watching his father's reactions closely. The prince was not exactly sure how his father felt toward the Pandavas. He first suggested that they be sent to Varanavata for the upcoming festival, on the pretext of giving them a holiday. Duryodhana spoke in a low voice, looking around the king's chamber to see if anyone else was present. "Once the brothers are in that distant city, who knows what may happen? Perhaps they will never return."

Dhritarashtra immediately understood. Quickly raising a hand, he checked his son, exclaiming, "No! Such thoughts are highly sinful. How could I ever allow you to harm Pandu's sons? My brother was kind and generous toward me. He gave me this very kingdom that I now enjoy. I bear neither him nor his sons any ill will. Indeed, I loved Pandu, and his sons are equally dear to me."

But even as he spoke, Dhritarashtra again felt the uncertainty he had been wrestling with since Yudhishthira's installation. His voice became more subdued. "Besides, what would the people say if we sent the Pandavas away? They may well rise up and remove us by force. And I am sure that Bhishma and the other Kuru elders would favor Pandu's sons."

Duryodhana smiled. He had already considered this possibility. "There need be no such fear, O king. Let us begin winning the people's favor by bestowing upon them wealth and honors. Once our position is established, we can send the brothers away. In their absence, we will continue to reinforce our standing with the people until the time is right for my coronation. When I have become king, the Pandavas could even return."

Dhritarashtra leaned forward. "This very thought has already crossed my mind, dear child, but I have kept it to myself out of fear of sin. Such a course of action would find no favor with Bhishma, Vidura, Drona, or Kripa. Those wise and virtuous men see no difference between the Kurus and the Pandavas. If they realize we are trying to deprive the Pandavas of their rights—even by harming them—then will they not consider us worthy of punishment?"

Duryodhana was unconcerned by this objection. He had spent some time carefully discussing every possibility with Shakuni. He moved closer to his father. "O king, Bhishma always remains neutral; indeed, he has sworn to protect the Hastinapura throne—and you now occupy that throne. As far as the others are concerned, Drona's son Ashvatthama is my staunch supporter, and Drona will certainly not oppose his own dear son. Kripa is our paid employee and his sister has married Drona—we are therefore assured of his support. Vidura may oppose us, but what can he do? He depends upon us for his livelihood and possesses little power."

Duryodhana repeatedly exhorted his father to send the Pandavas away. He described how in their presence he was suffering intensely. The king still felt reluctant, but his attachment for his son finally won out. Agreeing to the prince's proposal, he said, "Ensure that this is kept a secret from all but your most trusted counselors."

Duryodhana assented and then happily left the king's chamber to immediately begin making the arrangements, leaving his father still consumed by doubt.

Five

ॐ

ON THE RUN

BY GIVING ALL sorts of charity, the Kauravas began to gain favor among the people. They arranged for various ceremonies in which recognition and honor was given to many leading citizens. Gradually their popularity increased. As the time for the festival in Varanavata approached, Dhritarashtra had some of his ministers praise the city while the Pandavas were present. They mentioned its beauty and ideal climate, as well as describing the wonderful festival soon to be celebrated.

The young Pandava princes were attracted. Seeing this, Dhritarashtra said to them, "I have lately been hearing a lot about Varanavata and its many attractions. Normally, we send a delegation to their festival, and I thought that this year you brothers might like to go. It would be a pleasant vacation."

Yudhishthira immediately realized what was happening. He had already noticed how the Kauravas were trying to influence the people in their favor, and now it was clear why. It was obvious to him that some devious plan was afoot, but the prince knew there was little he could do. He and his brothers were not in a position of strength. The king was plainly a party to Duryodhana's schemes. He had control of the treasury, army, and ministers. It would be pointless and perhaps dangerous to oppose him. Concealing his feelings, Yudhishthira replied, "Let it be so. I think we would enjoy a holiday in Varanavata."

Duryodhana was thrilled to hear that the Pandavas had agreed to go. He spoke in secret with a close confidante named Purochana, instructing him to go at once to Varanavata. "Construct a house of highly flammable materials, making it appear perfectly normal. Bring the Pandavas there, and when they are settled and their guard is down..."

Duryodhana made a sign indicating fire. Purochana smiled in understanding and Duryodhana said, "This world and all its wealth are at my command. You shall want for nothing. Go now and carry out my order. I am fully depending on you."

Purochana gathered together a few trusted artisans and left at once for Varanavata. A few days later the Pandavas prepared to leave. They said their farewells to the elders and aggrieved citizens, who did not want them to go. Despite the Kauravas' many contrivances, the gentle Pandavas were still the most deeply loved by the people. Many of them suspected some evil-doing by the Kauravas.

As the Pandavas mounted their chariots to leave, Duryodhana stood by with his brothers and waved goodbye. "O sons of Pandu, may the gods bless you on your way. May not the slightest evil befall you."

The Pandavas, along with their mother, went out of the city followed by crowds of people. The citizens implored the brothers to remain in Hastinapura, censuring Dhritarashtra for sending them away. But Yudhishthira checked them. He stopped his chariot just outside the city gates and said, "Dear friends, Dhritarashtra is the king. He is our father, pre-ceptor, and superior. We must follow his commands without question. This is the eternal law laid down by God. Return now to your homes. When the time is right, you may render us some service."

The people reluctantly turned back, but Vidura came forward to speak with Yudhishthira. He addressed him in a language that only the two of them could understand. Through his spies, the minister had come to know of Duryodhana's plan. However, like Yudhishthira, he did not feel it wise to openly oppose the king. Taking hold of Yudhishthira's arm and speaking softly, he said, "Fire cannot harm one who hides in a hole or in the deep for-est. By the stars one can find his way at night. Even though oppressed by enemies, he who conquers his own senses will never be defeated. Indeed, he will come to rule the world."

Yudhishthira nodded in understanding. The Kuru minister then blessed the brothers and bid them farewell. When they were some way out of the city, Yudhishthira told his mother and brothers what Vidura had said. "He confirmed my own suspicions. It is plain that Duryodhana has somehow contrived to have us killed, seemingly by fire. Our uncle has given me a clue how we can escape."

Feeling apprehensive, they traveled to Varanavata, arriving by early evening. The citizens came out to greet them in large number, pleased to see Pandu's famous sons. There was a festive scene, as thousands of people appeared on many kinds of chariots, waving flags and playing instruments. The city elders greeted the brothers and led them into the city, where they were met by Purochana. He told them that, on the king's orders, he was arranging for a mansion to be specially constructed for their stay in the city. The brothers exchanged meaningful glances but said nothing.

Within two weeks of their arrival the mansion was complete. With a flourish, Purochana showed them around the large building. "Everything has been arranged for your comfort, O princes. You will not want for anything. I shall also stay here as your obedient servant."

When Purochana had gone, Yudhishthira went over to one of the walls and tapped it lightly. "This house is built entirely with highly flammable materials," he said to his brothers. "Can you not detect the odor of oil and lac? Without doubt, the sinful Purochana intends to burn us to death. He is nothing more than Duryodhana's instrument. The greatly intelligent Vidura has properly warned us of this danger."

Bhima snorted in anger. "Then let us leave here at once. I've had enough of Duryodhana's plots! We should deal with him."

Yudhishthira shook his head. "No, the time is not right. What can we five do against the state of Hastinapura, now effectively under Duryodhana's control through his weak-minded father?"

Yudhishthira also dismissed the suggestion that they flee from Varanavata. "If we run, Duryodhana will know that we have discovered him. He will dispatch many spies to seek us out and have us killed by any means possible. Better that we stay here for now. We should not let on that we know anything, and be especially careful about Purochana. If he suspects that we have discovered him, he may resort to anything to destroy us."

The other Pandavas, always obedient to their elder brother, agreed. Yudhishthira remembered Vidura's words. "We need to dig a tunnel under this place. If it is set on fire, we can take shelter there."

Yudhishthira suggested that they spend their days exploring the surrounding area. Then, when the opportunity came for them to escape, they would know their way around.

A couple of days after they had moved into the house, which Purochana had named 'Blessed Abode', a strange man appeared there, asking to meet with them. "I am an expert miner. Vidura has sent me here, saying you will have use for my skills."

Speaking in the same tongue used by Vidura when he warned Yudhishthira, the miner reminded him of that incident. Yudhishthira, at first suspicious that this may be yet another of Duryodhana's tricks, was then reassured. He greeted the miner warmly. "It is good to see you, noble sir. Any friend of Vidura is also our friend."

Yudhishthira told him about the house and Purochana's plan to burn them to death. The miner said he would be able to build a tunnel from the house that led into the nearby woods. "It can be completed in a month. I think Purochana will wait longer than that before he attacks. He will want to be sure that you are completely at ease."

Yudhishthira agreed, and the miner began his work at once, digging from a concealed place within the house. As the days and weeks passed, the Pandavas spent much of their time wandering around and becoming familiar with the surrounding countryside. They ascertained a route leading away from the town and marked it with pieces of white cloth that would be visible at night.

More than a month went by. The brothers and their mother gave the appearance of being peaceful, but they were always alert, waiting for Purochana to make his move. One of them would remain awake at night, listening for any unusual sounds, and they always had their weapons at the ready.

Seeing that Purochana suspected nothing and was confident that they were well settled in, Yudhishthira one day said to his brothers, "I feel we should act now, before Purochana has a chance. Let us set fire to this house ourselves, burning that wicked man along with the building. The tunnel is now complete and we can make good our escape, leaving everyone to think that we have perished."

Yudhishthira knew that news of their supposed deaths would soon reach Hastinapura. They would thus be able to travel throughout the country without fear of being pursued. Remaining incognito, they could get away from Varanavata and consider their next move.

The following day a festival was celebrated. Kunti arranged for food to be distributed from her house for the poor and needy in the city. By the arrangement of Providence, a tribal woman and her five sons came to the house. They ate heartily and drank a large amount of wine. Gradually they became drunk and fell asleep. Unable to rouse them, the servants left them where they lay.

When everyone had left the house that night, the Pandavas retired to their room. Purochana also slept in his usual place, in a room near the door. Outside, a storm blew up. The Pandavas sat silently till they were sure that Purochana was deeply asleep. Then, one by one, they entered the tunnel, placing their mother in the middle. Bhima waited till all the others were in the tunnel; then he took a torch and set fire to the house, starting with the door. He ran back to the tunnel, and within minutes, the house was fiercely ablaze.

Purochana had no chance to escape, as the house quickly became an inferno. Crowds of citizens, roused by the noise of the conflagration, came out onto the streets. When they saw the Pandavas' house ablaze, they cried out in distress. As the flames gradually subsided, they threw water over the burning embers and began searching. They found the charred corpses of the tribal woman and her five sons. Believing these to be the remains of Kunti and the Pandavas, they lamented loudly. "Alas, this is surely an act of the wicked and heartless Duryodhana! Always envious of his godly cousins, he has arranged for their destruction. No doubt his blind father was also a party to this; otherwise, how could it have been possible?"

The citizens had noticed the flammable materials used for the house's construction. Having helped search through the ashes, the miner had carefully ensured that the tunnel was not found. Messengers were then sent to Hastinapura to inform the Kurus of the tragedy.

*   *   *

Out in the woods, the Pandavas emerged from the tunnel into the blackness of night. Carrying torches, they searched out their cloth markers and began to follow the path through the woods. Tired from lack of sleep and from the effort of making their way through the long tunnel, they often stumbled. After walking for an hour or so, Kunti fell to the ground, unable to continue. The brothers gathered around her and gently fanned her face with some large leaves. They looked around fearfully at the thick woods. Then, to their amazement, Bhima lifted Kunti and all four of his brothers onto his huge frame. He placed his mother on his shoulders, the twins on his sides, and Yudhishthira and Arjuna on his arms. Keeping all five of them in these positions, he began to run through the forest.

Bhima soon reached the banks of the Ganges, where he set down his mother and brothers. They drank some of the clear water and splashed it on their faces, relieving their fatigue. They then started following the river to the south, looking for a shallow place to cross. As they made their way along the riverbank, they came across a large boat. A man on board called out to them, again speaking in the same dialect Vidura had used in his warning to Yudhishthira. Like the miner, the boatman stated that he was Vidura's emissary. "I was told to wait here on the water for your arrival. I have been here for over a month, expecting you at any time."

Relieved to know that this man was a friend, the five brothers and their mother boarded the boat, which was propelled by sails and an engine. As it set off, cutting swiftly through the dark waters, the Pandavas lay down to rest, and by sunrise the boat had carried them a long distance away from Varanavata. They disembarked on the other side of the river and, after thanking the boatman and giving him a message of gratitude for Vidura, they made their way into the thick forest.

Traveling south, the brothers struggled through the dense undergrowth. Kunti found it especially difficult. Prickly bushes grew everywhere. Tangled creepers and roots lay across the ground, and she repeatedly stumbled and fell. Bhima and Arjuna walked by her side, giving her support, as they gradually went deeper and deeper into the forest. They walked throughout the morning, and by the afternoon, all of them except Bhima were exhausted. Yudhishthira stopped in a clearing, and they all sat down to rest. Looking around in despair, he said, "What could be more painful? Here we are, utterly lost in these desolate woods. We do not know where to go or what to do. It is not even certain that Purochana perished in the fire. Perhaps he has informed the Kurus that we survived, and even now they may have spies searching for us."

The sounds of birds and various forest animals echoed around them. On many occasions, they had heard the growls of tigers in the distance as they walked. They had seen snakes coiled on tree branches and great apes moving through the high treetops.

Yudhishthira looked at Bhima. "O hero, of all of us, only you are free of fatigue. Born of the ever-energetic Vayu and blessed by the Nagas with their *rasa*, you possess limitless strength. O brother, we are dependent on you to save us now. Take us again on your arms and shoulders and carry us through this forest."

Bhima stood up, happy to be of service to his brothers. He resembled a young oak tree. His shoulders were as broad as a wide door and his whole body rippled with muscle. Following his brother's instructions, he again lifted everyone and rushed straight into the forest, not caring for any obstacle. Like a great elephant, he broke down trees with his chest and made a road through the woods. The wind created by the speed of his movement blew bushes over, and his mother and brothers practically fainted. He swam across wide streams, still carrying everyone and keeping them above the water.

When night fell, Yudhishthira told him to stop. Seeing a large banyan tree nearby, Bhima placed his family beneath it. Kunti slumped, exhausted, to the ground. Parched with thirst, she asked Bhima if he could find any water. Bhima stood up, craning his neck. "I hear waterfowl in the distance. There must be a lake nearby. Wait here while I go and see."

Bhima ran off into the woods. Some miles away, he found the lake. Taking off his upper cloth, he soaked it and ran back to his mother and brothers. When he got back, he discovered that they had all fallen asleep.

As he looked down at their faces, he began to lament loudly. "Alas, what more painful sight could there be than seeing my noble mother and brothers asleep on the bare ground? They who could not sleep on the best of beds in Varanavata are now sunk in slumber on the cold earth."

Bhima lamented at length and then began to curse the Kauravas. "O wicked-minded men, rejoice now while you can. Surely the gods are favoring you, otherwise I would already have sent you and your followers to Death's grim abode. What can I do, though, as long as Yudhishthira does not become angry?"

Breathing heavily and squeezing his palms, Bhima looked at the dark woods around him. They had traveled a long distance, and he felt sure there must be a town nearby. Resolving to remain awake till morning, he sat on a log close to his brothers.

Not far from the banyan tree lived a Rakshasa and his sister. The demon had heard Bhima crashing through the forest, and he sat high in his tree, sniffing the air. His huge mouth broke into a twisted smile, revealing rows of long fangs. He shouted to his sister, "O Hidimbi, I smell men. It has been too long since we feasted on human flesh. Go and seek them out. Rip out their throats and bring them here. We shall drink our fill of their frothing blood and rejoice together."

Hidimbi cackled and dropped down from the tree. She padded silently through the woods and approached the Pandavas. Peering through the trees, she saw Bhima sitting on the log. Her heart was at once attracted to the handsome youth, with his golden complexion, leonine shoulders, and lotus-petal eyes. The demoness had never seen such an attractive man. Any thought of killing him left her mind. There might be some momentary pleasure in eating his flesh, but there would be far more pleasure if she were able to enjoy conjugal union with him.

Hidimbi then exercised her mystic power and transformed herself into a beautiful maiden. Bedecked with celestial ornaments and wearing a tight-fitting silk sari that accentuated her thin waist, she moved slowly toward Bhima, glancing down bashfully.

The sound of her footsteps gave Bhima a start, but when he saw the beautiful woman, he sat back again. Smiling at the surprised Pandava, Hidimbi said, "O best of men, who are you and why are you here? Who are these godlike men asleep on the ground? And that lady of transcendent beauty there; who is she?"

Bhima looked at Hidimbi suspiciously. He knew that demons were able appear in any form they liked. Seeing his apprehension, Hidimbi reassured him. "Do not fear. I wish you no harm. Indeed, you have captured my heart.

Know that I am Hidimbi, the sister of Hidimba, a wicked Rakshasa who controls this region. That demon wishes to eat your flesh and has sent me here to fetch you. However, I would rather sport with you in wedded bliss. Become my husband, and I shall save you from my cruel brother."

Bhima shook his head. "Here lie my beloved mother and brothers. How can I abandon them, leaving them as food for a Rakshasa while I gratify my lust? It is not possible."

"Then wake them and I shall save you all. Carrying you through the skies, I shall take you to some celestial region, where we may enjoy in peace."

Bhima could not agree. "I shall not awaken them out of fear of your brother. O beautiful-eyed girl, no man, Rakshasa, or even celestial can stand up to my strength and prowess. O timid one, you may stay or go as you please; or, if you like, bring your brother here. It makes no difference to me."

While they were speaking, Hidimba became impatient. What was his sister doing? He jumped down from his tree and made his way after her.

Hearing his heavy steps, Hidimbi spoke urgently. "Here comes my brother now. O hero, doubtlessly you are brave and powerful, but I have many times seen the superiority of Rakshasas over men. Quickly—wake your family and I shall take you all away."

Bhima laughed derisively. "O fair one, you should not fear. Do not consider me weak, like an ordinary human being. I possess great power. Watch now as I crush the life out of this cannibal."

Suddenly Hidimba burst into the clearing where they stood. As tall as two men, with pointed ears and bright red hair, he was a frightful sight. Seeing his sister standing before Bhima in her voluptuous form, he let out an angry roar. His eyes opened wide in fury. "O foolish woman, how dare you disobey me? Do you not fear my anger? It seems you are ready to sacrifice all Rakshasa honor for the sake of lust! I shall kill you along with these humans, for whom you wish to do me a great injury."

The demon rushed with outstretched arms at his sister. Bhima at once stepped in front of her and exclaimed, "Stop!" Smiling scornfully, he said, "O wretch, why are you disturbing my peacefully sleeping brothers? Why also do you attack this innocent woman? Sent here by you, she has been overpowered by desire upon seeing me. For this, you should blame the god of love, not her."

The demon halted in his tracks and stared in disbelief at Bhima. How could any mere human be so rash as to stand before him?

Bhima went on, keeping his voice down so as not to disturb his mother and brothers. "Fight with me, O wicked-minded one. I will not stand by and watch you attack a woman. Step into the woods with me and I will send you to the land of the dead, pounding your head to pieces. Birds of prey will then gleefully feast upon your flesh. By slaying you, I shall render this forest safe for men to enter."

Hidimba laughed, throwing back his hideous-looking head. "O human, these are bold and boastful words. Make them good and then you may vaunt your power. You think yourself strong, but today you shall learn the truth. These others may sleep here at their pleasure till you are killed, and after drinking your blood, I shall kill them, followed by my sinful sister."

Hidimba ran straight at Bhima, who seized hold of his arms. He violently dragged the struggling Rakshasa well away from his sleeping family. Infuriated, the demon broke free and clasped Bhima in his massive arms. Sending forth a terrible yell, he squeezed the Pandava with all his power, but Bhima dragged him still further away. Expanding his great chest, he broke the demon's grip, and a fierce fight ensued. The two combatants aimed terrific blows at each other. With full force, they threw each other about. Trees were smashed and broken down as they cannoned into them.

The roars of the fighters woke the other Pandavas and their mother, who sat up and looked around in surprise. Seeing the beautiful Hidimbi standing nearby, they were astonished. Kunti asked, "Who and whose are you, O most fair maiden? Are you an Apsara or some other celestial girl? Tell me why you are here."

Hidimbi replied, "I live here with my brother in this great forest. He is called Hidimba, chief of all the Rakshasas in this region. I came here at his behest, seeking to kill you. However, upon seeing your golden-hued son, I have been brought under Cupid's control. Hence, I cannot suppress my passion."

The demoness pointed to where the fight was raging. "Your mighty son dragged my brother off to a distance. See them now, the roaring rivals, man and Rakshasa engaged in a frightful combat."

Yudhishthira and his brothers jumped up. They saw Bhima grappling with the demon, sending up a cloud of dust that hung suspended in the rays of the moon. Arjuna immediately ran over and smilingly said to Bhima, "Dear brother, O mighty armed hero, fear not. We are now here. We did not realize that you were becoming tired in this fight. Stand off now, and I shall soon finish this demon."

Jibed in this way, Bhima blazed up in anger. "O Arjuna, you are not needed here," he growled. "Having come into my clutches, this wretch will not escape with his life."

"Then act quickly," Arjuna urged. "Dawn is approaching and the demons gain strength from the twilight."

Bhima gazed at Hidimba, his eyes red with rage. The Rakshasa charged him and Bhima ducked down, tripping him. As the demon toppled over, Bhima seized him and lifted him over his head. He spun him around, saying, "Having lived a vain and sinful life, feeding on other's flesh, you deserve an unholy death. Smashing you and reducing you to nothing, I shall today free this forest of its most thorny bush."

Whirling him furiously around, Bhima dashed the Rakshasa to the ground. All of Hidimba's limbs were shattered and he let out a terrible howl. Bhima then broke his back in two.

Seeing the demon slain, Bhima's brothers joyfully surrounded him, embracing and congratulating him. Arjuna said, "O hero, I never doubted your ability to kill this one. Let us now depart. I believe there is a town near here."

The sun was rising and paths through the forest were visible. Deciding to head south, the brothers set off, with Kunti in their midst. As they walked away, Hidimbi began to follow them. Bhima turned round to her and said threateningly, "Rakshasas avenge themselves on their enemies by alluring deceptions. O Hidimbi, you may go the way your brother has gone."

Bhima wanted only to scare her away, but Yudhishthira reprimanded him. "O best of men, you should never kill a woman. Virtue should be preserved even at the cost of your body. Anyway, what can this woman do? You have slain her far more powerful brother. She is no threat to us."

Hidimbi stood with her head down. She folded her palms and looked up at Kunti. "O most noble lady, surely you know the pain of a love-stricken woman. I am feeling that pain now for your son Bhima. I have abandoned everything for his sake—my family, friends, and even my dharma. If this hero forsakes me, I will not be able to live. Please do not doubt it."

Hidimbi glanced at Bhima, who caught her eye and looked away quickly. She went on addressing Kunti, begging that she be permitted to marry the Pandava. She asked that she be allowed take Bhima with her to celestial regions where they could enjoy together. "O illustrious lady, pray have compassion on me, considering me your most obedient servant. After we have spent some time together, I will bring Bhima back to you."

Hidimbi argued that her marriage to Bhima would be quite in accordance with virtue, especially as it would save her life. "Protecting one's life by whatever means possible is always considered a prime virtue. Indeed, virtue itself protects life. He who keeps his virtue, even amid great distress, is the foremost of virtuous men."

Hidimbi looked hopefully at Kunti and Yudhishthira. Pleased to hear Hidimbi speaking about virtue and seeing that neither Kunti nor Bhima were objecting to her suggestion, Yudhishthira replied, "O lady of slender waist, you have spoken well. It must be as you say. Marry Bhima then, and take him with you to heavenly regions. But he must be returned each night."

Hidimbi's face blossomed into a great smile. She looked over at Bhima, who said, "I agree to this union, O blessed lady, on one condition only. As soon as a son is born to you, I shall leave you."

Hidimbi agreed, and they were married then and there in the forest, according to the Gandharva rites, by an exchange of garlands. Hidimbi took all of the brothers and Kunti to a delightful place high in the Himalayas. They constructed a wooden hut there and dwelt peacefully, living on the celestial fruits that grew all around them. By day Hidimbi went away with Bhima, showing him numerous heavenly regions. They sported together on the soft banks of crystal streams and by the sides of lotus-filled lakes. In meadows covered with many-colored flowers and in fragrant woods frequented by the denizens of heaven, they walked together, hand in hand. Hidimbi poured forth the sweetest song, dressing herself like a goddess. She gave constant delight to Bhima, who felt the days pass as if they were moments.

After some months, Hidimbi became pregnant. In the way of celestial women, she very soon gave birth to a son, who immediately grew into a youth. He stood before his parents, glowing like a god. His head was completely bald, his features fierce, and he had a powerful physique like his father. He bowed before his mother and father, and they went with him to see the other Pandavas. The boy, who was named Ghatotkacha, spent some time with the Pandavas, serving them in every way. The brothers soon became affectionate toward him.

Finally Yudhishthira said, "We have tarried long in this region. Now, as agreed, it is time for Bhima to leave Hidimbi. We must continue on our way."

Kunti and her sons said their fond farewells to Hidimbi and Ghatotkacha. Before leaving, Bhima's son said, "The very moment you think of me, I shall come before you. Always consider me your servant."

Hidimbi embraced Bhima tearfully. "Shall we meet again?" she asked.

Bhima said they would be reunited when he and his brothers were free from danger and settled in their own kingdom. They then parted, and the Pandavas continued making their way south. With their beards and matted hair, they resembled five ascetics. Although they passed through many towns and forest ashrams, no one recognized them. They spent much time hearing Vedic knowledge from the forest sages.

One day while they were seated in an ashram, Vyasadeva came to see them. Appearing there by his mystic power, the sage accepted their obeisances and blessed them. When they were seated before him, he said, "O best of the Bharata race, I have known for some time of your situation. You are being unjustly treated by the Kurus. I have therefore come here desiring to help you. Do not lament for your misfortune. It will all be for your ultimate good. Everything is under the Lord's supreme control."

Vyasadeva advised them to enter a nearby town called Ekachakra. He told them to remain there for some time, and in due course he would advise them further. The *rishi* consoled Kunti, "O daughter, take heart. Your son Yudhishthira will become the lord of this earth, virtuously ruling over all other kings. Assisted by his brothers, he will perform great sacrifices and distribute much charity to the brahmins."

After showing them the way to Ekachakra, Vyasadeva left. The brothers then found accommodation in a brahmin's house, where they began to live peacefully, undetected by anyone.

Six

THE FIRE-BORN PRINCESS

IN HASTINAPURA, THE messengers from Varanavata brought news of the Pandavas' supposed deaths. Dhritarashtra wailed in sorrow. Genuinely upset, his grief was compounded by feelings of guilt. He held his head and cried, "Today my illustrious brother Pandu, who had lived on through his sons, has died. This is a black day for the Kurus."

The king instructed that a funeral ceremony be performed. Thousands of grieving citizens entered the Ganges to make offerings to the departed souls. They lamented terribly, calling out the names of Kunti and her sons. Bhishma was particularly afflicted and he went to his rooms to grieve alone. Duryodhana and his brothers made a show of sorrow, but inwardly they rejoiced. Vidura also did not grieve much, but he knew he could not reveal the truth to anyone. Even Bhishma, who was favorable to the Pandavas, would be likely to inform the king, and then there would be much tension and disturbance in Hastinapura. It would be best to wait till the Lord revealed a more opportune moment.

The Pandavas lived for some time in Ekachakra. Presenting themselves as brahmins, they gleaned their livelihood by begging. By day they would go around the village collecting alms. They would return in the evening and Kunti would prepare their meal, dividing the food in half—one portion for Bhima and the other for everyone else.

While the Pandavas lived in Ekachakra, a traveling brahmin stayed for a night in the same house. He told them stories he had heard on his travels. They learned that there would soon be a *swayamvara* ceremony in King Drupada's capital, in which his daughter would choose a husband. They listened as the brahmin described Drupada's daughter, Draupadi. "This noble lady is incomparably beautiful. She was not born of any mortal woman. All the kings of the world will attend her *swayamvara*."

Fascinated, the Pandavas asked the brahmin to tell them more about Draupadi. "This story really begins with Drona's birth," the brahmin replied.

"It is rooted in the relationship between that great *acharya* and the mighty King Drupada."

The brahmin told them the history of Drona and Drupada's disagreement, which the Pandavas knew so well. They sat silently as he described how they had overpowered Drupada. "After this the king went away, seething with indignation. He wanted revenge on Drona. Realizing that only another powerful brahmin would be able to match Drona's strength, he entered the forest to search one out.

"He came across two brahmin brothers named Yaja and Upayaja. When he asked them if they could arrange for him to get a son who could kill Drona, they agreed to perform a sacrifice on his behalf. The king and his wife sat in the sacrifice, watching as the two brahmins made offerings into a great fire. Then, before their astonished eyes, a youth rose out of the fire. Dressed in golden armor, that effulgent warrior immediately mounted a chariot and rode about, roaring and wielding a bow. A voice was heard from the heavens announcing that he was born for Drona's destruction. He was named Dhrishtadyumna.

"After this, a girl also rose from the fire. With the complexion of a blue lotus, she was as beautiful as the Goddess of Fortune. Her eyes were dark and her hair hung down in long black ringlets. She emitted a sweet fragrance, her waist was thin, her hips were broad, and her limbs were exquisitely formed. A voice was again heard from the heavens: 'This divine beauty will be the best of all women. Accomplishing the gods' purpose, she will cause the destruction of countless warriors.'"

The brahmin told them that Drona, although aware that the boy had been born for his death, accepted him into his school and taught him the science of arms.

When the brahmin had finished speaking, the Pandavas sat silent. Their minds were bewildered. Hearing that their beloved guru Drona was to be killed, and also hearing the description of the celestially beautiful Draupadi, they felt stunned and unable to speak.

That evening, after they retired for the night, Kunti spoke to her sons. Seeing their anxious state, she said, "We have lived here long enough. I feel we should now leave and make our way to Drupada's kingdom, Panchala."

Yudhishthira agreed. He and his brothers dearly wanted to attend Draupadi's *swayamvara*. But he remembered Vyasadeva's instruction. "The *rishi* asked us to wait here for his return," he said to his mother.

But even as he was mentioning Vyasadeva's name, the sage suddenly appeared before them. They immediately bowed at his feet and he said, "I understood your minds, and thus have I come here to see you. You should certainly go to Panchala for Draupadi's *swayamvara*."

The sage said that Arjuna should enter the contest to win Draupadi's hand. "The princess is a worthy bride. Indeed, she is destined to marry you brothers."

Yudhishthira said, "O all-knowing *rishi*, we shall go at once to Panchala."

Vyasadeva then took his leave from Kunti and the brothers, and the next day they set off for Drupada's city, Kampilya, the capital of Panchala. Walking on the roads by day and night, they traveled in a northerly direction, and after three days' journey they reached the Ganges. It was night and they walked by the light of a torch held by Arjuna. As they approached the river, they were suddenly accosted by someone who shouted at them from out of the darkness.

"Halt! You men should not go any further. Know that I am Angaraparna, a Gandharva chief who is now bathing in this river. Night is the allotted time for celestials like us to use the river; men should bathe only during the day. If you come any closer you will be in grave danger. I am powerful and will not tolerate any abuse."

Arjuna held up his torch and peered ahead. He saw the Gandharva before him, seated on a shining chariot. Stepping forward, he laughed. "O fool, how can the Ganges be barred to anyone at any time? This is not in accordance with religious principles. Only one bereft of power would heed your warning. As for us, we care nothing for your words."

Angaraparna became furious. He immediately drew back his bow and released a succession of arrows that hissed like poisonous snakes. Arjuna was unperturbed. He fended off some of the arrows with the shield in his hand and struck down others with his torch. Laughing again, he called out, "O Gandharva, do not try to frighten those who are skilled in weaponry. You are wasting your time. Because you are a celestial, I shall fight you with celestial weapons. Stand now to receive the Agneyastra, the fire-god's missile."

Holding up his torch, Arjuna recited the mantras to invoke the celestial weapon. He then hurled the torch at Angaraparna. Charged with mystic power, it exploded against his chariot and reduced it to ashes. Stunned, the Gandharva fell headlong to the ground. Arjuna seized him by the hair, which was adorned with flower garlands, and dragged him over to Yudhishthira.

Angaraparna's shocked wife then ran forward with folded palms and begged Arjuna to release him. Yudhishthira smiled at Arjuna and said, "O hero, who would kill an enemy who is vanquished in battle, deprived of his fame, defenseless and, moreover, protected by a woman? Let him go."

Arjuna released Angaraparna, and his wife ran over and sprinkled water on his face. He came round and got to his feet, addressing Arjuna in a subdued voice. "Henceforth I shall give up my pride, for I have been humbled by a man. Still, I consider it my good fortune that I have met you heroes, who have at your command the gods' weapons. You have spared my life and I desire to give you something in return."

Angaraparna offered Arjuna the ability to see anything within the world, along with its essential nature. He also offered him the power to wield illusions in battle. "As well as this, I will give you celestial horses that can travel at the speed of the mind. Be pleased to take these gifts, O sinless one."

Arjuna held up his hands. "I cannot accept anything in exchange for your life. The Vedas ordain that one in distress should never be slain. Furthermore, my brother ordered me to release you. It was therefore my duty."

Arjuna asked why the Gandharva had seen fit to challenge them. "We are all learned in the Vedas, virtuous, and powerful wielders of weapons. What was our fault?"

Angaraparna replied that he had felt unable to tolerate their transgression. "No one possessed of power should brook any insult in front of his wife. Also, you are not accompanied by any priest, nor do you carry sacred fire; therefore did I censure you."

The Gandharva went on to explain that he had heard much about the Kuru race from the *rishi* Narada. He also personally knew all of the gods who had fathered the Pandavas. "I know that you men are all virtuous heroes. By the power of that virtue, you were able to overcome me, a celestial. However, it is essential that you find a qualified brahmin to be your guide. Kings without brahmins are soon overpowered, while those with brahmins as their advisors can conquer the whole earth and finally attain heaven."

Arjuna asked him if he could give them any advice about how to find a priest. Angaraparna replied, "Go north to the hermitage known as Utkacha. There you will find an effulgent *rishi* called Dhaumya. If you desire, you can accept him as your guide."

Thanking the Gandharva for his advice, the Pandavas took their leave from him and began following the path to the north. Before long they reached Utkacha. Going before Dhaumya, they bowed at his feet. The *rishi* received them with offerings of water and wild fruits. He was impressed with

their humility and could see that, like himself, they were Vaishnavas, worshippers of Vishnu. Thus, when they requested him to become their priest,
he readily agreed.

The brothers were overjoyed. With Dhaumya as their guide, they felt
their kingdom was already recovered, their enemies defeated, and the
Panchala princess won. For his part, Dhaumya, looking upon the five
heroes, felt that by virtue of their own accomplishments they would soon be
the lords of the earth.

*   *   *

The morning after they met, the Pandavas and Dhaumya set off for
Kampilya. On their way they saw crowds of brahmins who were also going
to the *swayamvara*. Traveling with them, the brothers appeared themselves
like five young ascetics. With their matted hair and long beards, no one
could recognize them amidst the throngs of brahmins walking on the road.
After a few days journey they reached a village on the outskirts of Kampilya.
There they found accommodation in a potter's house, where they began to
live as they had in Ekachakra, begging for alms.

The brothers heard from the villagers about the *swayamvara*. King
Drupada had set a stiff test for winning his daughter. A special bow had been
made, huge and fashioned of the strongest oak. Anyone hoping to win
Draupadi's hand would have to string that bow, then use it to hit a difficult
target. A small wooden bird had been placed at the top of a long pole.
Beneath it a metal plate rotated with a single hole punched in it. The successful archer would have to shoot his arrow through the hole at the exact
moment it passed over the target.

Hearing this, Arjuna was enlivened. He prayed he would get the
chance to try his hand at the test. If he could win Draupadi and thereby
secure Drupada's alliance, it would greatly strengthen Yudhishthira's position. He waited eagerly for the day of the ceremony.

In Kampilya, many kings and princes were constantly arriving from
various countries. Drupada had made lavish preparations. A vast stadium
had been erected, with one hundred broad gates set in its tall white walls.
On the day of the ceremony a stream of colorfully dressed people poured
through those gates and gradually filled the sloping terraces, making a sound
like the ocean. Jewel-encrusted seats stood on golden platforms in the front
rows, and one by one the visiting monarchs took their places. Kettledrums
resounded and thousands of conches were blown. The air was filled with fragrant incense, and within the arena, many brahmins loudly chanted Vedic

hymns. Crowds of ascetic brahmins entered the stadium, seeming to illuminate all sides with their bodily radiance.

Leaving their mother in the potter's hut, the Pandavas and Dhaumya entered the arena along with the brahmins. Unnoticed by anyone, they sat amid the ascetics and looked around the arena. At the head of all the kings sat Duryodhana, surrounded by his brothers, all of them dressed in brilliant gold armor and ornaments. Seeing the prince with his head thrown back, looking arrogantly around him, Bhima's anger rose. He felt like rushing forward and grabbing Duryodhana by the neck, but he kept himself in check. They could not risk discovery yet.

On one side of the arena sat Drupada with his sons and ministers. Before the ceremony began, he distributed heaps of gold and jewels to the brahmins, wanting to invoke all auspiciousness for his daughter. The Pandavas kept their places as the brahmins all around them went up to receive the charity. When all of them had received sufficient wealth, Drupada's son Dhrishtadyumna stood up to announce the start of the *swayamvara*. His powerful voice rang out like a drum.

"The princess Draupadi will now choose her husband. Anyone desiring her hand must pass the following test: Here is the bow and there is the target; any man of noble birth who can string this bow and, with it, shoot down the target will win Draupadi's hand. I say this truly."

Dhrishtadyumna pointed to the awesome bow on a table next to the target. As he took his seat again, Draupadi came into the arena. A gasp went up from the crowd as they viewed her astonishing beauty. Her features were faultless, her thin-waisted body perfectly formed, and she seemed to glow like the full moon. All eyes followed her as she slowly made her way to her place on the royal platform.

As the transcendentally beautiful princess passed before them, the kings and princes leapt up from their seats. They glared at one another and made loud declarations. "Draupadi shall be mine!" "Go home, all of you— I shall win this princess!" "Consider her already won by me!" Afflicted with desire, they felt envious of even their own friends.

As they boasted and vaunted their power, the monarchs made a great noise, and Dhrishtadyumna again stood to silence them. When everyone was settled once more, they saw above the arena numerous gods and other celestials arriving to witness the proceedings. Those divine beings stayed in the sky, seated upon their golden conveyances, and they dropped showers of celestial flowers on the arena.

Among the many kings sat Krishna and his brother, Balarama. Glancing around the crowd, he spotted the Pandavas. He smiled and turned toward Balarama, speaking to him in a whisper. "Dear brother, just look over there. Do you see Yudhishthira and his brothers?"

Balarama looked carefully at the five men sitting together, then turned with a smile to Krishna. They were joyful to see the Pandavas safe and well.

Drupada then indicated that the test should begin. He looked around at the kings. None of them looked like worthy husbands for Draupadi. Only Krishna and the other monarchs from Mathura seemed qualified, but they were not participating in the test. There was only one person that Drupada wanted to have as his son-in-law—Arjuna. Hearing rumors that the Pandavas had survived the fire in Varanavata, the king had devised a test that he felt sure only Arjuna could pass. He had even been told by the brahmins at Draupadi's birth that she would become Arjuna's bride. Would those words prove false? Where was Arjuna? The king looked around anxiously.

Having at last seen Draupadi, the Pandavas were struck by Cupid's arrows. They gazed at her with wide-open eyes. Surely, she would not be won by Duryodhana or any of his cronies. How could those wretches deserve such a prize? Arjuna looked intently at the massive bow meant for the test. He doubted that any of the Kauravas would succeed. No doubt he would soon get his chance to try for the princess.

Dhrishtadyumna began to call out the monarchs' names and they stepped up to the bow. But when they tried to string it, they were utterly confounded. Some could hardly lift it. Of those who could, it took their full strength to bend the great bow even slightly. Straining and struggling to the limit of their power, they were tossed to the ground and lay there groaning. One by one the kings and princes were humiliated, and they returned slowly to their seats, their hope of winning Draupadi shattered.

After more than twenty monarchs had tried and failed, Karna rose up and marched forward. A gasp of admiration went up as he lifted and strung the bow in a matter of moments. He placed an arrow on the string and took aim. Seeing him resolved to shoot the target, Yudhishthira and his brothers felt that it had already been struck down. Suddenly, Draupadi stood up and called out, "I will not wed a charioteer's son."

Karna turned angrily toward her. There was nothing he could say. The princess had exercised her prerogative, and Dhrishtadyumna had already stated that the test was meant for those of noble birth. Throwing the bow aside, he glanced up at the sun, masking his vexation with a crude laugh. The crowd was silent as he stormed back to his seat.

Duryodhana then stood up. He went over to the table, where the bow had been replaced by Drupada's servants. Like Karna, he deftly strung it and placed a golden-shafted arrow on the string. The crowd held its breath as he took careful aim. Draupadi was seized with apprehension. What would she do if Duryodhana succeeded? How could she marry that obviously arrogant prince? She glanced around at the other monarchs. Seeing Krishna, she prayed to him that Duryodhana might fail. Krishna watched with a smile as Duryodhana stood motionless, aiming the fully stretched bow at the target. There was a great twang as he released the arrow. It shot upwards and passed cleanly through the hole but missed the target by a hair's breadth.

The prince angrily threw the bow down. Seeing even the great prince of Hastinapura fail, everyone else remained seated. No one felt able to pass this test. The princes who had come from Mathura with Krishna had heard from him that Draupadi was destined to marry Arjuna, so they did not make any attempt. King Drupada felt increasingly anxious. Would Arjuna come? Was he even still alive?

Krishna and Balarama looked over at the brahmins' compound. If Arjuna were to attempt the test, it would have to be now. Realizing this, the Pandava turned toward Dhaumya, who nodded in assent. Arjuna then stood up and strode out into the arena. Seeing him make straight for the bow, the brahmins cheered and waved their shawls. Some were dismayed, fearing that this brash young brahmin would bring ridicule on their order. "How will he ever succeed when mighty men like Duryodhana have failed?" they exclaimed.

But others were confident. "Just see his stride, like a powerful lion. Look at those broad shoulders. Why should he not succeed? A brahmin's power is always greater than a warrior's."

Going before the royal platform, Arjuna bowed to Drupada and asked, "Is it permissible for brahmins to try this test?"

King Drupada looked at him curiously. "Brahmins are always superior to the royal order," he replied. "Indeed, we depend upon their power for our protection, even as the gods depend upon Vishnu. You may try the test."

Arjuna turned and walked over to the bow. He folded his palms and walked around it in respect, then lifted the bow and weighed it in his hand. In one skillful movement, he bent and strung it, swiftly placing an arrow on the string. The whole stadium was absolutely silent as the unusual brahmin stood stock still, the stretched bow held firmly in his powerful hands. Suddenly, he released the golden shaft and it shot upward, piercing the target right through its middle. With a great clatter it fell to the ground.

Seeing this, the stadium was in uproar. Brahmins danced around in glee, throwing their upper garments into the arena. The crowd roared in joy, and thousands of musical instruments sounded. From the sky, the celestials rained down flowers and beat their drums. Draupadi went forward with the nuptial garland in her hands. She placed it over Arjuna's head and caught his eye, then looked down shyly. He was now her husband and the formal ceremony would soon follow.

Drupada looked closely at Arjuna. There was no shame in his daughter marrying a brahmin. But who was he?

With their pride smashed by a brahmin, the monarchs were horrified. They stood up and looked at each other in dismay. "How has Drupada allowed this?" they exclaimed. "Does he have no respect for the royal order? By bestowing his daughter on a brahmin, he has simply insulted us. How can it be tolerated?"

Seeing the kings rising up in anger, Yudhishthira began making his way out of the stadium, followed by his brothers and Draupadi. The kings were shouting and arguing among themselves. Some suggested they attack Arjuna, but others declined, saying that a brahmin should never be assaulted. Drupada was the real culprit, they argued. On account of his disrespect for them, he deserved to be killed.

With weapons at the ready, the kings advanced menacingly toward Drupada. Yudhishthira saw this and he said to Bhima and Arjuna, "Drupada is now our father and worthy of our protection. You two should check these belligerent kings, even as the shore checks the ocean."

The two princes ran back into the arena. Arjuna took up the bow with which he had struck the target and called out a challenge to the kings. By his side stood Bhima, who had pulled down a tree and was brandishing it like a colossal club. The kings looked at them in surprise. What kind of brahmins were these?

Krishna had remained unmoved as the kings rose up against Drupada. Seeing the two Pandavas in the arena, he said to Balarama, "These two are undoubtedly Bhima and Arjuna. Only Bhima could have uprooted that tree, and who but Arjuna could have passed Drupada's test?"

Krishna indicated the other Pandavas waiting by the gate. "That one there, a full four cubits tall, with eyes like lotus petals, a fair complexion, and prominent features, who bears himself with all humility—that is Yudhishthira. By his side are the handsome sons of the Ashvinis, Nakula and Sahadeva. As sure as I am Vasudeva's son, this is the truth."

Balarama agreed, "How wonderful that our cousins have survived the fire, along with our aunt Kunti."

The kings had turned to face Bhima and Arjuna. "Although brahmins should not be attacked, if they are aggressors there is no sin in fighting them," some of them declared, raising their weapons.

Drupada quickly had his soldiers provide Arjuna with a number of long-shafted arrows. Karna, particularly angered that he had been refused the opportunity to try the test, stepped forward and shouted, "O brahmin, stand ready to receive my shafts." He sent a cluster of swift arrows at Arjuna, who immediately countered all of them with his own. A fierce exchange took place between the two warriors. Their arrows collided in mid-air and fell to the ground, shattered. Penetrating Karna's guard, Arjuna stunned him with a cluster of forceful arrows that struck his limbs all over. Karna was astonished to witness Arjuna's speed and power. He stepped up his own attack, letting go many hundreds of silver-winged shafts that filled the air like a flock of birds. He invoked celestial weapons that caused a vast number of arrows to fly from his bow. Arjuna expertly resisted the attack, invoking other weapons to check Karna's. He stood unharmed, laughing at his opponent.

As the duel went on, King Shalya from Madras rushed at Bhima. The powerful monarch caught hold of Bhima's tree and hurled it aside. The two men began grappling in furious hand-to-hand combat, resembling a pair of angry male elephants contending for a female. They wrestled for some time, throwing each other about and shaking the earth as they stomped around the arena. With his superior strength, Bhima soon gained the advantage. He lifted Shalya above his head and slammed him to the ground, leaving him dazed. The prince did not use his full power on the king, knowing him to be Madri's brother.

All the other kings watched in amazement as the two so-called brahmins exhibited the strength and skill of heroic warriors. Realizing that he could not gain the upper hand, Karna lowered his bow and called out to Arjuna, "O brahmin, I am highly pleased by your prowess. It is without compare. Who are you? Very few warriors could resist my attack. I think only my guru, Parasurama, or Indra, or the infallible Vishnu are capable—or perhaps Arjuna, the son of Kunti. Are you by chance any of these?"

Arjuna smiled tightly. "Know me to be a simple brahmin who has become expert in arms by his guru's grace. I am ready to vanquish you in battle. Attack me if you dare."

Karna found it hard to accept that this was an ordinary brahmin. But he knew that a brahmin's power was always to be respected. It would be better to desist from battle. Draupadi was already won, and there was nothing left to gain from fighting. Bowing slightly to Arjuna, he turned and walked away.

Duryodhana had looked on in amazement as both Karna and Shalya had been matched in prowess by the two brahmins. Turning to the other kings, he said, "These two are no ordinary men. They must surely be either great rishis or heroes from some mighty line of kings. Let us first establish their lineage, and then the fight may continue."

Krishna then stepped forward and spoke. "O rulers of the earth, I see no point in any further conflict here. Draupadi has been fairly won in a wonderful fashion by this brahmin. Let us not blight this auspicious occasion by bloodshed—and especially by assaulting brahmins."

Arguing persuasively, Krishna managed to calm down all the kings. One by one they began to put down their weapons and make their way out of the arena. Taking their opportunity, Arjuna and Bhima rejoined Yudhishthira at the gate. Along with Draupadi, they quickly went back to the potter's hut.

Seven

A KINGDOM DIVIDED

As KUNTI WAITED alone at the hut for her sons to return, she felt anxious. What if they had been discovered? Duryodhana and his brothers would be at the *swayamvara*. If they saw the Pandavas alive, they would certainly try to have them killed. Kunti remembered Vyasadeva's predictions. Surely that illustrious sage could not have been wrong. But the course of destiny was always difficult to fathom. The Supreme Lord was the ultimate controller—and no one could know his plan.

Kunti busied herself in preparing her sons' evening meal. As she bustled about the hut, she suddenly heard Arjuna's voice greeting her. "Dear mother, we are back. Come and see the wonderful alms we have received today."

Feeling a surge of relief, Kunti called back, "I am so glad you are safe. Share the alms equally among you."

Arjuna then entered the hut with Yudhishthira. Draupadi came between them, and when Kunti saw her, she was shocked. "Oh! What have I said?" The Kuru queen felt her religious principles threatened. She valued truth above everything. Even in jest she would not speak a falsehood. But she had said that all her sons should share Draupadi. How was it possible? No woman could have five husbands. She looked anxiously at Yudhishthira.

"Do not worry mother," Yudhishthira replied. "You shall doubtlessly be saved from sin."

Yudhishthira turned to Arjuna. "You have won this maiden, and thus, you should now take her hand in sacred marriage."

Arjuna looked at his brother in horror. "Please do not cast me onto the path of wicked men. What virtuous man would accept a maiden's hand in the presence of his unmarried elder brother? You should be the one to marry her, not me. After that Bhima should marry, and only then myself, and finally the twins."

The other Pandavas had entered the hut and, hearing Arjuna's words, they all glanced at Draupadi, who smiled and returned their looks. All five brothers felt their hearts leap, and their minds became bewildered. The Panchala princess glowed with beauty, and she filled the hut with her natural bodily fragrance. The brothers could hardly take their eyes away from her.

Seeing the condition of his brothers, Yudhishthira feared that Draupadi would cause disunion among them. After reflecting for some moments, he then said, "This chaste girl shall become the wife of us all. This is our mother's order and, in my view, it is what Vyasadeva meant when he told us of her destiny."

The brothers had wondered about the sage's words, but now they understood. All of them felt great joy. Draupadi was a prize beyond compare.

At that moment there was a knock on the door, and Krishna entered. Seeing Yudhishthira seated on the floor and surrounded by his brothers, like Indra amid the chief gods, he went over and touched his feet. "I am your cousin Krishna. Here, too, is my brother, Balarama."

Krishna and Balarama offered their respects to Kunti by bowing before her and touching her feet. Yudhishthira was surprised to see them. "How did you find us?" he asked.

Krishna smiled. "Fire is easily detected, even when covered. Who other than yourselves could have performed such feats in the *swayamvara*? By good fortune you have escaped the fire in Varanavata, and by good fortune has Duryodhana's evil desire been thwarted. Be blessed. May you grow in prosperity like a fire in a cave that gradually spreads all around."

The brothers folded their palms and thanked Krishna, who then said he had better leave at once, before anyone noticed him. Along with Balarama, he went furtively out of the hut. Having seen their cousin from Mathura and heard his reassuring words, the brothers felt confident that they would soon recover their kingdom. Like their mother, they had faith in him as the all-powerful Supreme Person.

Not far from the hut, Dhrishtadyumna had observed Krishna and his brother come and go. Curious to know who had won his sister, the Panchala prince had followed the Pandavas from the stadium. He crept up to the hut and peered through the window. Inside he saw the five brothers and Kunti being served their meal by Draupadi. He watched as she gave equal portions to four of the men and a huge portion—equal to all the others put together—to the one who had thrown down Shalya. As they ate, the brothers began to discuss arms and warfare. Dhrishtadyumna listened as they spoke in the language of warriors, laughing together as they described the fight at the *swayamvara* and how they had routed the monarchs.

The Pandavas then lay down to rest. Draupadi, smiling with great happiness, lay humbly at their feet, and Kunti lay at their heads. Dhrishtadyumna had seen and heard enough. These men were clearly not brahmins. They were certainly great warriors, probably royalty in disguise. Were they the Pandavas? The prince slipped away and went quickly to the palace to inform his father of everything he had seen.

*   *   *

Drupada sat anxiously in his palace. It had been some hours since his son had gone after the brahmins. Where had they taken his daughter? Why had they not stayed in the city? There still had not been a proper marriage ceremony. The king bit his lips and gazed out from his balcony. Soon, to his relief, he saw Dhrishtadyumna hastily approaching. He ran down to greet the prince, immediately quizzing him about Draupadi. "Where is my beloved daughter now? Who was it who won her? Was it indeed a high born brahmin—or perhaps a great warrior from the royal order? Surely she has not been taken by a man of low birth. O son, my deepest desire is that she has been won by Arjuna. Alas, where now are the Pandavas? Do those heroic men still live?"

Dhrishtadyumna spoke with a smile. "O father, I saw those five men take Draupadi with them to a potter's house near the city. There, a lady as beautiful as a blue lotus, who seems to be their mother, greeted them. Draupadi was joyfully serving them and took her place at their feet."

As they spoke, Drupada and his son made their way into the palace. The prince described how he had heard the five brahmins speaking on martial subjects. "Their voices are deep like thunderclouds and they resemble five effulgent gods. I am sure they belong to the royal order. From the way in which the target was struck down, from the fact that they are five and traveling with their mother, and from their language and appearance, I believe that your desire has been fulfilled. They can only be Kunti and her sons."

Drupada looked up at a painting of Vishnu hanging from the palace wall. He prayed that his son's words were true. The king hardly dared believe that it had actually been Arjuna who had passed the test. But who else could have succeeded?

Drupada looked thoughtful. "O son, when morning comes, send our priest to the potter's hut. He should try to ascertain their identities.

Meanwhile, have a great feast prepared and ask the brahmins to calculate an auspicious day for the marriage."

Early the next day Drupada's priest went to the Pandavas. Yudhishthira received him with respect. After he had been comfortably seated in the hut, the priest, accepting the brothers as brahmins, said, "O worshipable ones, having seen his daughter won in the assembly by a wonderful feat of arms, Drupada's joy is boundless. But he is anxious to know who you are. The king believes you may be the Pandavas in disguise. Is this true? His ardent desire has always been that Arjuna would marry his daughter. Has it been fulfilled?"

Yudhishthira turned to his brothers. "Bring water and wash this man's feet. He is Drupada's holy priest and worthy of our respect in every way."

Bhima quickly followed Yudhishthira's instruction, who then said, "O brahmin, the king set a price for winning his daughter. That price has been paid, and he therefore has nothing to say about our lineage. All his questions have been answered by the striking down of the target with his bow."

Hearing Yudhishthira's firm rebuttal, the priest's eyes opened wide, but Yudhishthira reassured him. "Do not fear, gentle sir. The king's long-cherished desire will soon be fulfilled. Could any lowborn or unqualified man have passed his test? Go back and tell Drupada that he need not grieve."

As the priest was leaving, another messenger from the palace arrived to announce that a feast had been prepared in the city. "The king requests that you all attend. He said that a proper wedding ceremony can now be performed, if it so pleases you."

Yudhishthira smiled and nodded in assent. The messenger showed them to a fine golden chariot, and they climbed aboard with their mother and Draupadi. Soon they reached the great white palace in Kampilya and were led into a hall where a sumptuous feast awaited them. Headed by Yudhishthira, they walked into the great chamber, which was spread with costly rugs and decorated all around with fine paintings. Golden seats furnished with silk had been set out for the feast. Clearly comfortable with their opulent surroundings, the brothers took their places without any hesitation. Well-dressed servants immediately attended them and began to lay out gold and silver dishes containing fine food of every description.

After eating their fill, the Pandavas washed their hands and stood up. They saw that a number of tables had been set out along the walls. Some of them were spread with paraphernalia used by brahmins in sacrifices, and others held items used by traders and merchants, while on other tables there were weapons and armor.

The brothers immediately went over to the weapons and began examining them with interest. Seeing this, and noting their lion-like gaits as they strode across the chamber, as well as their powerfully built bodies, the king felt joyful. There was no doubt that these men were warriors of the royal order. Drupada walked up to them and, with a broad smile, asked, "Are we to know you as warriors or brahmins? Or are you perhaps celestials disguised as brahmins who have come to win my daughter's hand? Truth is the highest virtue, dear sirs. Please, therefore, settle my doubts."

Yudhishthira looked the king in the eye. "O Panchala monarch, be of good cheer. Your desire has been fulfilled. Know us to be kshatriyas, warriors of the royal order. We are the sons of the illustrious Pandu. I am Yudhishthira, this is Bhima, he who won your daughter by a stupendous feat of archery is Arjuna, and these two are the twins Nakula and Sahadeva. The lady who accompanied Draupadi to the inner chambers is our mother, Kunti. O king, like a lotus flower transplanted from one clear lake to another, your chaste daughter has gone from one royal house to another. You are now our revered father-in-law and our guru. I have told you everything."

Drupada was unable to reply for some moments. Tears flowed from his eyes and his limbs trembled with ecstatic emotion. Suppressing his joy with difficulty, he finally said, "What greater good fortune could there be? Hearing about the fire, we had feared the worst. Now we see that our prayers have been answered. Tell me, O hero, how you escaped from Varanavata."

Yudhishthira explained everything in detail. Drupada angrily censured Dhritarashtra. "How could the blind king permit all this?" He assured the Pandavas that they could live with him for as long as necessary. Looking at Arjuna, he then said, "Let this mighty hero take Draupadi's hand with all due rites. Today is an auspicious day."

Yudhishthira replied, "O king, as the eldest brother, I must marry first."

"Then you should take her hand, or let her be given to any of you whom you deem fit." The king felt that all five brothers were equal to the gods.

Yudhishthira shook his head. "Draupadi shall not marry any one of us. She shall be the wife of us all."

Drupada caught his breath. He took a step back. "Is this consistent with virtue? O descendant of Bharata, I have never heard of a woman having five husbands."

Yudhishthira spoke reassuringly. "I have considered this carefully, O king. My mind always turns from sin and I find no fault in Draupadi's becoming the joint wife of us all. Our mother, the sinless Kunti, also approves of this. You have nothing to fear. It is certainly in line with virtue."

Drupada was still doubtful. "Pray forgive me, but I would like further consultation on the matter. Let us speak with learned brahmins and decide what should be done. Tomorrow I will do whatever is proper."

As the discussions took place, Vyasadeva arrived at the palace. Seeing the effulgent *rishi*, everyone stood up and then bowed before him. Holding up his hand in blessing, he saluted everyone present and then took his seat.

Drupada immediately asked him about Yudhishthira's proposal, and the sage replied, "I have come here specifically to clear up this doubt. In my opinion, there will be no sin in your daughter accepting the five brothers as her husbands. I shall explain why."

Vyasadeva asked to speak alone with Drupada. They went into the king's chambers, and the sage began to narrate an ancient history. He described how the five Pandavas had all been powerful gods in their previous lives. They were destined to marry an incarnation of the goddess Laxmi, and Draupadi was that incarnation. She had also been blessed by the great god Shiva that she would have five husbands. "There cannot be any fault in the acts of such gods," concluded Vyasadeva. "Therefore, permit your daughter to marry the Pandavas."

Drupada felt his doubts dispelled by the all-knowing *rishi*. He cheerfully agreed and made arrangements for the ceremony at once. The palace was decorated with countless flower garlands and adorned everywhere with precious stones. Troops in spotless armor lined the courtyard as the sacred fire was kindled by Dhaumya. Holy mantras were melodiously chanted to the accompaniment of music, and the people cheered as the Pandavas accepted Draupadi's hand. On each of five consecutive days she married a different one of the brothers, amid much celebration throughout the city.

Krishna, hearing of the occasion, sent vast amounts of wealth as wedding gifts for the brothers. Gold, jewels, costly robes, soft blankets and skins, horses, elephants, chariots, and all sorts of other valuable items arrived from Mathura. Wishing to please Krishna, Yudhishthira accepted all those presents and sent a message of thanks to him.

Feeling great happiness, the five brothers and their wife and mother began to live comfortably in Kampilya.

*   *   *

News of the Pandavas' survival soon traveled around the world. Learning of the Kuru's treachery toward the brothers, many kings censured

Dhritarashtra and the other Kuru leaders. "Why do they not show any love to those virtuous heroes?" was the most common feeling.

Spies brought the news to Duryodhana even as he was still traveling back to Hastinapura. He struck his head in disbelief and horror. Understanding that his mortal enemies had not been killed but had rather become stronger by forming an alliance with Drupada, the prince seethed with frustration. Severely depressed, he cursed Purochana. Dushasana criticized Arjuna. "The Pandava cheated in the test by disguising himself. If he had revealed his identity, he never would have succeeded, for then we would have captured him. Surely destiny is supreme and man's endeavors useless."

Duryodhana felt uneasy. "We have cause for concern now, dear brother. Our cousins have mighty warriors on their side. We have already seen Drupada's power, and his son Dhrishtadyumna is predicted to be Drona's slayer. We need to speak to Father."

Entering the city, the Kauravas hastily made their way to the palace. Elsewhere in Hastinapura, feelings were different. Bhishma and Vidura rejoiced when they heard the news. Vidura went at once to Dhritarashtra and said, "O king, by good fortune the Kurus are prospering."

Thinking that Vidura was referring to Duryodhana's success in the *swayamvara*, the blind king exclaimed, "What good luck!" He immediately ordered, "Have ornaments made for the Panchala princess. Give her the finest jewels."

The king reached out for Vidura's hand. "O wise man, have Duryodhana and Draupadi come before me in great pomp. This is a joyous day."

Vidura laughed. "O king, you do not understand. The princess has been won by Arjuna. He and his brothers survived the fire and are now in Kampilya."

Dhritarashtra sat back on his throne. He clapped his hands. "How wonderful! Pandu's sons are dearer to me than they were even to him. This news fills me with joy."

Vidura looked intently at his blind brother. "O king, may this feeling stay with you for a hundred summers."

As they spoke, Duryodhana and Karna came into the room. Seeing Vidura, they smiled and bowed their heads slightly. They greeted the king but remained silent until Vidura left. When Duryodhana was sure he was out of earshot, he said to the king, "O Father, how are you seeing our enemies in such a favorable light? Why are you joyful to hear of their success? O best of men, their success is our great danger. We should act quickly to

ensure that we are not soon swallowed by them, with all our wealth and followers."

Dhritarashtra reached out for his son's hand. "My desires are the same
as yours, dear child. I did not want to reveal such feelings to Vidura. Tell me,
what do you see as being in our interests now?"

Duryodhana glanced at Karna with a smile. "Here is what I think we
should do. Let us immediately send some trusted and skillful brahmins to
Kampilya who can sow seeds of dissent among the brothers. They could
foment a quarrel between Kunti's and Madri's sons. Or let us offer vast
wealth to Drupada so that he will abandon the Pandavas and come to our
side. Again, I am sure we could incite Draupadi against her husbands—that
cannot be difficult with a woman who has five husbands. Perhaps we could
even tempt the Pandavas with beautiful women, causing Draupadi to spurn
them."

Duryodhana became enlivened as he went on suggesting his ideas. He
slashed at the air with an imaginary sword. "If we can somehow have Bhima
killed, our problems are solved. Without him, the Pandavas are nothing.
There must be some spies who could find a way to eliminate him."

Duryodhana laughed at the thought of Bhima's death. Concluding his
speech, he said, "If all else fails, we could just have them brought back here
and then use our immense resources and power to wipe them out. Who
could check us? What do you think, Karna?"

Duryodhana turned to his friend, who was shaking his head as he
replied. "O Duryodhana, I do not think your ideas are well considered. No
intrigue will work against the Pandavas, nor any machinations or treachery.
You have already tried this without success, even when they were young
boys without a friend or ally. Then they were living right here in the city.
Now they are grown up, powerful, living at a distance, and allied with the
mighty Drupada."

Karna went on dismissing Duryodhana's other proposals. In his view,
there was no chance of creating disunion among the five brothers—they
were like one person. As for Draupadi, she had accepted them when they
were in poverty and near exile; how would she reject them now? "She has
five powerful husbands—what more could she desire? And her father is virtuous and truthful. He will not forsake his sons'-in-law for the sake of
wealth."

Karna strode back and forth as he spoke. He stopped in front of
Dhritarashtra, his hands on his hips. "Here is my idea, O king. Gather up
your army and have it march on Kampilya now. With myself and
Duryodhana at their head, your vastly superior forces will soon crush the

Pandavas and Drupada. Forget any more trickery. Only prowess can succeed here. And it must be done soon, before Krishna can come with the mighty Yadava hosts to support his cousins. If that happens, we will face a highly difficult task. Let us display our strength now. After killing your enemies, you will rule this wide world as its undisputed emperor."

Dhritarashtra praised Karna. "O suta, you are a mighty hero, without doubt. Your speech is worthy of you alone. But before I can undertake any such move, I need to consult Bhishma and the other Kurus. We cannot possibly enter into open hostilities with powerful foes without their support."

Karna's head fell. He looked across at Duryodhana, who grimaced. How would Bhishma and Drona ever agree to attack the Pandavas? He tried to argue, but Dhritarashtra was firm. He would call an assembly to discuss what should be done.

When all the leading Kurus were seated in the hall, the blind king told them what Karna had suggested. Bhishma immediately got to his feet. Tears flowed from his eyes as he spoke. "Pandu's sons are our own. They are as dear to me as your sons, O king, and equally deserving of our protection. I can never agree to a fight with them. We should make a treaty with them and hand over half the kingdom. This is the only virtuous course. Why, if they have no claim to the kingdom, then how do the Kauravas? Indeed, their father Pandu had first claim to the throne; what then of his sons?"

Bhishma paused and looked around the assembly. No one could argue. They all remained silent as he continued, making it clear that there should be no delay in restoring the Pandavas to their rightful position. "Otherwise, sin and infamy will be our lot. Since I heard they had perished in the fire, I could not face any living being. Their survival saves our house from a terrible stain. By God's grace our reputation is saved. Let us not forsake that grace. Embrace the Pandavas. Do not confront them in battle. They are virtuous and united. Not even Indra, king of the gods, could deprive them of their paternal kingdom by force."

Drona then stood up and added, "A true friend when consulted will always speak the truth, whether or not it is agreeable. O king, I share Bhishma's opinion. Pandu's sons should be given their kingdom. This is eternal virtue."

Drona suggested that messengers be sent at once to Kampilya, bearing many valuable gifts for the Pandavas and Drupada. "Your own sons should go. They should bring the Pandavas back to Hastinapura. Receive them with love, O king, for they are just like your sons."

Hearing this, Karna's face darkened. He jumped to his feet, gesturing toward Bhishma and Drona. "These two are not to be trusted! O king, although maintained by you, they show no gratitude. Siding with the enemy, they speak as if they were your friends. You should certainly ignore their advice."

Drona laughed. "You are a wicked man, Karna. Your desire is simply to harm the Pandavas. My advice was meant only for the Kurus' welfare. If it is ignored, then in my view, the Kuru house will be destroyed."

Karna snorted and started to reply, but Vidura stood up and silenced him by raising his hand. The Kuru prime minister then said, "O king, you should pay heed to Bhishma and Drona. Even after careful consideration, I cannot think of a better friend than these two. They are equally disposed to both the Kauravas and Pandavas. They are wise and learned in all scriptures. Their words are meant only for your good. Those who disagree with them, seeking to excite your attachment for your sons, offer advice fraught with evil."

Vidura looked across at Duryodhana as he went on. "Who but one cursed by the gods would try to achieve through war that which can be had by peaceful means? The Pandavas can never be vanquished in battle. They are equal to the celestials and have on their side the all-powerful Krishna. Know for certain that wherever there is Krishna there will certainly be victory."

A murmur of approval came from the assembly as Vidura spoke. Only Duryodhana, Karna, and Dushasana disapproved, turning their heads away from Vidura and scowling.

Everyone looked at Dhritarashtra. The blind king remained silent for some moments, then said, "In my view, Bhishma, Drona, and Vidura have spoken the truth. There is no doubt that those great heroes, the Pandavas, are as much my sons as they are Pandu's. Their survival has removed my great grief. It is fortunate indeed that they and their mother are alive and that Purochana is dead. Fortunate, too, is their alliance with Drupada. O Vidura, go to Kampilya and bring them here. They are certainly entitled to the kingdom, no less than my own sons."

The king dismissed the assembly, as he had made his final decision. Duryodhana and his brothers stormed out of the hall, striding across the wide mosaic floor with their silk robes flowing behind them. As everyone dispersed, Vidura assisted the king as he descended from his throne and then led him toward his chambers.

*   *   *

The next morning Vidura left for Kampilya. He carried with him numerous jewels and all kinds of other riches. Accompanied by a division of soldiers, he traveled along the forest paths to Drupada's kingdom. Vidura had heard that Krishna was in Kampilya to visit the Pandavas. The Kuru minister felt excited at the prospect of seeing him. Many times he had heard from the rishis about Krishna's divine identity. He had no doubt that Krishna was God, come to the earth for his own inscrutable purposes.

After a three-day journey, he saw the tall buildings of Kampilya in the distance. With the sun reflecting from its golden temple domes, the city resembled a great cloud pierced by lightning bolts. When he reached the outskirts of the city, messengers ran to inform Drupada. The Panchala king personally came out with the Pandavas to greet him. They received Vidura with affection and respect, worshipping him with offerings of *arghya*, and the Kuru minister presented them with all the valuable gifts from Hastinapura.

When at last they were all seated in Drupada's chambers, Vidura said, "O king, Dhritarashtra sends you his warmest greetings. He and all his ministers were overjoyed to hear about our alliance with you. Every one of them, and indeed, all of Hastinapura's citizens, long to see Pandu's sons again. They also very much desire to see the virtuous Queen Kunti and the divine Draupadi. O sir, kindly permit them to come back with me."

Drupada smiled and nodded. "O greatly learned man, I too am pleased by our alliance. It is proper for the princes to now return to their ancestral kingdom, but it is not my position to order it. Here is Krishna, the greatest authority. If he permits it, and if Yudhishthira and his brothers so desire, then they may go."

Drupada was unsure what kind of reception awaited the Pandavas in Hastinapura. If it was anything like the treatment they had so far received, they had best keep away. But Krishna would surely know what was right. Drupada looked over at him.

Krishna turned toward Yudhishthira, gesturing for him to speak, and the Pandava said, "O king, we are now dependent on you. We shall gladly do whatever you command."

Krishna, who sat next to Drupada on a tall seat encrusted with gems, said, "I am of the opinion that they should go. O king, you are the eldest and most learned man here, tell us what you think."

Drupada agreed with Krishna. "There can be no better well-wisher of the Pandavas than you, O Krishna. Your decision will certainly be in their best interests. Let preparations be made for their departure in the morning."

The following day, after saying fond farewells to Drupada, the Pandavas mounted a great golden chariot with Draupadi and left the city, headed by Vidura and the soldiers from Hastinapura. The king and his wife followed them on foot, shedding tears to see their beloved daughter leaving. Krishna accompanied the princes on his own splendid chariot, and a contingent of powerful warriors marched behind him. The procession went out of Kampilya like a line of celestials leaving Indra's capital, Amaravati.

Citizens lined the streets as they entered Hastinapura. The people crowded around the Pandavas, joyfully greeting them. "Welcome back! Today King Pandu has returned to life."

Brahmins blessed them as they went by. "If we have ever performed any religious acts, then let the Pandavas live in our city for one hundred years."

The people bowed their heads to the ground as Krishna passed. They threw flower petals and rice grains on the ground, and wealthy people threw gems from the balconies of their houses.

Standing on the terrace of their chariot, the Pandavas waved at the citizens. The brothers shed tears of delight to see their city again. Dhritarashtra sent out Drona, Kripa, and other important ministers to meet the procession on the road. They took the Pandavas and Krishna to the great palace assigned to them by Dhritarashtra, informing them that there would be a royal assembly the following morning. The king would settle the matter of the kingdom, once and for all.

The next day the Pandavas took their places in the vast assembly hall. Krishna was given a seat of honor near the king and he sat comfortably, seeming to light up the hall with his bodily effulgence. When everyone was settled, Dhritarashtra spoke. "Surely we are favored by the gods to have Pandu's sons with us again. So that no further dispute may arise between them and the Kauravas, I wish to divide the kingdom into two parts. O Yudhishthira, dear child, go to Khandava. This shall be your half of the kingdom."

The assembly remained silent after the king had spoken. Bhishma and Vidura looked at one another. Dhritarashtra had certainly given half the kingdom—Khandava was a huge area of land—but it was completely unoccupied. Having been cursed long ago by a *rishi*, it had been abandoned and was now nothing more than jungle and desert.

Yudhishthira was not concerned. He was happy to accept any settlement if it would mean peace. The Pandava had seen Krishna smile when he heard the name of Khandava. He would know what to do. Furthermore, Dhritarashtra was the ruling monarch and, as such, he represented God.

Yudhishthira would never question his order. Folding his palms, he said, "It shall be as you desire, O king. We shall leave tomorrow."

The next morning Dhritarashtra had Yudhishthira crowned as king of Khandava. Vyasadeva performed the rituals, and when it was time for the Pandavas to depart, he went with them. Krishna also accompanied the brothers. Reaching the vast Khandava region, he asked Vyasadeva to select an auspicious site to found a city. Krishna then summoned Indra. When the deity appeared, shining like the sun, Krishna said, "O king of the gods, sprinkle your heavenly nectar on this land. Make it rich and fertile. Then, construct a celestial city for the Pandavas."

Indra set about the task. He called for the heavenly architect, Vishvakarma, to begin work building the city. Soon many great mansions were standing along the sides of broad highways. Tall palaces of white marble rose up from the center of the city, and there were beautiful gardens and orchards everywhere. The god built hundreds of temples dedicated to Vishnu and the principal deities. Vast granite walls surrounded the city, with a wide moat encircling them. By the power of Indra's nectar, the surrounding country became green and fertile. Delightful woods filled with blossoming and fragrant trees spread out around the city. Within those woods were lakes filled with lotuses and frequented by swans and cranes.

The Pandavas took up their residence in the central palace, which resembled the heavenly Mount Meru, abode of the gods. The city soon attracted many thousands of saintly brahmins, who began to live in houses built for them around the royal quarters. People from all the other orders of life also came in great numbers to populate the city, which became known as Indraprastha.

Out of friendship for the Pandavas, Krishna remained in the city for some weeks. He and Arjuna were especially close and they spent much time together. Draupadi also took every opportunity to serve Krishna, and she became very dear to him.

Eight

THE CELELSTIAL HALL

SOME TIME AFTER moving to Indraprastha, the Pandavas were visited by the celestial sage Narada. He was served by Draupadi, and after seeing her divine beauty, he feared that dissension might arise among the five brothers. He told them an ancient history about two asuras, celestial demons, who had fallen out over a woman. Although they had been inseparable and devoted to one another, out of envy they had finally killed each other in a terrible fight. Narada cautioned the Pandavas. "Do not let this happen to you. Establish a rule concerning Draupadi so that no disagreement may arise."

The brothers then decided upon a rule. They would each have a certain amount of time with Draupadi. If any of them intruded upon another who was alone with Draupadi, there would be a severe consequence; the offender would have to go to the forest for one year, having no contact with her during that period of exile.

As time went by, Indraprastha became famous even among the gods. The virtuous rule of the Pandavas kept all the citizens on the path of piety. Always guided by the brahmins, Yudhishthira ensured that all his people were cared for in every respect. His kingdom flourished greatly, and many other kings accepted his leadership.

Draupadi served her five husbands with unswerving devotion. According to their agreement, they each had their allotted time with her. One day, as Yudhishthira sat alone in his rooms with Draupadi, a brahmin came to the palace in distress. He cried out to Yudhishthira, "O king, save me! Wicked robbers have taken my cows. Do not allow virtue to be destroyed in this way. It is always the king's duty to protect his citizens."

Yudhishthira did not hear the brahmin's cries, but Arjuna heard them and immediately called out, "Fear not, gentle brahmin. I shall soon apprehend the robbers."

But when he ran to fetch his weapons, he discovered that Yudhishthira was alone with Draupadi in the room where they were kept. He stopped at the door and thought carefully. How could he break the rule? But if he did not catch the thieves, Yudhishthira's virtue would suffer. People would censure the king for failing to protect a brahmin. For entering the room, however, the only consequence would be that he, Arjuna, would have to enter the forest for a year. Even if he died there, it would be better than allowing sin and calumny to touch his brother.

Arjuna knocked hard on the door and entered. Looking straight ahead of him, he went toward the weapons. Yudhishthira sat up in surprise and greeted him warmly. Saying he would explain later, Arjuna quickly took his weapons and went after the robbers. Before long he caught them and recovered the brahmin's cows. He then returned to the city and went before Yudhishthira. Bowing at his feet, he told him why he had entered his room, then said, "Permit me now to go to the forest, in accordance with our agreement."

Yudhishthira raised his hands. "Why? You have not committed any sin. You were simply wishing to uphold virtue. Do not go."

Arjuna was firm. "You have often told me that virtue should be practiced without equivocation. I must adhere to truth, for it is my greatest strength. The agreement was broken and I must go."

Tears fell from Yudhishthira's eyes, but he could make no argument. His brother was right. The Pandava king nodded in assent and Arjuna immediately left to make preparations for his departure. Soon he was ready and, watched by his sorrowful brothers, he walked out of the city, followed by many ascetic brahmins who were taking the opportunity to go on a pilgrimage with him. On Yudhishthira's order, many servants also accompanied him, bearing wealth to distribute in charity to the rishis he met on his way.

Arjuna decided to follow the coastline, visiting the many holy places that lay along that route. Eventually he came to Dwaraka, which lay on the western coast, where he stayed for some time. There, with Krishna's assistance, he was able to win the hand of Subhadra, Krishna's exquisitely beautiful sister. At the end of the year he returned to Indraprastha, taking the princess with him. His delighted brothers surrounded him as he entered the city. They congratulated him on winning Subhadra and listened in wonder as he told them about his adventures during his travels.

A few days after Arjuna's return, Krishna and Balarama came to Hastinapura. They were accompanied by all the leading personalities from Dwaraka. They entered the city in state, admiring its wondrous architecture. Indraprastha appeared like a jewel among cities. The streets were washed spotlessly clean and sprinkled with perfumed water. All of the tall white mansions were adorned with garlands of wild flowers and decked with rows of brightly colored flags. As the procession from Dwaraka passed by, wealthy men threw sparkling gems on the road. Thousands of conchshells were blown, and brahmins chanted auspicious hymns, praising Krishna and his associates.

The Pandavas greeted their guests with respect and love. Yudhishthira had them housed in his own magnificent palace. Krishna and Balarama then presented him with the wealth they had brought as Subhadra's dowry. Heaps of gold bricks were laid out, along with countless precious stones and many costly rugs and blankets. The two Yadu chiefs also gave thousands of cows decorated with gold ornaments, a thousand moonlike, white horses, a thousand mules, and a thousand first-class war chariots. They had also brought a thousand great elephants, each raised on the sea beach and resembling a hill decked with bells and ornaments. Having been laid out, the wealth presented to the Pandavas looked like a sea stretching in all directions.

Yudhishthira graciously received all the gifts. He and his brothers spent many days with the Yadus, sporting and talking together in great happiness. Finally the Yadus returned to Dwaraka, but Krishna decided to stay on a bit longer. He wanted to spend more time with Arjuna. The two friends went on hunting trips together in the forest surrounding Indraprastha, laughing and joking together as they tracked the wild animals that posed a threat to the rishis who lived in the forest.

On one particularly hot day, they were sitting together beneath the shade of a large banyan tree when, to their surprise, a strange-looking brahmin emerged from the woods. He had a copper-colored complexion, with bright yellow hair and beard. His reddish eyes were like lotus petals and his body was powerful and well formed.

Seeing this brahmin, who shone like fire, Krishna and Arjuna immediately stood up in respect and folded their palms. "What can we do for you?" Krishna asked.

"I know you two to be the best of men," the brahmin replied in a resonant voice. "I have come to beg my food. However, I am not an ordinary brahmin. Know me to be Agni, god of fire. I wish to eat this entire forest by which we stand. Please assist me."

The god explained that he had made numerous attempts to consume the forest, but it was under the protection of Indra. "There is a Naga living here who is Indra's friend. Each time I blaze up to swallow this wood, Indra sends down torrents of rain. Only you two can prevent him. I must eat this forest, for it contains many medicinal herbs."

Agni told them how he had become ill after consuming too much ghee in a great sacrifice performed by King Swetaki, an ancestor of Arjuna. Eating the forest herbs would cure him. The great creator, Brahma, had told Agni that he should ask Arjuna and Krishna to help him. "These two were formerly Nara and Narayana, the divine rishis," said Brahma. "Now they have appeared on earth to accomplish the gods' purposes. Therefore, ask for their help."

Arjuna folded his palms to the god. "I would surely like to help you, and indeed, I possess many powerful weapons with which I can check even the celestials. However, I have no bow capable of bearing their strength. And even if I have such a bow, I will also need an inexhaustible supply of arrows and a suitable chariot on which to stand as I do battle."

Agni smiled. "It shall be done." He thought of Varuna, god of the nether worlds and the waters. The deity quickly appeared, and Agni said, "O lord of the deep, please give me the bow and quivers which formerly belonged to King Soma, as well as his chariot that is decorated with an ape banner. Arjuna needs them in order to achieve great deeds on behalf of the gods."

Varuna was the custodian of all kinds of celestial weapons, which he kept hidden in the ocean's depths. He immediately made the chariot and weapons appear, and Agni gave them to Arjuna. The Pandava gazed in wonder at the bow, which Agni said was called the Gandiva. As tall as a man, it shone like a rainbow and was studded with sparkling gems. It was flawless, with no sign of weakness in any of its ornately formed parts. After bowing down to Agni, Arjuna took up the bow and approached the great chariot that Varuna had produced. It was filled with celestial weapons, including two inexhaustible quivers of arrows. The chariot was yoked to a team of silvery steeds from the land of the Gandharvas. Resembling an evening cloud and reflecting the splendor of the sun, it was dazzling and was furnished with a tall golden flagstaff. Its flag bore an image of Hanuman, Rama's famous monkey servant, who emitted fierce cries.

As Arjuna mounted the chariot and donned the suit of celestial armor he found there, Varuna presented a discus weapon to Krishna. "Here is your eternal weapon, Sudarshana," he said, handing him the effulgent disc, which looked like a circle of fire. "Hurled from your hand, this razor-edged weapon can slay any creature within the three worlds. Here, too, is your club, the Kaumodaki, which is capable of crushing the hordes of Daityas and Danavas."

Varuna, having given the two weapons to Krishna, then bowed before him and vanished from the spot. Standing on the chariot cased from head to toe in his armor, Arjuna shone brilliantly. Krishna climbed into the driver's seat and took up the reins, saying he would guide the chariot for Arjuna. In heroic tones, Arjuna said to Agni, "O great deity, blaze up to your full extent. With the Gandiva as my weapon and Krishna as my charioteer, I am ready to withstand even the entire celestial host."

Agni at once assumed his fiery form and surrounded the forest. Huge flames leapt upward and dense clouds of black smoke spread throughout the sky. The crackling of burning wood was deafening and the air was filled with a choking stench. The lakes and ponds in the vast forest were boiled dry and the rocks glowed white-hot.

In the heavens, Indra became alarmed. His Naga friend Takshaka seemed to be in dire danger. The king of the gods then sent massive clouds over the forest that began to thunder and release volumes of water. But the conflagration was so intense that the rain simply turned to steam in the sky. Indra caused even larger clouds to appear, and great columns of water began to douse the flames.

Seeing this, Arjuna invoked the Vayavya wind weapon and, firing it upwards, he dispersed all the clouds. Indra became angry and he summoned many celestial fighters to challenge Arjuna. Thousands of Asuras, Gandharvas, Yakshas, and Nagas all appeared in the sky and released their weapons at Arjuna.

The Pandava countered their attack with consummate skill. With the Gandiva constantly drawn to a circle, he released countless arrows charged with the force of celestial weapons. Due to Krishna's expert driving, his chariot wheeled about and evaded the weapons that rained down on him from the sky.

Seeing Arjuna successfully holding off the heavenly army, Indra then appeared personally, accompanied by all the principal gods. Although impressed by his son's power, he was determined to show his own superiority.

One by one the deities threw their personal weapons at Arjuna. Yamaraja threw his death-dealing staff, Surya his dart, Varuna his noose, and Indra himself took up his fearsome thunderbolt. Dozens of other gods also released their weapons, but Arjuna stood unmoved on his chariot. With his swift arrows he checked all those missiles. So many shafts were fired by Arjuna that they seemed to be leaving his bow in one continuous line. Simply by the strength of his arms and the Gandiva, he checked the gods' attack. They all praised his prowess.

Then a voice was heard in the sky, saying, "O Indra, your friend Takshaka is not here. Desist from battle. The burning of this forest and the sinful beings within it has been ordained by fate. You will not be able to overpower Arjuna and Krishna."

Recognizing the voice to belong to Brahma, the gods retired from the fight. Agni continued to devour the forest for fifteen days. As it burned, hordes of Rakshasas and other demons rushed out in terror. Arjuna cut them all down with his arrows. Krishna drove his chariot round the forest with such speed that it seemed to be on all sides at once. No demon was able to escape from Arjuna.

There was a leader of the Danava race of demons named Maya who had hid himself underground during the fire. When the flames began to die, he came out and tried to make his escape. Using his powers of illusion, he evaded Arjuna but was seen by Krishna, who raised his discus weapon to kill him. The intelligent demon then ran to Arjuna and fell at his feet, saying, "O hero, I seek your protection."

Bound by his principles, Arjuna could not refuse. He raised his hand to stop Krishna from killing Maya. The demon thanked him with folded palms and said, "O Arjuna, you have saved my life. What can I do for you in return?"

"I will not take payment for doing my duty," Arjuna replied at once.

Maya insisted. "You need not see it as payment. Let me just do something to please you."

"O Danava, if you wish to please me, then kindly do something for Krishna."

Maya turned expectantly toward Krishna, who said, "O Danava, there is one thing you can do that will be highly pleasing to me. Construct a celestial assembly hall for Yudhishthira in Indraprastha. Let it be the finest hall within this world."

Krishna knew that Maya's building skills were superb. He had constructed many wonderful edifices in the higher planets. Agreeing to Krishna's request, the Danava accompanied him and Arjuna back to Indraprastha. After some thought, he drew a design for the hall and then left for the Himalayas to collect the materials he would need. "I have left there large amounts of celestial gems unknown to this world," he explained. "I will soon fetch these and then begin work."

After Maya had gone, Krishna approached Yudhishthira and asked his permission to leave. All of the Pandavas were sorrowful at the prospect of his departure. Krishna embraced them with love and said that he would come again before long. He said his fond farewells to Kunti, Draupadi, and

Subhadra. They all fought back their tears as they watched him go, not wanting to cause any inauspiciousness at the moment of his leaving.

As Krishna rode out of Indraprastha, the Pandavas accompanied him for some way. Yudhishthira personally took the reins of his chariot, while Arjuna stood fanning him with a golden-handled whisk. Bhima held a parasol over his head and the twins walked ahead, clearing a way through the crowds that had assembled to see him off. When at last they parted, the five brothers stood watching the chariot till it was nothing more than a speck in the distance. They then slowly returned to the city, thinking only of their intimate friend from Dwaraka.

*   *   *

Within a few days, Maya returned with many Rakshasas carrying the materials for the hall. As well as the gems, he brought with him a great club, which he presented to Bhima, and a celestial conchshell known as the Devadatta, which he gave to Arjuna. "This club is equal to a hundred thousand other clubs, and the sound of this conchshell will instill terror in any enemy."

Then, on a day marked with auspicious stars, the Danava began work. He marked out an area of five thousand square cubits and, using his celestial powers, started construction. It took him over a year. Thousands of golden pillars were erected to support the splendid hall. It resembled a mass of new clouds rising in the sky. Giving off both terrestrial and celestial light, it seemed to be on fire. It was spacious, cool, charming, and soothing to the mind. Adorned with jeweled walls and gates, it was decorated with countless pictures and heavenly ornaments. With its crystal stairways, golden arches, and beautiful ponds, the hall surpassed even the Sudharma hall of the Yadus, which had been brought from the heavens.

Yudhishthira then entered the hall. To invoke auspiciousness, he distributed much charity to thousands of brahmins. A festival was declared in the city, with athletes, actors, bards, wrestlers, and musicians all displaying their skills. Many ceremonies were performed in which Vishnu and all the gods were worshipped with costly paraphernalia.

When Yudhishthira was sitting in state in the great central hall, many celestial rishis came there from all over the universe. They were given seats of honor, and they looked like so many moons lighting up the hall. Foremost among them all was Narada, who was worshipped by Yudhishthira and his brothers with all respect.

After taking his seat next to the Pandavas, Narada inquired from Yudhishthira, "O king, are you properly protecting the people? Is your mind fixed in virtue? Do you pursue life's four aims—religion, profit, pleasure, and liberation—each in its proper time?"

Narada questioned the attentive king at length, his questions effectively constituting a number of instructions on the art of kingship. The *rishi's* wisdom and knowledge were famed throughout the universe. He was also famous as a great servant of Vishnu, familiar with the Lord's divine plan. His movements were always arranged to assist that plan. The Pandavas and their whole assembly remained silent as he spoke. Narada explained that the essential duty of a king was to protect all living beings within his jurisdiction, not just by providing them with their material necessities but also by ensuring that they advanced toward life's goal of spiritual emancipation.

When Narada finished speaking, Yudhishthira replied, "O all-knowing sage, you have perfectly described true religion and morality. I shall do all that you have said. My knowledge has increased by your instructions. By the Lord's grace, I am endeavoring to do my duty, striving to follow in the footsteps of my noble ancestors, but I do not possess the same ability as they."

Seeing Narada admiring the celestial hall, Yudhishthira asked him if he had seen any to equal it anywhere in the universe. He knew the sage was a frequent visitor to all of the higher planets of the gods. Narada then began to describe all of the assembly halls he had seen, starting with that of Indra. In the course of his descriptions, he mentioned the names of many of Yudhishthira's forefathers who had ascended to heaven. Yudhishthira heard how his father Pandu was living in the great assembly hall of Yamaraja. Hearing also that the great king Harischandra was dwelling with Indra, Yudhishthira became curious. He asked Narada, "How is it that my father did not attain the abode of the king of gods, as did Harischandra? What pious acts did that king perform that my father did not?"

Narada explained that Harischandra had performed the great Rajasuya sacrifice, which entailed subjugating all other kings and establishing its performer as the world emperor. During its performance, vast charity had to be distributed to hundreds of thousands of brahmins. Any king who successfully performed this sacrifice, setting the whole world on the path of virtue, became qualified to attain Indra's abode.

Narada then said, "O king, your father asked me to pass a message on to you. He desires that you perform the Rajasuya. You will thereby elevate both yourself and him to Indra's heavenly planet."

Both Narada and Pandu knew that the gods wanted Yudhishthira to perform the sacrifice. It was part of a divine plan meant to free the world from demonic influences. Since Pandu's demise, many evil kings had been growing in power and were exploiting the earth for sinful purposes. Yudhishthira would need to overpower them before he could perform the Rajasuya. Narada understood that Yudhishthira and his brothers were dear to Krishna, who wanted to use them as instruments in his plan to re-establish religion in the world.

The sage concluded, "O king, consider, then, the performance of the Rajasuya. But be warned; it will not be easy. Darkly powerful spirits will oppose you. A war may result that will destroy all the world's kings and warriors. Knowing this, do what you feel is best."

Narada said that he would soon be visiting Dwaraka to see Krishna. Fearing that he did not have the power and resources to perform the Rajasuya, Yudhishthira said, "Please ask the infallible Lord to soon come again to Hastinapura. More than ever I need his help and guidance."

Narada assented and then got up from his seat. Along with the other rishis, he rose up into the air and vanished.

Seated in his wonderful assembly hall, which was called the Mayasabha, Yudhishthira ruled over Indraprastha with justice and compassion. His virtuous rule attracted the cooperation of all the gods, and therefore his kingdom was not even afflicted by any natural disturbances. The rains fell at the proper time and the earth gave forth abundant produce. Men lived to a ripe old age, free from disease and anxiety, and they had everything they desired. All the people followed their religious duties properly and were devoted to God. No one entertained any hostility toward Yudhishthira, and he became famous as Ajatashatru, "one without an enemy."

The years passed by as the Pandavas ruled from Indraprastha. Draupadi bore each of them a son, who, like their fathers, flourished like the gods in heaven.

But Yudhishthira was not content. He thought continuously about the Rajasuya. Recognizing that it was the desire of the gods, and thus of the Lord himself, he intensely desired its performance. Narada's caution, however, had made him apprehensive, and he bided his time. When at last he felt that he had sufficiently established his rule, he decided to go ahead with it. He called a full assembly to discuss what had to be done. When everyone was present, he said, "I think I must perform the Rajasuya. Although I do not long for dominion over this earth for myself, I wish to carry out the Lord's desire."

Yudhishthira considered that the sacrifice would be an opportunity to establish Krishna's supreme position throughout the world. If everyone recognized Krishna's supremacy and thus worshipped him, they would be well on the path to liberation. This was the only proper aim for an emperor to achieve.

The ministers were all in full agreement. They could think of no better person than Yudhishthira to become emperor. If his virtuous rule could be extended across the earth, it would become exactly like heaven. Dhaumya stood up and spoke in response. "O great king, you are surely worthy of performing this sacrifice, which will bestow upon you universal sovereignty. First, though, you must gain the acquiescence of all other kings."

Yudhishthira had decided to send his four brothers in the four directions in order to win over the kings. Those who would not accept his rule would have to be overpowered. The Pandava knew there would be some who would put up a fight. He discussed with his ministers the best way to proceed; everyone agreed that they should first consult with Krishna. Yudhishthira prayed to Krishna within his heart, knowing that Krishna would certainly understand his desire. And Narada would also have informed him. If he wished to come, he would no doubt soon arrive in Indraprastha.

Nine

VIRTUE ESTABLISHED

NEWS REACHED DWARAKA about the Pandavas' incomparable halland increasing opulence. Krishna heard with pleasure how Yudhishthira was righteously ruling his people. He also heard that Subhadra had given birth to a son, who was named Abhimanyu. Hearing all this news, Krishna again desired to pay a visit to Indraprastha.

Each day, Krishna would go to his own assembly hall, the Sudharma, to meet with the citizens. Vishvakarma, the architect of the gods, had originally constructed this hall for Indra, and it had been presented to Krishna when he built Dwaraka. It had the special quality of being able to free the people within it from all material suffering. Krishna would enter the hall and bow before King Ugrasena, who ruled over Dwaraka. He would then take his seat on a jeweled throne near the king. Although he was not the king, Krishna was respected as the most important person present. Everyone in Dwaraka was aware of his divine position and they accepted him as their natural leader, especially after he had personally slain Kamsa, Ugrasena's evil-minded son who had seized the throne from his father.

When everyone was settled in the hall, jesters, dancers, and musicians would entertain them. Brahmins would then recite Vedic hymns, and the sounds of *mridanga* drums, flutes, and bells could be heard throughout the hall. After the various performances, the day's business would commence.

One day a messenger arrived at the hall from a distant country. After being respectfully received, he introduced himself as a king who had escaped from Jarasandha, the ruler of the Magadha province. Jarasandha, in alliance with other kings, had been attacking all the surrounding kingdoms. After defeating the monarchs there, he would capture and imprison them. The messenger explained, "This evil man intends to offer all the captive kings as human sacrifices to the goddess Bhairava. I have therefore come here to seek your shelter and protection. O Krishna, all-powerful Lord, please save these kings and end Jarasandha's reign of terror once and for all."

It was well known that Krishna had fought and defeated Jarasandha many times, but the Magadha king had somehow managed to escape with his life. Jarasandha hated Krishna for having killed his friend Kamsa, who had also been the husband of his two daughters. Taking a vast army, he had marched on Dwaraka repeatedly, but Krishna had repeatedly crushed him in battle.

Krishna consoled the messenger and offered him a seat in the hall. He turned toward Ugrasena and his ministers to discuss what action they should take, but just as he was about to speak, Narada entered the hall. Everyone in the assembly stood in respect. Narada was given a seat of honor and personally worshipped by Krishna. When the ceremony was complete, Krishna said, "O godly sage, your presence here is welcome. Surely, everything is known to you. Please tell us how Yudhishthira is faring. What are his present plans?"

Narada smiled. "My Lord, what can be beyond your knowledge? Yet you come to this world and act just like an ordinary man. I can therefore tell you that Yudhishthira is flourishing in every respect. He resembles Indra in Amaravati. Now he desires to perform the Rajasuya and is praying that you will assist him. He has asked that you go soon to Indraprastha."

Krishna thanked Narada for the information. He then turned to his chief advisor, Uddhava. "What do you think, O wise man. How can we satisfy this distressed king and also the pious Yudhishthira?"

Uddhava stood up to reply. "I think, O Krishna, that both things can be achieved at once. If you go to Indraprastha, you will enable your cousin Yudhishthira to perform the Rajasuya. To do this, he will have to defeat Jarasandha. Thus, the kings will also be released."

Uddhava cautioned that Jarasandha would not be easy to conquer. "We have intelligence that he has amassed an immense army. To avoid a difficult encounter in which millions will die, I suggest that he be challenged to a one-to-one fight. And in my view, the person to fight with him is Bhima. He should go to Jarasandha disguised as a brahmin and beg a fight from him. Jarasandha is proud of his charitable nature. He never refuses a brahmin's request. And, O Krishna, if you go with Bhima I am sure he will be victorious."

The Yadu assembly voiced their approval. They had been considering how to deal with Jarasandha. It could only be a matter of time before he again marched on Dwaraka.

Krishna agreed, saying he would leave for Indraprastha at once. He told the messenger to return to the imprisoned kings and reassure them that they would soon be released. Then, taking permission from Ugrasena, he made arrangements to depart.

A great procession left Dwaraka the next day. Krishna traveled in state with all the principal Yadus and their wives. Thousands of soldiers went with them, protecting them on all sides. The slow-moving procession resembled the sea rolling onto the shore.

When messengers informed Yudhishthira that Krishna's procession had reached the outskirts of Indraprastha, he cried out in joy and ran out of the city with all his brothers to greet the visitors. As the royal musicians played and brahmins chanted hymns, the procession made its way along the crowded city streets.

When all the Yadus had been settled in various palaces, Yudhishthira approached Krishna to ask him about the Rajasuya. Sitting with Krishna on a broad golden couch, Yudhishthira said, "Although I strongly desire to perform this great sacrifice, I am apprehensive. It will not be easy. Do you think I should go ahead? O Krishna, your advice is always impartial and full of sublime wisdom. Please tell me your opinion."

Krishna looked round at Yudhishthira and his brothers, who sat surrounding them. It was a warm day, and servants fanned them with long-handled peacock feather fans. The sounds of brahmins worshipping in nearby temples drifted in, creating a soothing air of auspiciousness. Raising his hand, which was adorned with brilliant gems, Krishna said, "O Yudhishthira, with your four powerful brothers you are worthy in every way to perform the Rajasuya and become emperor of the earth. I think the chief obstacle will be Jarasandha. That dark-hearted king has formed an almost invincible alliance with other similarly inclined monarchs. His influence is now spread throughout the middle portion of the world, and he has designs on the rest. You will need to curb him without delay."

Krishna asked Yudhishthira how he felt he should deal with Jarasandha. Yudhishthira turned to his brothers. Bhima then said, "In my view, it would be unwise to engage in warfare with this wretch—especially in his own territory. Too many lives would be lost. When dealing with a strong enemy, one needs to employ cunning strategies. Between Krishna's skillful diplomacy, my strength, and Arjuna's ever-victorious nature, I think we can finish off the wicked Jarasandha."

Krishna agreed. "Jarasandha must indeed be checked by whatever means possible. He, too, desires to become emperor, and he now has more than eighty kings held captive. When that number reaches one hundred, he will offer them in sacrifice, aiming to establish himself as supreme in this world."

Yudhishthira was still apprehensive. He did not like the idea of sending just three men to face the very powerful Jarasandha, even if Krishna was one of them. Yudhishthira's love for Krishna overpowered any thought of his divinity. The Pandava king voiced his concern. "How can I risk your lives for the sake of my own selfish desires? Bhima and Arjuna are like my two eyes, and you are like my mind, dear Krishna. I could not possibly live without you. In my view, Jarasandha would be hard to overcome even for Yamaraja, what to speak of ourselves."

Arjuna then spoke, his voice filled with heroic determination. "I do not think we should cower before Jarasandha. We have energy, strength, weapons, allies, and dominions. We belong to a race famous for its valor. What can be achieved by one who lacks courage? Our fame and virtue will surely perish if we do not challenge Jarasandha. On the other hand, simply by confronting him they will be enhanced, even if we are defeated."

Krishna praised Arjuna's speech. "This is the proper mood for one born in the Bharata race. We should either kill Jarasandha or, being killed by him, ascend to heaven."

Yudhishthira asked Krishna about Jarasandha's history. Krishna described how he had been born in two pieces from the two wives of King Brihadratha. "The king was blessed by a *rishi* to get a son, and the *rishi* gave him a charmed mango for his senior wife. But the king cut it in two and gave it to both wives, desiring two sons. When he saw the resulting two half babies, he threw them in the forest, where a Rakshasa woman named Jara found them. She joined the parts into one baby, who then came to life with a great roar. Jara returned the child to his father, who named him Jarasandha, "joined by Jara."

Krishna concluded, "Let us leave at once. Jarasandha's time has come. I am sure Bhima will defeat him in single combat."

Yudhishthira relented. "Seeing your determination, O Krishna, I consider him already killed, the imprisoned kings released, and the Rajasuya completed. What is impossible for one who has you as his guide? Leave with my brothers whenever you wish."

On Krishna's suggestion the three heroes dressed themselves as brahmins and immediately began to make the journey on foot. They walked for some days, begging their meals as they traveled and sleeping on the ground. At last they reached the Goratha hill, from which they saw in the distance Jarasandha's capital, Girivraja. Sitting amid beautiful parkland and woods, it was splendid, with many mansions and palaces.

Pointing toward the city, Krishna said, "This unassailable city is protected on all sides by five hills. Let us enter it now by passing over the largest of them, called Chaityaka, which stands before the main gate."

Krishna led them to the top of the hill and they began to tear down its peak with their bare hands, hurling down boulders and creating a landslide. They then ran down its slopes with loud shouts. At the bottom of the hill was a great drum made from the skin of a Rakshasa that Jarasandha had slain. When struck, it would vibrate for a full month, and Jarasandha had it continuously sounded to warn off any potential attackers. Arjuna and Krishna smashed the drum to pieces.

The three of them then clambered over the city wall and made their way toward the king's palace. The guards stood back in surprise as the three apparent brahmins strode along the main highway. Awed by their obvious power, the soldiers made no attempt to check them. Even the palace guards froze in astonishment as they burst in, marching fearlessly into the courtyard where Jarasandha was seated. Having been warned by his brahmins of fearful omens, the king was performing a sacrifice to ward off evil. When he saw the three brahmins approaching, he hastily rose up and said, "Welcome. Please be seated and accept my worship."

Jarasandha immediately arranged for his visitors to be worshipped with a footbath and offerings of *arghya* and other auspicious articles. He also offered them cows in charity. But Krishna held up his hands and refused all the offerings, saying, "We cannot accept your charity, O king, but we wish you well. May you soon attain salvation."

Jarasandha looked carefully at his unusual guests. They did not resemble any brahmins he had seen before. Powerfully built and fearless, they bore the traits of kshatriyas. Noting the bowstring scars on their forearms, he felt sure they must be warriors. But as they had appeared before him as brahmins, he said, "I cannot allow you to come before me without giving you something. It is always a king's duty to bestow charity on brahmins."

As Jarasandha spoke, his guards came and quietly informed him of what his visitors had done on their way in. The king became even more curious. "I do not think you are brahmins. You bear all the signs of warriors. Why did you enter my city by climbing the wall, as enemies enter? And your acts of violence outside the city were also inimical. Who are you? What do you want?"

Krishna replied, "We are here representing one who desires the imperial dignity. It is true that we consider you an enemy. If you will not acquiesce peacefully, accepting our demands, then you shall witness our prowess today."

Jarasandha was surprised. "What have I ever done to you, or indeed, anyone else? I always follow my duties as a king. What injury have I done to any living being?"

Krishna smiled and shook his head. "This is not true. O king, you have captured many men and intend to make human sacrifices of them. Even now, they are suffering in captivity, persecuted by you. How is this not sinful? If you are virtuous, you should release them at once. Otherwise you will witness our prowess today. You offered us charity, but all we desire from you is battle. We shall soon dispatch you to Death's abode. Know me to be Krishna, and these two are Bhima and Arjuna."

Jarasandha laughed. "Of course—my old enemy Krishna! So you have been forced to resort to trickery, having failed to slay me in any other way. I disagree with you that I am sinful. All the kings held by me were first defeated in a fair fight. Their lives are forfeit to me. I will certainly not release them out of fear of you. Rather, I will fight. Whatever you prefer—troops against troops, one on one, or me against two or even all three of you together."

Krishna laughed. "Your pride will soon be crushed, O king. We ask from you a fight in single combat. Choose any one of us you please."

Jarasandha nodded slowly, carefully eyeing his three antagonists. Finally he said, "I select Bhima, for only he is a suitable match for me."

Bhima bit his lips and glared at Jarasandha. "I am ready."

The Magadha king had two huge maces brought out, and he allowed Bhima to choose one. Then he led him to an arena on the edge of the city. Many citizens followed them and crowded around, eager to watch the fight, which soon began in earnest.

They came together with upraised maces, creating showers of sparks as the weapons collided. Before long, the maces were smashed and the combatants fought hand-to-hand. Both men were expert wrestlers and displayed many wonderful moves, dexterously seizing and throwing each other around the arena. First Bhima and then Jarasandha seemed to have the advantage. They roared and smashed each other with their palms and fists, causing great cracking sounds to reverberate around the city. Both greatly enjoyed fighting, and they laughed in delight as they grappled together, appreciating each other's strength and skill.

They fought throughout the day, and when evening came they retired, agreeing to meet again the next day. In this way, the fight went on for twenty-eight days. Neither showed any sign of fatigue. By the twenty-eighth day, Bhima began to wonder if the fight would ever end. They seemed to be equally matched in every respect. Noting this, Krishna thought about how he could help Bhima. There was no question of assisting him in the fight, but he could offer him some useful advice. Taking up a blade of grass, Krishna waited till Bhima was looking at him and then he bifurcated it, throwing the two pieces aside.

Bhima immediately understood Krishna's sign. Knowing that Jarasandha had been joined at birth, he realized that he would be weak at the seam. When an opportunity came, he threw Jarasandha to the ground and quickly grasped one of his legs, standing on the other one. With a great roar, he tore his opponent in two.

The citizens, seeing their king slain, cried out in sorrow. Arjuna and Krishna cheered loudly and embraced Bhima. They went with him back into the city and consoled Jarasandha's son, Jayatsena, whom they then installed as king of Magadha. More pious than his father, Jayatsena agreed to accept Yudhishthira's rule and said he would attend the Rajasuya. He had the imprisoned kings released, and they all came to offer thanks to Krishna and the two Pandavas. Jayatsena then arranged to transport them back to Indraprastha.

When they arrived, Krishna went straight to Yudhishthira. He bowed at his feet and said, "O king, by good fortune Jarasandha is slain and your brothers are well."

Yudhishthira joyfully embraced Krishna, who asked for permission to depart, promising to return when the sacrifice commenced. The Pandavas would first have to gain the compliance of all other kings. Krishna wished them well in that endeavor and then left for Dwaraka.

Yudhishthira spoke with his brothers. It was time for them to make their expeditions. Taking large numbers of troops, Arjuna went to the north, Bhima to the east, Sahadeva to the south, and Nakula to the west.

As the brothers spread out from Indraprastha, they encountered hundreds of kings ruling over various provinces. Most monarchs happily acquiesced, being aware of Yudhishthira's virtue remembering fondly their own or their fathers' previous encounters with the Kuru dynasty. Some, however, were averse to Yudhishthira's rule. In those cases, the Pandavas first tried diplomatic means to win over the kings, but if this failed, a battle would always ensue. Some kings, even though not antagonistic to the Pandavas, fought anyway, as a matter of pride. But eventually all were subdued by the might of the four brothers and the Kuru army. No one could stand before them, and before long the entire globe was under Yudhishthira's control.

Ten

THE GREAT SACRIFICE

YUDHISHTHIRA RECEIVED NEWS of his brothers' conquests and began making arrangements for the sacrifice. One by one they returned, bringing with them the vast wealth they had either been given or won. Yudhishthira's treasury became like a vast ocean that could not be emptied, even in a hundred years.

As the time for the sacrifice approached, Krishna came again to Indraprastha, accompanied by his wives and ministers and surrounded by the great Yadu and Vrishni armies. The clatter of their horses' hooves and chariot wheels filled the city. Krishna presented Yudhishthira with still more wealth, and the Pandava received him with love. Embracing him warmly, he said, "O Krishna, for your sake only has this earth been brought under my control. Indeed, it has been possible only by your favor. By your mercy, I am now opulent beyond limit. I wish to engage my wealth in the service of the brahmins and in worshipping Vishnu. O Lord, install yourself in the sacrifice. If it is performed by you, I shall be freed from all sin."

Krishna praised Yudhishthira's virtues. "O best of kings, doubtlessly you deserve the imperial dignity. Let the sacrifice commence, led by the brahmins. Appoint me to some lesser office. I shall obey your commands."

Tears flowed from Yudhishthira's eyes. "O Krishna, Lord of the senses, because you are here and agreeable to my wish, I consider my success in this endeavor to be certain."

When Vyasadeva arrived in Indraprastha, he was placed in charge of the sacrifice. He appointed the many priests who were required to tend the six sacrificial fires and chant the sacred mantras. A great compound was marked out on the edge of the city, and the altars were carefully constructed.

Many hundreds of kings arrived in Indraprastha and were accommodated in mansions that Yudhishthira had built especially for the sacrifice.

Brahmins streamed into the city, and they were given spacious living quarters, furnished with every desirable thing, and attended by many servants.

When the Kurus arrived from Hastinapura, Yudhishthira greeted them personally. He was overjoyed to see Bhishma, Drona, Kripa, and all his other beloved elders. He fell at their feet and said, "Everything I own is yours. Indeed, I am your servant. Please guide me."

Bhishma raised Yudhishthira and embraced him. His voice was choked with happiness as he praised the Pandava. All the Kuru elders were highly pleased that he was performing the Rajasuya. Even Dhritarashtra, who could not attend, was happy and had sent word of his approval. After all, the Pandavas were extending the glories of the Kuru dynasty by once more establishing their position as world emperors.

Bhishma said, "This is a fortunate day. O child, my heart swells with joy to see your success. We are here today to serve you. Give us some post and we shall happily carry it out."

In consultation with Vyasadeva, Yudhishthira asked Bhishma and Drona to take charge of organizing the sacrifice. Duryodhana oversaw the receiving of the many gifts that were being brought for Yudhishthira. Dushasana took charge of distributing food, and Ashvatthama looked after the brahmins. Other important jobs were given to the other senior Kurus. When all the tasks were assigned, Krishna, desiring to gain the brahmins' blessings, volunteered to wash their feet as they arrived.

The sacrificial compound was soon crowded with effulgent rishis. They chanted hymns from the Sama Veda and poured offerings into the blazing fires. Chief among them was Narada, who gazed around the arena in wonder. He knew that some divine plan was being enacted. The gods had come in person to witness the sacrifice and were seated on the gold platforms that had been set up around the arena. Many of the kings present were expansions of the celestials, and the Supreme Lord himself was also there.

For many days the sacrifice proceeded, with offerings being made to all the chief celestials. Tall columns of smoke rose up from the six fires as the ladles of ghee were poured into them. Expert priests chanted the mantras, and they were checked by other brahmins, who listened carefully to ensure that no fault was committed that would allow evil forces to sully the sacrifice. Powerful warriors surrounded the compound, equipped with every kind of weapon and fully alert to any possible danger.

When at last the rituals were complete, Yudhishthira was crowned as emperor. The brahmins prepared the juice of the soma plant to offer to the great personalities in attendance. Traditionally, the first offering was made to the most important person present, and when the time came, Bhishma said to Yudhishthira, "O king, you should select the foremost of all personalities present. Offer him the first worship, then worship the others as they deserve."

Yudhishthira turned to his counselors. "Whom do you consider fit to receive the first worship?"

There was some uncertainty. Some thought that Brahma, the powerful creator of the universe, should be first. Others suggested Shiva, while some thought it should be Vyasadeva or another of the great rishis. Yudhishthira knew whom he wanted to worship, but he did not want to make an independent decision and be accused of favoritism. He turned to Bhishma. "O grandsire, who do you think is most worthy among all the luminaries assembled here?"

Bhishma had no doubt. "As the sun shines among all luminous objects, so Krishna shines among all men. His effulgence, strength, knowledge, and prowess are without equal. He should receive the first worship."

Yudhishthira beamed in agreement. He signaled to Sahadeva, who stood up and announced that Krishna would receive the first worship. Addressing the gods and rishis in particular, he asked for their endorsement, citing Krishna's many glories. "By worshipping Krishna, who is the Lord in the heart of all beings, we will satisfy everyone."

A shout of approval went up from the gods and sages. "Let it be so!" they exclaimed.

Yudhishthira got down from his throne and personally began the worship of Krishna. Out of love for the Pandava, Krishna was agreeable and he smilingly received the offerings of *arghya* and soma juice.

Among the monarchs present was the king of Chedi, Sishupala. He was an avowed enemy of Krishna, particularly hating him because he had kidnapped his intended bride, the beautiful princess Rukmini, and married her himself on the very day she was supposed to wed Sishupala. When the Chedi monarch saw Krishna receiving the first worship, he became incensed. He jumped to his feet and spoke vituperatively. Waving his arms, he exclaimed, "Stop this ridiculous worship at once! Clearly, O Bhishma, you lack any discrimination. How on earth can Krishna be the most important person here? He is not even a king! Nor is he the eldest, wisest, or anything else. There are so many others here who are far more worthy of worship than he."

Sishupala turned toward Krishna. "As for you, Janardana, how do you have the nerve to accept the worship? Like a dog that has stolen sacrificial offerings and licks them up in solitude, so do you sit there enjoying this misplaced honor that the ignorant Yudhishthira offers you. He has shown us what kind of man he is today—mean-minded and ill-motivated, as are Bhishma and, indeed, Krishna himself. I cannot stay here any longer."

As Sishupala began to stride away from the sacrifice, a murmur went up from the assembly, some agreeing with him and others censuring him. Yudhishthira ran after him and tried to reason with him, pointing out how Bhishma was the most learned man in the assembly, and that his decision was supported by the many rishis present. But Sishupala was unmoved. He looked round at Bhishma and laughed.

Bhishma then began to justify his selection of Krishna. He described Krishna's transcendental position. There could be no doubt that he alone was worthy of the first worship. Keeping his anger in check, Bhishma said, "Blinded by envy of Krishna, Sishupala cannot understand his actual position. Therefore he criticizes him, everywhere and always. This Chedi king is like a foolish child. No heed should be paid to him at all."

Yudhishthira returned to complete the worship, as Sishupala watched in dismay. Turning toward the assembled kings, he boomed, "How can you sit here and tolerate this madness? Rise up! With me as your leader, stand in battle, arrayed against the Pandavas."

The assembly of kings appeared like an agitated ocean. Most had approved of Krishna's worship, but there were many who had been incited by Sishupala. They began to argue with each other, slapping their powerful arms and reaching for their weapons.

Seeing his sacrifice about to be spoiled, Yudhishthira became alarmed, but Bhishma reassured him in a loud voice. "Fear not, O best of Kurus. This Sishupala can rant only as long as Krishna does not act. Krishna is like a sleeping lion, and the kings who would challenge him are like so many barking dogs. Plainly, the Lord desires to take back the energy he has vested in Sishupala. Thus has Sishupala's intelligence become so perverse. A man on the verge of death will say any foolish thing."

Sishupala exploded at Bhishma. He began to insult him with harsh language, even as he continued to criticize Krishna, who looked on in silence. After all, Sishupala was his cousin. Krishna recalled how he had made a promise to Sishupala's mother, who had heard a prophecy that Krishna would kill her son. "O blessed lady, I shall spare his life, even if he insults me most grievously. Indeed, I shall tolerate one hundred insults from him."

Krishna patiently listened to Sishupala's torrent of abuse. The Chedi monarch finally concluded, "I, for one, will not stand by as this injustice is perpetrated. You are a slave and a wretch, Krishna. No worship should be offered to you. Get up and fight with me. I shall send you, Bhishma, and all the Pandavas to Death's abode."

Krishna then replied in a calm voice. "This man is my relative, yet he always wishes me ill. Once he came to Dwaraka while I was away and set fire to the city. He killed and captured many citizens, even stealing some of their wives. On another occasion, he cunningly disguised himself in order to rape an innocent princess. No virtue is to be found in him. I have promised to tolerate a hundred insults from him. Now he has gone beyond that number and will die at my hand."

Hearing Krishna speak, the assembly reproached Sishupala, who again rebuked Krishna. "Why should I fear one so weak? What harm can you do to me?"

Sishupala pulled out his sword, still hurling abuse at Krishna. In an instant, Krishna raised his chakra weapon and threw it. The brilliant disc streaked toward Sishupala, who tried desperately to fend it off with his sword. But it caught him on the neck and severed his head. The slain king fell heavily, like a cliff's edge falling onto a beach. Then, to everyone's astonishment, a shining light left his body and merged with Krishna. From the clear sky, rain fell and claps of thunder were heard. The assembly was silent. Sishupala's supporters were angered but, out of fear, they said nothing.

The rishis broke the silence by praising Krishna. "Well done! Well done! This person thoroughly deserved to die. Now, by your grace, he has achieved liberation."

Gradually the assembly became peaceful. Yudhishthira ordered his brothers to perform Sishupala's last rites. Sishupala's son was then installed as the king of Chedi. The Rajasuya was brought to a successful conclusion, and it ended with Yudhishthira distributing vast amounts of charity.

Gradually, all the monarchs left for their own kingdoms. Yudhishthira begged Krishna to stay on for a few more days and he agreed, sending his party on ahead. During his stay in Indraprastha, Krishna was personally served by Draupadi, and he developed much affection for the Pandava queen. One day, while he was paring some fruits she had served him, the sharp knife in his hand slipped and cut his finger. Seeing blood flow from the finger, Draupadi quickly tore off a strip of her fine sari and handed it to Krishna. Taking the cloth, Krishna said, "O blessed lady, I will surely repay this gift of yours."

Draupadi looked down modestly and thanked Krishna, who wrapped the piece of silk around his finger and then left the room.

*　　*　　*

Duryodhana had decided to remain in Indraprastha for a few days after the Rajasuya. He had been amazed to see the Pandavas' opulence. Consumed by envy, he walked through the streets, gazing open-mouthed at the hundreds of great palaces and mansions. The prince was especially fascinated by the wonderful Mayasabha, and he had the royal servants show him around. Shakuni had remained with him, and the two men gradually toured the great hall, stunned by its opulence. They felt as if they had entered Indra's assembly hall in heaven. The hundreds of rooms within the spacious hall were lit by countless celestial gems inlaid in the marbled walls. Golden archways wreathed with fragrant garlands stood alongside crystal-clear lakes. Exquisitely carved statues of gods and goddesses seemed alive, and everywhere the strains of heavenly music could be heard.

Seeing the celestial workmanship, Duryodhana felt his envy increase more and more. He snapped angrily at the servants and strode around with an air of indifference. Gradually, he came to the large lake in the center of the hall. Perfectly still, it was like a sheet of glass and had been designed in such as way as to reflect its marble bottom. It appeared like a continuation of the floor leading up to it, and Duryodhana failed to realize this fact. Not noticing that the servants had gone to the sides, he walked straight into the lake, his golden helmet flying off as he fell in with a great cry.

The Pandavas were watching from a balcony nearby. Seeing Duryodhana going headfirst into the water, his arms and legs akimbo, Bhima guffawed. Many ladies were also present, and they too laughed out loud, with their hands over their mouths. Without looking up at them, Duryodhana hauled himself out of the lake and stood dripping by its side. Seeing his acute embarrassment, Yudhishthira told his brothers to stop laughing. He quickly arranged for dry clothes to be brought for Duryodhana. The Kaurava prince was seething. He could hardly bear the humiliation, especially the laughter of Bhima and Draupadi. He was still smarting from his failure to win the Panchala princess in the contest.

After changing his clothes, the prince completed his tour of the hall. Maya's deceptive designs caught him again when he came to an apparently open door that was actually shut. With his head held high, he walked straight into it, bumping his head on the clear crystal. When he reached out to open a similar door that was already open, he stumbled forward, cursing. The servants struggled to contain their laughter as the angry prince strode out of the hall.

Yudhishthira was sorry to see his pain, and he hurried to console him, but Duryodhana simply laughed and stormed off. Krishna told Yudhishthira not to worry—Duryodhana had only gotten what he deserved. The Kaurava prince then left with Shakuni for Hastinapura, thinking only of revenge.

Krishna also decided to leave at that time, and he bade a fond farewell to the Pandavas, saying, "Cherish your subjects as if they were your own children. Be a refuge to them, as a large tree is to the birds."

After Krishna's departure, Yudhishthira approached Vyasadeva and asked him if he felt the Rajasuya had been successful. "I heard previously from Narada that great danger can arise when this sacrifice is performed. Was this averted when Krishna slew Sishupala? Have you seen any other fearful portents?"

Vyasadeva replied that the signs were ominous. "It seems that, thirteen years from now, there will arise a war that will destroy the kshatriyas. Destiny will make you the cause, through Duryodhana's fault. O king, do not grieve for this, for none can surmount the inevitable influence of time. Know that it is God's will."

After blessing Yudhishthira, the sage took his leave and went to the Himalayas to practice asceticism. Alarmed at his words, Yudhishthira said to his brothers, "If I am to be the cause of so much death, then perhaps I should end my own life now."

Arjuna replied, "O king, take heart. The sage has said that it is God's will. Do your duty with a firm mind."

Yudhishthira was thoughtful. "From this day on I shall not make a quarrel with anyone, for that is always the root of war. I shall never use harsh words and shall always practice virtue. Ever obedient to the order of my elders, I will carefully avoid all conflict."

Having made this vow, Yudhishthira felt more peaceful. Along with his brothers, he continued to rule his kingdom. He realized that some plan of the Lord must be unfolding. Yudhishthira knew there were many demonic kings who had only reluctantly accepted his rule, after being subjugated by his brothers. He had seen how they had risen to support Sishupala at the sacrifice. And no doubt Duryodhana would not be happy in a subordinate position to the Pandavas—especially after his recent humiliation. Yudhishthira realized Vyasadeva's words would surely prove true.

Eleven

EVERYTHING IS LOST

AS HE TRAVELED BACK to Hastinapura, Duryodhana was miserable. Repeatedly sighing, he gazed distractedly at the passing countryside, not even seeing the people who stood by the roadside, waving at the royal procession. Shakuni touched his shoulder and asked, "What ails you, O king? You appear greatly depressed."

Duryodhana turned his vacant eyes toward Shakuni. "O uncle, my heart is on fire. Seeing Yudhishthira's wealth and influence, I cannot contain my jealousy. The whole world now fears the Pandavas. When Sishupala was so unrighteously killed, there were none who had the courage to challenge them. The kings of the world brought them tributes, acting as if they were tax-paying citizens."

The Kaurava prince took off his gem-studded helmet and threw it on the seat of his chariot. He played with the many rings that adorned his fingers. "I feel like ending my life. What man possessed of any power could live like this, seeing his foes so prosperous? I will never be able to equal the Pandavas; nor have I found any way to destroy them. Surely, fate is supreme and mans' exertions useless."

Duryodhana felt tears of anguish running down his face. He asked Shakuni to represent his plight to Dhritarashtra. Shakuni placed an arm round his shoulders. "Why do you envy the Pandavas?" he asked, a slight edge of sarcasm to his voice. "By good fortune they have prospered, winning Draupadi as their wife and conquering the earth. What is there to be sorry about? All your attempts to subdue them have failed. Why, then, do you lament?"

Duryodhana looked curiously at his uncle. What was his point?

Shakuni smiled. "O king, their wealth, the Kuru wealth, can also be yours. You say there are none who have the courage to challenge them, but this is not true. On your side, you have many mighty heroes: all your brothers,

Drona, Karna, Kripa, Somadatta, and so many others. With their assistance, you could surely rule the entire world."

Duryodhana looked ahead. Hastinapura was visible in the distance, like a dark cloud on the horizon. Turning back to Shakuni, he said, "Perhaps you are right, Uncle. Who can defeat us? Let us challenge the Pandavas. By overpowering them, we shall ourselves become rulers of the earth. And I shall own their wonderful assembly hall, so full of riches."

"No, that is not the best policy," Shakuni replied quickly. "The Pandavas, assisted by Krishna, are unconquerable. Some other means will be needed to dispose of them. Then you may hold sway over the earth." Shakuni fingered the dice he always carried, clicking them together as he spoke. "Indeed, O king, I know just the means."

Duryodhana leaned forward eagerly. "Then tell me, Uncle. How can we get rid of my enemies, once and for all?"

"I believe that Yudhishthira is fond of dice." Shakuni replied, twisting the end of his dark mustache. "However, he is not so expert at the game."

Duryodhana smiled in understanding. No matter how good Yudhishthira might be at dice, he would be no match for Shakuni. The Gandhara king spent all his time practicing with other experts at the game. He could make the dice do practically anything he wished. Duryodhana had even heard it said that Shakuni had been blessed by his father that he would never lose at dice. The prince could certainly not recall any instance where that blessing had failed.

"Just challenge him, O king, and I shall do the rest," Shakuni continued. "Let me play on your behalf, and I will win for you this whole world. Have no doubt."

The chariot had reached the city and the huge gates were swung back. The guards shouted respectful greetings to Duryodhana as he rode past. As the chariot sped along the main highway toward the palace, he suggested to Shakuni that they go at once to Dhritarashtra. "Tell him what you have just told me. Let us get his permission."

Shakuni agreed, and the two men went straight to the royal chamber, where Dhritarashtra was seated alone. After bowing before him, Shakuni said, "O great king, your son is pale and afflicted with grief. If you think it fit, inquire from him as to the cause."

Dhritarashtra looked surprised. "O Duryodhana, O son, why are you so depressed? What possible reason could there be for your sorrow? All my vast wealth is at your disposal. Thousands of servants await your command. You have the best food, the best chariots and horses, finely furnished palaces, and excellent gardens. Many beautiful damsels are ready to serve you. I think even the celestials do not have more opulence. Why, then, do you grieve?"

Duryodhana immediately told his father how much he envied the Pandavas, because their wealth and influence far exceeded his. The prince described what he had seen in Indraprastha. "Yudhishthira received so much tribute at the Rajasuya that some had to be turned away—there was simply nowhere to put it! Millions of elephants, horses, cows, and camels were given, as well as heaps of gold and gems, piled up like mountains. One hundred thousand brahmins were fed at a sitting during the sacrifice, and this went on continuously."

Duryodhana said his mind had been completely stunned by the opulence he had seen. Even the gods had come to the sacrifice and offered gifts to Yudhishthira. There was now no limit to his wealth. Duryodhana's voice almost choked as he described it to his father.

Dhritarashtra remained silent, and Shakuni then said, "I know a way by which we can win all this wealth. O truthful one, challenge Yudhishthira at dice. He will not be able to refuse. Then, let me play against him, and I will win everything. O king, you may then enjoy this earth without a rival."

Before the king could respond, Duryodhana immediately added, "O father, please grant your permission. Shakuni will not lose."

Dhritarashtra was uncertain. "Perhaps, but let me first consult with Vidura. He always knows what is best."

Duryodhana's face contorted in annoyance. "You know Vidura favors the Pandavas. How will he agree to this? O father, I cannot live while my enemies are so prosperous! I would rather kill myself. Then you may live happily with Vidura. What need do you have for me, anyway?"

Duryodhana knew he could manipulate his father. The blind king always gave in to him. As expected, Dhritarashtra was moved by his threats and said, "All right, I shall convince Vidura. You should order the royal builders to construct a hall equal to Yudhishthira's. Let me know when it is completed; then we shall arrange for the game."

When Duryodhana and Shakuni had left, smiling together, Dhritarashtra summoned Vidura. He knew his brother would object to the dice game, but the king still could not do anything without first discussing it with him. When he arrived, Dhritarashtra told him what he had in mind. Vidura immediately protested. "O king, gambling always causes dispute. I cannot approve. You should be careful not to exacerbate the tense relationship that already exists between your sons and the Pandavas."

Dhritarashtra's response was firm. "My mind is made up on this, dear brother. Whether right or wrong, the game will go ahead. Everything depends upon fate. If fate favors us and the gods are with us, then no dispute will arise. Otherwise, what can we do?"

Vidura rose from his seat and walked to the window, looking out at the beautiful palace gardens that the king had never seen. "This reasoning is false, O descendant of Bharata. We cannot deny responsibility for our acts, for we always have free will. Surely everything lies in God's hands, but He is giving us the consequences of our own acts. It is up to us how we act. Consider carefully why you want this gambling match. If you are acting out of impure motives, the results will not be auspicious."

Dhritarashtra said nothing and Vidura began to walk away, pensively shaking his head. He prayed that the king would come to his senses—but he was not very hopeful. Although he was not a fool himself, Dhritarashtra was virtually controlled by his foolish and covetous son. Disaster loomed. Vidura knew the dark age of Kali was imminent. If the gambling match occurred, it would almost surely usher in that fearful time, for it would lead to the annihilation of the world's rulers. Dhritarashtra's words were not entirely false, however. The Supreme Lord was ultimately controlling everything. If it was his desire that there be a great war, then, without doubt, it would take place. Trying to fathom the Lord's inscrutable plan, Vidura left the room.

* * *

As the hall in Hastinapura was gradually built, Dhritarashtra began to feel apprehensive. Generally, he disregarded Vidura's advice at his peril. It was true that gambling was fraught with danger—especially a match between his sons and the Pandavas. A war between them, involving as it would all of the world's kings, would be catastrophic.

The king decided to make one more attempt to change his son's mind. Sitting alone with him, he said, "My son, there is no need for playing dice. Vidura does not approve and I, too, am highly doubtful. Gambling leads to dissension, bringing in its train terrible conflict. What need is there for you to gamble, anyway? You have everything. A vast kingdom is at your command. What more could you want?"

Duryodhana sat kneading his hands. He had expected his father to object to the gambling, especially after consulting with Vidura. But the prince saw the impending match as his best, and probably only, hope of overcoming the Pandavas. He spoke in a pitiful voice. "My existence has become wretched. How can I live, O king of kings, while our enemies prosper like the gods in heaven? At the sacrifice, it was my job to receive the tributes. Day after day, I became completely exhausted from handling the gems and jewels that were brought. I had never seen such opulence before! Our wealth is not a fig by comparison."

Duryodhana described the incidents in the hall when he fell into the lake and walked into the door. "After smashing my head on the solid crystal, I stood with my brains swimming. The twins then ran up and held me by my arms, saying, 'The door is over here, O king.' I could have died, then and there."

Dhritarashtra listened silently as his son went on describing the opulence of the Rajasuya. His voice became pleading. "How can I live in this state? Is it not the accepted duty of kshatriyas to challenge their enemies? If we leave the Pandavas alone, they will continue to flourish, eventually consuming us, along with all our wealth. However, if we challenge them to open warfare, our fate will likely be the same as Sishupala's. A dice game is the safest and surest means of defeating them."

The king was still not convinced. "Enmity with the powerful is not sound policy, O son. Nor do I like harboring such feelings toward Pandu's sons. It cannot lead to any good. You think you will achieve your ends by gambling, but mark my words—it will result in a frightful war."

Duryodhana dismissed his father's doubts. "We are simply arranging for a friendly match. If Yudhishthira chooses to stake his wealth, then how will we be to blame? But, O father, if he does, then he will certainly lose. Shakuni is undefeatable at dice."

As usual, Dhritarashtra felt unable to deny his son. He rose from his seat and rang a bell to summon his servants. As they entered the room, he said, "Do as you will, then. My doubts remain, for I cannot see how impious deeds will ever yield lasting prosperity. But I shall order Vidura to bring the Pandavas here."

Duryodhana smiled as the servants led his father out of the room. The prince went immediately to Shakuni to tell him the good news.

Ordered by the king, Vidura soon left for Indraprastha, his mind filled with foreboding. As he entered the Pandavas' city, he saw that it had become unlimitedly affluent. Passing through jeweled golden arches, he marveled at the prosperity visible everywhere. The citizens, dressed in fine silks and decked with many ornaments, moved about on various shining chariots. Seven-storied mansions of diverse designs lined the long and smoothly paved roads, which sparkled with precious stones. Vidura saw many elephants, adorned with jeweled dresses, sprinkling the roads with perfumed water. He heard the blast of conches and the sound of bells and drums as brahmins worshipped Vishnu in great marble temples. Seeing the

Mayasabha from a distance, he felt his bodily hair stand on end. It shone like a palace of the gods and emanated an exquisite fragrance. Servants led him in, and he was brought before Yudhishthira, who sat in the central hall, surrounded by his brothers and ministers.

Seeing their uncle, all the Pandavas quickly got up and bowed at his feet. Overjoyed, Yudhishthira greeted him with tears in his eyes. Vidura embraced him with affection, but Yudhishthira could see that he was worried. He asked, "Something seems to be bothering you, Uncle. Do you come in peace? Is everything well in Hastinapura?"

Vidura looked down. "All is well with us, O king. I have come here to invite you to see the assembly hall the king has just built. He suggested that you may like to play some dice with your cousins."

Yudhishthira glanced over at his brothers. Seeing this, Vidura nodded and said in a low voice, "I think, O son of Kunti, that you understand well enough his intentions."

"Indeed, uncle, and I know well how gambling produces quarrel and conflict. How, then, can I consent to play?"

Yudhishthira was torn. He felt unable to refuse Dhritarashtra's invitation and was also bound by the moral code that dictated that a kshatriya not refuse any challenge, whether to fight or to play at dice. But he sensed that the game would result in disaster, especially when he recalled Vyasadeva's words.

Vidura raised his hands in a gesture of helplessness. "I tried to dissuade the king, but he was determined. Duryodhana and Shakuni have convinced him. Even now, Shakuni is spending his time practicing dice with many highly skilled players in preparation for the game. It is he you will have to face."

"If I am challenged, I will not refuse," Yudhishthira replied. "This is my vow. I am unwilling to gamble, but I will come with you to Hastinapura in obedience to Dhritarashtra's desire."

Yudhishthira looked over at his brothers, who all appeared apprehensive, and said, "This whole universe moves by the Lord's will. Bound by duties and obligations as if by ropes, we are helplessly carried by fate. We shall leave tomorrow."

The next morning Yudhishthira mounted his blazing chariot, along with his brothers and Draupadi. Appearing like the god of wealth leaving his celestial abode, he went out of Indraprastha with brahmins, chanting sacred hymns, walking before him.

When the party reached Hastinapura that evening, they were greeted by the Kuru elders and escorted into Dhritarashtra's palace, where they rested for the night.

The following morning the five brothers were brought to the new assembly hall. Occupying the same amount of space as the Mayasabha, it was supported by thousands of many-colored marble pillars worked with gold leaf. Fine hand-woven rugs were laid out along the floor, and beautifully carved seats were arranged in the many alcoves. Sunlight streamed in through countless windows and, escorted by the Kurus, the Pandavas admired the workmanship, although the hall was obviously not the equal of theirs.

The huge building was crowded with the many kings and princes who were visiting Hastinapura. The Pandavas greeted them, bowing before their elders and saluting their peers. They then sat down on new seats, which were covered with costly cloth and studded with gems. Seated opposite them were Duryodhana and his brothers, along with Karna and Shakuni. When everyone was settled, Shakuni said, "O king, we have been waiting for you. Let us enjoy some friendly dicing together. Shall we establish the rules before we begin?"

Yudhishthira looked at the grinning Shakuni. "O Gandhara monarch, what virtue is there in gambling? Deceitful play is especially sinful and is always avoided by the wise."

Shakuni laughed. "Those who know the skills of the game need not fear anything. In any event, it is excessive staking that leads to injury, not the game itself. Let the stakes be fixed and we need have no worries."

"I have always been advised by the rishis to avoid gaming with experts. O Shakuni, do not try to take from me the wealth with which I wish to serve the brahmins. For myself, I have no desire to win anything at gambling; therefore, why should I play?"

Shakuni leaned back with a smile. "I understand, O king. If you are afraid of losing, then we need not play. Obviously, one approaches a contest with a desire to win—that is only natural. But if you feel I am being dishonest in some way, then let us desist from the game."

Yudhishthira looked across at the Kuru elders. Dhritarashtra sat at their head, hearing everything but seeing nothing. He made no remark. By his side sat Bhishma and Vidura, who both appeared uncomfortable. The whole hall remained silent as Yudhishthira looked around. Turning back to Shakuni, he said, "O king, when challenged, I never refuse. I shall play, but who is a suitable match for me? Who can stake equally?"

Yudhishthira knew that Shakuni could not match him in staking and thus, could not fairly play against him, even though he may be more skillful at the game. But Duryodhana quickly spoke up. "Let my uncle play, O king.

I shall provide him with the stakes. Bet whatever you will, gems, gold, or any other wealth."

The Pandavas looked at one another. This was what they had expected. Plainly, it was no friendly game. Yudhishthira said, "I have not heard of one man playing while another stakes, but if everyone thinks it is acceptable, then let the play begin."

Yudhishthira looked toward the Kuru elders, but still no one spoke. Shakuni took up his bone-white dice. "What, then, will you stake, O king?" he asked.

Yudhishthira took from his neck a long, golden chain studded with immaculate pearls. "Here is my first bet."

"It is matched," said Duryodhana, fingering the heavy gold chains that hung round his own neck.

Shakuni closed his eyes and rubbed the dice together, then threw them across the large wooden board that had been set up for the game. "Kali!" his voice rang out as the dice skittered across the board. As they came to a stop on the desired throw, he shouted, "Lo, I have won!"

"You should not be so proud of yourself, Shakuni. This game has been contrived only for my defeat. But it is not yet over. I will now stake my hundreds of thousands of jars of gold, each filled to the brim. Let us see if you win again."

Yudhishthira rarely played dice. He had no real liking for the game, which he knew to be a weakness of kings that often caused their destruction. But having accepted the challenge, he would not back down. Powerful kshatriyas always fought fearlessly, whether in battle or at gambling.

Hearing Yudhishthira place such a huge stake, Shakuni glanced over at Duryodhana, who smiled and waved his hand. Yudhishthira gathered up the dice and rolled them, calling out his desired throw, but they fell differently. "Unlucky," said Shakuni with false sympathy, as he picked up the dice and made his throw. Again they landed according to his call, and he cried out, "I win again!"

"Then I shall stake my priceless celestial chariot, adorned with gems and gold, covered with tiger-skins and yoked to eight milk-white steeds. Make your throw, Shakuni."

Once again Yudhishthira lost, as the dice fell as if commanded by Shakuni. The Pandava, seemingly caught up in the fever of the game, went on raising the stakes, losing every throw. Gradually, he lost all his wealth. All that could be heard was the calling out of the bets, then the clatter of the dice, followed by Shakuni's shout of, "Lo, I win again!"

Duryodhana and his brothers laughed and urged Yudhishthira to keep on playing. "What else will you stake, O king?" they taunted. "Your wealth is limitless."

Each time Shakuni shouted, Dhritarashtra leaned forward and eagerly asked Vidura, "What has been won?" Vidura felt increasing distress as the game continued. He could hardly tolerate watching Yudhishthira being practically robbed. The Pandava had little chance of beating Shakuni at dice. That was obvious, but no one was protesting, least of all Dhritarashtra. Everyone sat silently. Surely all-powerful destiny was moving them according to some higher plan.

Again and again the dice landed exactly according to Shakuni's call. Each time, Yudhishthira remained impassive and made another huge stake. Playing with Shakuni's unfamiliar dice, he was unable to win a single throw.

Yudhishthira's brothers writhed in agony as they watched him losing. Bhima was especially suffering. He found Duryodhana's sneering demeanor unbearable. The powerful Pandava squeezed his hands together in frustration, longing to jump up and challenge Duryodhana to an open fight. But without Yudhishthira's order, he could say nothing. Arjuna and the twins also remained still, looking on in horror as their elder brother kept losing.

Suddenly Vidura jumped to his feet. He could stand it no longer. The game had to be stopped. He spoke out loudly. "O great king, leader of the Kurus, listen to my words, which will be as disagreeable to you as medicine is to a dying man. Even when this sinful wretch Duryodhana was born, I warned you that he would destroy our dynasty. That time is close. Act now before it is too late. Have Arjuna kill him at your command. This is the proper course of action. An unworthy son should always be abandoned for the good of the house. Otherwise, you will sink into an ocean of grief."

Everyone looked at Vidura. Duryodhana frowned and ground his teeth together in anger. But the blind king said nothing. Vidura continued, "The virtuous Pandavas will provide you with far more happiness than the evil-hearted Duryodhana. Purchase those five tigers at the cost of this jackal. Do not be like the king who once possessed a bird that could vomit gold but, out of greed, cut it open, thus killing it."

Vidura further described the benefits of maintaining friendship with the Pandavas, but seeing that this was having no effect on Dhritarashtra, he began to describe the dangers of forming an enmity with them. "A great fire has blazed forth, O king, and you are about to enter it willingly. These five heroes are like enraged serpents, with venom in their eyes. Do not provoke them further. When they stand in battle, not even the celestials can face them. Driven by your covetous son, you are rushing toward a terrible conflict that will destroy the Kurus to their roots. Who will be your refuge in that hour of confusion?"

Suddenly Duryodhana exploded. Glaring at Vidura, who had never had a good word to say about him, he boomed out, "O Vidura, you are nothing but an enemy in the guise of a friend. You always praise our foes and criticize us. We are foolishly maintaining you, like a man keeping a serpent in his lap. Who do you think you are, offering us such vicious advice? Why do you find fault with me? I am what God has made me. If I am acting wrongly, then it is God you should blame, not me, for I am under His control. You simply blather uselessly. Your opinion is not needed here. Go wherever you please. An unchaste wife, however well treated, always forsakes her husband."

Vidura shook his head in despair, finding Duryodhana's sarcastic words about God particularly painful. The atheistic prince was simply mocking Vidura's faith. Having vented his anger, Duryodhana sat down again, with a smug smile. Vidura turned again to Dhritarashtra. "O king, judge for yourself the merit of your son's words. I am trying only to offer advice meant for your good. Many men can be found who will speak agreeable words, seeking to win their master's favor, but rare are those who will speak disagreeable truths. O descendant of Bharata, act now with intelligence and humility. Stop persecuting the Pandavas, and reject your son."

Still Dhritarashtra remained silent. Vidura sat down, burying his face in his hands. What would it take for the king to see sense?

Duryodhana laughed and waved at Shakuni, who then said, "O Yudhishthira, you have lost much wealth. Do you wish to stop now, or do you still have something left to stake?"

Yudhishthira looked steadily at Shakuni. "I have riches counted in the millions, tens of millions, billions and hundreds of billions, and even more. Why do you ask? With all this wealth do I play. Roll the dice."

Shakuni smiled. The dice once more clattered across the board as he made his call. Again they fell as he desired, and again his laughing voice rang out, "I win!" Yudhishthira staked his land, animals, army, and servants, losing them all. When the entire kingdom was lost, Shakuni looked at him quizzically. "It seems you have lost everything, O king. How shall the game continue?"

Yudhishthira was breathing heavily. Somehow he had lost every single throw. It was almost inconceivable. Nothing remained of his vast wealth. All of it now belonged to Duryodhana. Had it been willed by the Lord? Yudhishthira was perplexed. How would he now be able to perform his duty as a king, protecting and serving the brahmins? He had to try to win some-thing back. What, though, could he stake?

Yudhishthira looked round at his brothers. Perhaps there was still a way back. He turned toward Shakuni. "These princes are also my wealth. With this fair-skinned Nakula, then, the mighty-armed and virtuous son of Madri, do I play."

Seconds later Nakula was also lost. Yudhishthira shook his head in dis-belief. Things had really gone too far. But there could be no turning back now. His voice was strained as he made his next stake. "Here is Madri's other son, the equally powerful Sahadeva, so dear to us all. He should not be risked, but I shall wager him."

Within moments Shakuni's voice was again ringing out in glee. "Lo, I have won!" He looked at Yudhishthira with a slight smile. "It seems that Bhima and Arjuna are more dear to you than the twins."

Yudhishthira blazed up. "Fool, do not try to create disunion among us, who are all of one heart. The game is not yet over. Here is Arjuna, who is ever energetic and who always takes us to the other shore of the sea of battle. He shall be my next stake."

The hall was completely silent as the dice were thrown again. Duryodhana leaned forward in eager anticipation. Winning Yudhishthira's wealth was one thing, but taking possession of his brothers had been beyond his wildest hopes.

As the dice came to a halt, Shakuni's monotonous voice was again heard. "I have won! O king, three of your brothers are now lost. Will you stop there?"

Yudhishthira thought again of Krishna. Was he testing him in some way? It seemed incredible that the Lord could allow even his dear friend Arjuna to be lost. Could things still be turned around? He looked down as he spoke, "Although he does not deserve to be staked, although he is our leader and our shelter, still do I wager this lion-like Bhima, the foremost of all mace fighters and the grinder of foes."

Shakuni closed his eyes and made his throw. Bhima was lost. Yudhishthira sat perspiring freely. There was only one thing left for him to do. He could not leave the hall with his four brothers lost into slavery to the Kauravas, which would no doubt be their fate. Taking a deep breath, he said, "I am still left, the eldest of the Pandavas. Let me be the next stake. If I am lost, I shall do whatever a slave is obliged to do."

The kings watching the game gasped as Yudhishthira spoke. They watched in astonishment, as the dice yet again seemed to obey Shakuni's command. "You are lost!" he exclaimed. "Surely an act worthy of a sinful man, for you still had wealth with which to bet. You still have one more stake dear to you. Why do you not bet Draupadi? By betting her, you can win yourself back."

Yudhishthira sat in silent anguish. How could he bet Draupadi? It was his duty to protect her, not deliberately place her in danger. But what choice was left? Everything else was gone. If the Lord was going to save him, it could only be through Draupadi.

"She who is neither short nor tall, who is perfectly formed, who has eyes like lotus petals, who emanates the fragrance of lotuses, who has a wealth of beauty, grace, and virtue, and who is possessed of every feminine accomplishment—with her at stake, I shall now play."

When Yudhishthira said this, his brothers looked at each other in disbelief. The Kuru elders cried out, "Fie! Fie!" Many kings bowed their heads in sorrow, with tears flowing from their eyes. Bhishma, Drona, and Kripa were covered with perspiration, and Vidura sighed repeatedly, staring in hopeless despair at his blind brother. But Dhritarashtra leaned forward, eagerly asking, "Is the stake won? Is it won?"

Shakuni was flushed with excitement. By his side, Duryodhana, Dushasana, and Karna were all laughing loudly as he threw the dice, with the inevitable result. His voice resounded throughout the shocked hall. "She is won! She is won!" He stood up and began to dance around, repeatedly saying in a sneering voice, "You still have one more stake dear to you. Bet Draupadi, O king." The grief-stricken Yudhishthira sat mute, breathing heavily.

Duryodhana, relishing his moment of victory, turned to Vidura and said, "Come, O uncle, bring Draupadi here. Let that dear wife of the Pandavas be engaged in some menial work."

Vidura could hardly look at Duryodhana. He immediately retorted, "O wicked man, fool, do you not see that you are standing on the edge of a steep precipice? Deadly snakes are on your head. Do not provoke them further and thus go to Death's abode."

Vidura turned to address Dhritarashtra and the rest of the assembly. "In my view, Draupadi cannot be lost, since Yudhishthira had already lost himself when he bet her. This son of Dhritarashtra, like a bamboo that bears fruit on the point of death, wins treasures at dice, not seeing the frightful terrors that will soon follow. He will certainly cause the Kurus' destruction. When the words of wisdom spoken by friends are ignored, when temptation and lust hold sway, know for sure that a fearful and universal destruction is close."

Duryodhana waved his hand dismissively at Vidura, "Fie on you," he laughed. Looking around, he saw the chief palace servant and called out to him, "O Pratikamin, bring Draupadi here. There is nothing to fear. It is only Vidura who raves crazily. He never wishes for our success."

The Pandavas sat with their heads bowed. Yudhishthira seemed stupefied with sorrow. He was consumed by remorse. How had he let himself get so carried away? He had gambled away everything, casting his brothers and even Draupadi into slavery. That had been a terrible mistake. But what could he now do? The Kuru elders, with the sole exception of Vidura, were silent. It seemed they did not disapprove of the gambling, nor of the fact that Draupadi was being brought to the assembly as a slave. Their silence amounted to tacit approval. Yudhishthira felt helpless. It was plainly his own fault that he and his brothers were now in such an awkward situation.

Seeing their elder brother subdued and Dhritarashtra also saying nothing, the other Pandavas kept themselves in check. All of them longed to challenge the gloating Duryodhana to open combat on the spot. But they would not do anything without Yudhishthira's order. They watched in silent dread as the Pratikamin left the hall for the ladies' quarters.

Twelve

EVIL TAKES A HOLD

DEPRESSED AT HEART, the Pratikamin went quickly toward Draupadi's chamber. He stood before her with folded palms and said in a trembling voice, "O queen, you have been lost at dice by Yudhishthira. I have come here with Duryodhana's order to bring you to the assembly."

Draupadi put down the cloth she had been embroidering. Her expression was disbelieving. "O Pratikamin, how can this be true? Who would stake his own wife in a gambling match? Could he find nothing else to bet?"

"O queen, the king had already lost everything, including his brothers and even himself. He then staked you."

Draupadi could understand that yet more Kaurava treachery must be afoot. Still, it was strange that she should have been lost. She felt her anger rise. "O servant, go back to the assembly and ask one thing for me. Ask that gambler whom he lost first: himself or me? Having ascertained this, you may then take me with you, if indeed it is my husband's desire."

The Pratikamin bowed and left Draupadi's room. Arriving back at the assembly, he addressed Yudhishthira with Draupadi's question. Yudhishthira made no reply. He sat sighing, his head hanging down, seemingly deprived of his senses.

Duryodhana laughed. "Let Draupadi place her question directly to Yudhishthira, so that we may all hear the words that pass between them. Go, Pratikamin, and fetch her here."

The servant unwillingly made his way back to Draupadi. With tears in his eyes, he relayed Duryodhana's message. "O queen, it seems the Kurus' destruction is close at hand. When the weak-brained Duryodhana is intent on humiliating you, he will not be able to maintain his prosperity for long."

Draupadi felt compassion for the distressed servant. She spoke gently. "Surely the Lord has ordained this. In accord with destiny, happiness and distress come, one after the other. We should therefore pursue only religion, seeing that as life's highest goal. If cherished, it will pour blessings on us. Let not the Kurus abandon religion now by abusing me, a helpless woman in an embarrassed condition."

Draupadi was referring to the fact that she was in the period of her menses. Wearing only a single cloth, she was keeping herself in seclusion, as was the custom. To be brought before a public assembly in that condition was unthinkable. "Go back to the assembly one more time, O servant, and ask the virtuous Kuru elders their opinion. If they think it conformable to morality that I be brought before them, I shall go."

The servant returned to the hall and repeated Draupadi's words. Everyone sat with downcast faces. Duryodhana's eagerness and Dhritarashtra's complicity left them feeling helpless. Yudhishthira looked up. "We are now under Duryodhana's command. He has ordered that Draupadi be brought here, so let it be so. Tell her to come here and stand before her elders, even though she is attired in a single cloth and should not be seen by anyone."

Yudhishthira looked across at Dhritarashtra and Bhishma. The blind king was leaning forward slightly, but Bhishma appeared deeply pained. He slowly shook his head from side to side, but remained silent as Duryodhana again commanded the servant, "Go once more to Draupadi and bring her here immediately. She now has her husband's order."

The servant shifted from foot to foot, perplexed. He feared Draupadi's anger, which he felt could burn the world itself to ashes, but did not want to disobey Duryodhana. The Kaurava prince became impatient. He turned to Dushasana. "This foolish servant is afraid of Bhima. Go, brother, and bring Draupadi yourself. What can the Pandavas do? They are now our slaves."

Throwing a smiling and disdainful glance at the Pandavas, Dushasana rose up and went out of the hall. Like a dog entering a lion's den, he went into Draupadi's quarters and said to her, "Come, O princess, you are fairly won by us. Show yourself to your new lords, the Kauravas."

Draupadi shrank back from the leering prince. She got to her feet and ran from the room, calling out for Gandhari. Dushasana bellowed in anger and ran after her. Catching her by the hair, he began to drag her toward the hall. Draupadi trembled like a sapling caught in a gale. She cried out and struggled, but Dushasana pulled her even more forcefully, caring nothing for the fact that she had five great heroes as her protectors.

Seeing that she could do nothing to stop him, Draupadi spoke to Dushasana in a low and contemptuous voice. "O rude one, O wretch, how dare you drag me before the assembly? Can you not see that I am indisposed?"

"So what?" Dushasana harshly replied. "You are now our slave. What does it matter if you are attired in a single cloth or naked? Come and take your place among the serving women."

Dushasana dragged the piteously wailing Draupadi through the palace corridors and into the hall, where he threw her before Duryodhana. She lay with her cloth and hair disheveled, praying ardently to both Krishna and Arjuna.

Seeing Draupadi's pitiful condition, Vidura, Bhishma, and Drona wept openly. They looked despairingly at Dhritarashtra, but he only said, "What is happening? Is the Panchala princess here?"

Draupadi then realized that not even her husbands were able to say anything. Gathering her cloth around her and covering her hair, she rose up in anger, like a flame, and began chastising the Kurus. "In this assembly are many learned men, devoted to sacrifice and possessed of godly virtues. Some of you are my elders and, indeed, my gurus. How, then, have you allowed me to be dragged before you in this state?"

She turned toward Dushasana, her eyes blazing as she spoke. "Cruel wretch! Keep your hands off me. The Pandavas will not forgive you, even if Indra and all the celestials protect you!"

Turning back to the Kurus, she went on, "Yudhishthira is constrained by the subtle laws of morality. Only men of his high caliber can understand those laws. I will not admit even an atom of fault in him. Surely, all you Kurus are of the same mind as Dushasana and his evil brothers, otherwise how could you sit silently as I am abused so? Alas! The Bharata race has lost its greatness today."

Draupadi threw a glance at her husbands, who sat like five enraged tigers ready to strike at any moment. Catching that glance, filled with modesty and anger, they felt more pain than they had by losing their wealth, kingdom, and everything else.

Dushasana also saw Draupadi glancing at her husbands. Laughing loudly, he seized her again and dragged her even more violently. Duryodhana, Karna, and Shakuni laughed along with him and applauded him. Apart from those four and the blind king, everyone else in the hall grieved with loud cries.

Draupadi pulled away from Dushasana and looked imploringly at Bhishma. The old Kuru leader took a deep breath and said, "O blessed lady, your question is difficult to answer. Surely a slave has no wealth of his own and cannot, therefore, stake anything. But then, a wife is always under her husband's control. Yudhishthira will abandon the world and all its wealth, but he will never abandon morality. He knew that Shakuni is matchless in dice; still he agreed to the play and lost everything. Knowing all this, I cannot decide on the matter."

Draupadi shook her head and her long braid moved about like an angry snake. "How can you suggest that Yudhishthira played voluntarily? Everything was arranged for his defeat. Although not expert himself, he was enticed into playing with skillful, wicked, and deceitful gamblers. What virtue was there in this?"

Dushasana told Draupadi to keep quiet, rebuking her with harsh words. She fell to her knees and covered her face with her hands, weeping silently. Bhima could take no more. Afflicted with unbearable agony at seeing Draupadi's condition, he finally gave vent to his boiling anger. Looking toward Yudhishthira, he said, "What gambler, however desperate, would stake his own wife? Even though you lost our wealth, kingdom, and our very selves, I felt no anger, for you are our lord. But seeing how the innocent Draupadi is suffering as a result of your gambling, I am unable to control my wrath."

Bhima turned his massive shoulders toward the twins. "Sahadeva, bring fire. I shall burn the king's hands."

Arjuna was alarmed. He reached out and caught Bhima by the arm. "O Bhima, in the association of immoral men, you are losing your own high morality. Do not fulfill the enemy's desire. Yudhishthira is without fault, and he is your worshipable elder. Brought here and forced to play against his will, he has only added to his fame and virtue."

Arjuna's reproach made Bhima feel ashamed and sorry for his outburst. His head dropped and he replied, "You are right, Arjuna. Forgive me; my anger for Draupadi overpowered my reason."

Among Duryodhana's hundred brothers, one of them, Vikarna, was outraged. He could not believe what he was seeing and felt impelled to speak out. Seeing his chance, he stood up and said, "Draupadi's question deserves a proper answer. If we, as an assembly, cannot decide the matter, then great sin will overcome us. Let us hear everyone's impartial opinion."

Vikarna looked around the assembly, appealing to Bhishma, Dhritarashtra, Drona, and Vidura to say something, but they remained silent. He then said, "If no one else has any opinion, then here is mine. I consider that Draupadi is not won. It is said that four vices afflict kings: hunting, womanizing, drinking, and gambling. The actions of one who is under the influence of any of these four sins cannot be taken seriously. Mad with the fever of gambling and urged on by the wicked Shakuni,

Yudhishthira staked the Panchala princess. And that was after he had lost himself. Therefore, how can she be considered won by the Kauravas? It is not right."

Vikarna's words were received with uproarious acclaim. Many kings stood up and praised him, at the same time censuring Shakuni. Karna became furious. He jumped to his feet and waved his well-muscled arms to silence the assembly. His powerful voice filled the hall. "Vikarna, you speak like a fool! What do you know of morality? Many great personalities are here, all of them far more learned than you, and they are silent. Clearly, they consider Draupadi as fairly won. How, then, do you think otherwise? Obviously, Yudhishthira lost her along with all his other possessions. This can hardly be doubted."

Karna looked down at the weeping Draupadi. Her words to him at her *swayamvara* were still vivid in his mind. He would never forget that humiliation. Feeling his anger rise as he recalled that moment, he said, "If you think this woman does not deserve such treatment, then consider these excellent words of mine. A chaste woman would never marry five husbands, contrary to the ordinance. She is practically a prostitute, and it would not matter if she were brought here naked, never mind in a single cloth. O Dushasana, remove her cloth, and those of the Pandavas as well. They are all our property now."

Duryodhana cheered Karna and lifted a hand toward Dushasana, urging him on. Dushasana reached down and pulled Draupadi to her feet, taking hold of the end of her cloth. Before the eyes of the mortified assembly, he began to forcefully strip her.

Draupadi tried to resist Dushasana, but it was useless. Her cloth slipped through her hands as the Kaurava warrior pulled even harder. She looked desperately at her husbands, but they did not move. The princess could understand that she had no protector in that assembly. She thought of Krishna. Surrendering fully to his shelter, she threw up her arms and prayed, "O Govinda! O Krishna! O Lord! O protector of the people and destroyer of all affliction, save me! O soul of the universe, see me sinking in the Kuru ocean. I am losing my senses in this wicked assembly. Please rescue me."

Hearing her piteous plea from where he was standing many miles away, Krishna immediately responded. He expanded himself by his inconceivable power and ran toward Hastinapura. Reaching the hall in a matter of moments, he entered it invisibly. At once he began to supply an unlimited amount of cloth to Draupadi. As Dushasana pulled and pulled, he saw to his amazement that Draupadi remained fully clad. Her many-colored cloth piled up on the floor in an increasingly large heap. The prince continued trying to strip her, but after some time he became exhausted and saw that his efforts were useless.

The assembly was again in an uproar. All the kings applauded Draupadi. They rebuked Dushasana, shouting at him to leave the Panchala princess alone. Perspiring heavily, he slumped down next to Duryodhana, shaking his head in astonishment.

Bhima glared at him steadily, as if to burn him with his very glance. As the assembly calmed down, he got to his feet and spoke out in a thunderous voice. "O kings, listen to my words. I shall now make a vow, the likes of which has never before been made. If I do not tear open the chest of this wicked-minded scoundrel on the field of battle, drinking his life-blood, then may I not attain the path of my ancestors."

As Bhima uttered his terrible vow, Duryodhana and his brothers looked at him in horrified disgust. But all the other kings loudly praised him. They called for the Kurus to answer Draupadi's question. Their angry voices echoed round the hall. "Shame on Dhritarashtra. Why is he silent? Where is his morality?"

Vidura then got to his feet and raised his arms to silence the assembly. He spoke again. "In this assembly religion is being persecuted. It is the duty of good men to relieve, by means of truth and morality, the suffering of any distressed person who approaches them. Those who sit in an assembly and fail to speak out against a sin are themselves afflicted by that sin. So far, only Vikarna has spoken. Now it behooves everyone else to give their honest opinions in response to Draupadi's question."

Vidura looked pointedly toward Dhritarashtra as he spoke. He cited an ancient story from scripture illustrating the importance of speaking the truth to a supplicant. Still the blind king said nothing. Seeing that no one was heeding Vidura's words, Karna said to Dushasana, "Take the servant woman Draupadi to the inner quarters where she belongs."

Dushasana again took hold of Draupadi and began pulling her out of the hall. Folding her palms, she looked up toward the Kuru elders and said, "Before I am taken away by this worst of men, I must offer you my respects. Forgive me for not doing so earlier, but I was sorely afflicted and deprived of my senses."

As Dushasana continued to violently drag Draupadi by the hair, she beseeched the Kurus, "It seems that a dark age of evil has surely come upon us. How do you tolerate seeing your daughter treated in such a way? Where are your morals? I should not even be seen by the sun or the wind in my present state, but here I am being cruelly persecuted before an assembly of kings."

Draupadi placed her question again. "O Kurus, tell me truthfully, am I a servant woman or not? I, the chaste wife of Yudhishthira, born in a royal order, Krishna's friend, and your own relative. Tell me what is morally right, and I will cheerfully follow your order. I can no longer tolerate the touch of this destroyer of Kuru fame."

Bhishma, with tears running down his face, then said, "O blessed lady, O noble one, that you should turn to religion even under such trying circumstances only adds to your great virtue and fame. The ways of morality are subtle, and I find it difficult to answer your question. However, as the Kurus have given way to lust and ignorance, I can say that their destruction will come on no distant date. Seeing them sitting here with downcast faces, I think they will not give you a reply. In my view, only Yudhishthira is able to respond."

All eyes turned toward Yudhishthira, who still appeared stunned and unable to speak. Everyone in the assembly remained silent, apparently afraid of Duryodhana's power. Smiling, the Kaurava prince signaled Dushasana to let go of Draupadi. He then rose up and said, "O Draupadi, I think Bhishma is correct. It is your husband who must answer your question. If he declares that he spoke falsely when he wagered you and that he is therefore still your lord, then you shall be free. And if his brothers declare the same thing—that they, too, were falsely staked—then they shall also be free. The magnanimous Kurus are all grieving at seeing your condition, brought about by Yudhishthira. Now let him settle the matter."

A clamor arose among the assembly, as many kings applauded Duryodhana. Others loudly lamented, with cries of "Oh!" and "Alas." Again, they turned their eyes toward Yudhishthira, eager to hear his reply. But before he could say anything, Bhima, sorry for his previous outburst against Yudhishthira, jumped to his feet and said, "If this high-souled son of Dharma were not our lord, we would never have pardoned the Kurus. He is our guru and the lord of our lives. If he considers himself won, then we are all won."

Bhima turned his reddish eyes toward Duryodhana and his brothers. "It is only because Yudhishthira does not command me that I have not slaughtered these wretches with my bare hands, even as a lion kills a number of small animals."

Seeing Bhima's fury about to explode, Bhishma, Drona, and Vidura became alarmed, and they exclaimed, "Be peaceful, O Bhima! You are capable of anything."

Karna immediately began to criticize the three Kuru elders, accusing them of always supporting the Pandavas against the interests of their master. Turning toward Draupadi, he then said to her, "O beautiful lady, select for yourself another husband. The Pandavas are our slaves and cannot possess you any longer. The Kauravas are now your lords. Go to their servants' quarters and await their command. Clearly, Yudhishthira considered his life, prowess, and manhood useless, for he gambled you away in the presence of this assembly."

Bhima, still on his feet, glowered menacingly at Karna. He slowly took his seat again next to Yudhishthira, appearing like a smoldering fire about to burst into flames.

Duryodhana laughed and exchanged a glance with Karna. He then turned to the Pandavas and said, "Come now, O heroes, tell us whether Draupadi is truly won or not."

Reveling in his moment of triumph and wanting to encourage Karna, Duryodhana uncovered his right thigh, which resembled a tree trunk. He showed it to Draupadi with a smile, indicating that she should take her place on his lap, as his wife.

Bhima roared in anger. His voice thundered around the hall. "If I do not smash that thigh in a great battle, then let me not attain the higher regions!" He looked like a burning tree with sparks and flames emitting from every crevice.

The whole assembly was becoming agitated, and Vidura rose again to address them. "A very great danger has now arisen from Bhima. O Dhritarashtra, a calamity sent by destiny threatens to overtake us. Your sons have gambled in this assembly, disregarding every moral law. Now they are quarreling over a lady. Alas, the Kurus' prosperity is at an end."

Vidura declared that Draupadi was certainly not the property of the Kauravas, since Yudhishthira had lost her when he himself was already lost.

Duryodhana smiled at the grief-stricken Pandavas. "I will abide by the words of Yudhishthira's brothers. If they declare that Yudhishthira is no longer their master, then Draupadi will be free."

Arjuna at once retorted, "The son of Dharma was certainly our lord before the game began. But he has lost himself, so let the Kurus decide whose master he is now."

As Arjuna spoke, many inauspicious omens were suddenly seen and heard. A jackal cried in Dhritarashtra's nearby sacrificial chamber. Asses brayed and fearful birds uttered fierce cries. Alarmed, Bhishma, Drona, and Kripa cried out, "All peace!" Vidura urged the king to do something before disaster overtook him.

Realizing at last that things had gone too far, Dhritarashtra chastised his son. "Duryodhana, wicked-minded wretch, by insulting Draupadi you are bringing certain destruction down on your head."

The king then tried to console Draupadi. "O Panchali, you have suffered enough. Be peaceful. Chaste and devoted to virtue, you are the foremost of my daughters-in-law. Ask from me any boon you desire. I wish to make amends for the despicable treatment you have received here."

Draupadi turned her tear-streaked face toward the blind king. "O best of the Bharatas, if you really desire my well-being, then release Yudhishthira from slavery."

"It is done," replied Dhritarashtra. "Now ask from me a second favor. My heart desires to give you something more."

"O king, release also the other Pandavas, and give them back their chariots and weapons."

"O greatly blessed girl, it shall be so. O daughter, ask yet another boon and that too shall be granted."

Afraid of the omens, and of Vidura's repeated warnings, Dhritarashtra was prepared to give everything back to the Pandavas, but Draupadi said, "O king, greed destroys virtue. I will not ask a further boon, for my husbands will be able to secure all prosperity by their own virtuous acts."

Karna laughed derisively. "What kind of men are the Pandavas? They have been saved by a woman!"

Bhima flared up in anger, but Arjuna checked him, saying, "Desist, O hero. Great men never take seriously the harsh words of inferiors. They always try to remember whatever little good may have been rendered them by the offending party."

Bhima's fury did not abate. He turned to Yudhishthira. "O king of kings, grant me leave to slay all these foes here and now. Or shall I do it outside the palace? What consideration is required in the matter?"

Bhima glared at the Kauravas, like a lion casting its glance over a herd of deer. Arjuna held his arm and tried to calm him with appealing looks, but Bhima remained feverish. Yudhishthira embraced him, saying softly, "Be peaceful, dear brother."

Yudhishthira then went before Dhritarashtra and said, "O king, you are our lord. Command us now; what should we do? We desire to always remain obedient to you."

The Kuru king replied, "Go in peace, O Ajatashatru. At my command, rule your kingdom with all your wealth. Live in peace and try to forget the harsh words that were uttered here today. Pious men such as yourself remember only the good deeds of their enemies, not their hostile acts."

Dhritarashtra spoke at length in an attempt to appease Yudhishthira. He begged him to maintain friendly relations with the Kauravas. "Have pity on me, your old and blind uncle, and on Gandhari, your aunt. Think of us as your father and mother. I meant no malice in allowing this match. I merely wished to see the respective strengths and weaknesses of you Pandavas and of my own sons. You have proved yourself to be highly virtuous. Return now to Indraprastha with my blessings. Let there be brotherly love between you and my sons."

Duryodhana looked angrily at his father but remained silent. There was little he could say. Dhritarashtra had accorded boons to Draupadi, which he could hardly reverse now. The Kaurava turned his dark eyes toward Karna and Dushasana, who both sat shaking their heads.

After bowing before Dhritarashtra and the other Kuru elders, the Pandavas ascended their chariot with Draupadi and headed back to Indraprastha. Dhritarashtra rose to leave the hall, and the assembly broke up. Some kings went away praising Yudhishthira, while others commended Duryodhana. The blind king was led away by Vidura. Thinking of the heinous treatment given to Draupadi by his sons, he was gripped by anxiety. How would the Pandavas ever forgive and forget such abuse? Especially Bhima, who had made such terrible vows. It was unlikely that he would forget them. The Kuru monarch entered his chamber and sat for his evening prayers, his mind filled with remorse. Why had he not acted sooner?

Thirteen

THE KURUS SEAL THEIR FATE

WHEN EVERYONE HAD dispersed after the dice game, Duryodhana sat alone with Shakuni, Karna, and Dushasana. They condemned the king for his weakness. He had certainly blundered by showing favor toward powerful enemies, especially after they had already been subdued.

"The old man returned all the wealth we had gained with so much endeavor," Dushasana lamented. "Now our hated foes are strong again."

Duryodhana appeared thoughtful. "You are right, brother, but I think we can still turn things around."

The prince had seen how his father had inquired so eagerly about the gambling, as it was going on. Obviously, he had been enjoying his son's success. It was only fear that had finally made him intervene. Perhaps they could play on that fear to make him think again.

"Let us go to the king at once," Duryodhana suggested. "We should point out the very grave danger he has now caused. By allowing the Pandavas to go back to their kingdom with all their wealth, he has placed us in great peril."

"Then let us take up our weapons and pursue them," Karna interjected. "Taking them by surprise, we can annihilate them before they reach their city."

"No, dear friend, the time is not yet right," Duryodhana replied. "We need to consolidate our position, gain more allies, and build our armies. Only then should battle be joined with Pandu's highly powerful sons. Let us start by using strategy to weaken them."

Shakuni agreed. "This is intelligent, O king." He toyed with his dice, rolling them about in his hands. "I think you should speak with your father."

Duryodhana looked at the dice and nodded. This time there should be no mistake. Taking Karna with him, he immediately left for his father's chamber, where he found him concluding his evening prayers. The prince said, "O king, I am fearful. The Vedas clearly state that a dangerous enemy should be utterly destroyed, by any means whatsoever. The Pandavas are like five deadly serpents; by grievously offending them, we have placed them on our heads. There is no doubt that they now pose a dire threat. We have to act quickly before everything is lost. If they are given time, they will assemble a vast force and crush us."

Dhritarashtra said nothing. This was also his fear. The Kurus had ignited a fire during the gambling match that could well consume them to their roots. But what could be done now?

Duryodhana could see he had his father's full attention. He spoke softly. "Here is my idea, O king. Summon Yudhishthira back for one final game. Let there be one decisive wager. The loser should be made to retire to the forest for twelve years. For the final year they may come out of the forest and live incognito in a town of their own choosing. If they are discovered, then a further twelve years in exile will be their lot. Otherwise, they may get their kingdom back when they return."

Dhritarashtra immediately shook his head. The gambling had already produced fearful consequences. How could he permit another game? What would Vidura say?

But Duryodhana was insistent. "This is the wisest policy, Father. Shakuni will certainly win. Then we will have time to make our position strong—using Yudhishthira's wealth. While the Pandavas stay in the forest, we can amass such a force that not even they will present any threat. Permit this final game and let us settle the issue now."

Dhritarashtra again felt his mind being swayed by his son's influence. Twelve years was a long time. Enmity had already been created with the Pandavas. It would be hard now to avoid a conflict. But if they were out of the way, the danger would be gone. Maybe it would be best for everyone. Certainly his own sons would be better off, as there seemed little doubt that Shakuni would win the game.

"All right, have the Pandavas recalled and arrange for the final game." The king spoke with a sigh. He still had misgivings, but this seemed like the best immediate solution. At least there would be time for things to cool down.

But when the other Kuru elders heard that the Pandavas were being summoned for another game, they were shocked. Every one of them disapproved. They tried hard to dissuade the king, but he would not listen. He had made up his mind.

Gandhari was also anxious. She went to her husband when he was alone and said, "Vidura long ago advised us to abandon Duryodhana, but you did not take heed. Now it seems he will destroy us all. O descendant of Bharata, do not approve the counsel of foolish men who are no better than boys. Do not rekindle a great fire that has been extinguished. Control your sons and become their leader, leading them on the path of virtue. You are intelligent and must surely see the consequences of acting otherwise."

After hearing his queen's counsel, Dhritarashtra remained in thought for some moments. Finally he said, "If the destruction of the Kurus has arrived, what can I do? If it is God's will, how can it be opposed? Let it happen at once. O noble lady, the match will go ahead; consider it as ordained by destiny."

The blindfolded queen tried for some time to change her husband's mind, but he was determined. Finally she gave up, shrugging her shoulders in helplessness. It seemed that the end of the Kurus truly was ordained by destiny. The king's attachment for Duryodhana had entirely overpowered his intelligence. Calling for her servants, Gandhari left for her own quarters.

On Dhritarashtra's order, the Pratikamin was dispatched on a swift steed to catch up with the Pandavas. On reaching them, he bowed before Yudhishthira and said, "O son of Pandu, I carry the king's order. He requests you to come and throw the dice one more time."

Yudhishthira was not surprised. He had been more surprised when Dhritarashtra had returned his wealth and kingdom. Guessing at once that the king had been influenced by Duryodhana, he turned to his brothers and said, "All creatures receive the fruits of their own work, whether good or bad, as ordained by God. Whether I play this game or not, we shall receive those fruits. This is a challenge to play at dice, and it is also a summons by the king. How, then, can I refuse, even though I know it will be destructive to me? Surely men's minds become bewildered when the hour of calamity approaches."

With heavy hearts the Pandavas retraced their steps back to Hastinapura. Seeing them returning, their friends and well-wishers felt pain. It was plain what was about to happen. Entering the assembly hall, the brothers saw everyone seated as before. The blind king was on his throne, with the Kuru elders by his side, and the dice game was set up in readiness.

When the Pandavas had again taken their places, Shakuni smiled and said, "Welcome back, O Yudhishthira. The king has returned all your wealth and that is all well and good. But let us play one final game, for a stake of high value."

Shakuni explained the stake. Hearing that the losers would be exiled for thirteen years, a great gasp went up from the kings in the hall. "This cannot be allowed!" some of them cried. "Duryodhana should be stopped before he destroys himself and his whole house."

But those cries went unheeded, and the game began. Yudhishthira took up the dice and said, "O Shakuni, how can one like me, who always desires to do his proper duty, refuse a challenge? I accept the stake."

A strange sense of fatality filled Yudhishthira's mind. Obviously, he was about to lose everything and be consigned to the forest. Equally obvious was the fact that the Kurus would soon be destroyed due to their loss of virtue. Yudhishthira thought again of Krishna. Was all this his desire? What would he do when he discovered what had happened?

Filled with foreboding, Yudhishthira threw the dice. They clattered against the side of the board and yet again landed wrongly. The Pandava watched in silence as Shakuni made his throw. "I have won!" came the inevitable cry, as the dice came to a stop.

Once more the watching kings cried out in distress, "For shame! For shame!" But Duryodhana and his brothers jumped to their feet in glee. Dushasana was completely overjoyed. "Now Duryodhana is the absolute sovereign of this world," he effused. "The Pandavas are defeated and plunged into misery. Whatever anyone may say about us, the gods have favored us. Kunti's sons, who, from the pride of wealth, laughed at Duryodhana in his suffering, must now enter the forest, deprived of everything."

Dancing around in great happiness, Dushasana railed at the Pandavas for some time. He told them to take off their royal robes and put on the deerskins that Duryodhana had immediately ordered his servants to fetch. After hurling various kinds of insults at the Pandavas, who silently tolerated the abuse, Dushasana then turned to Draupadi and said, "Your father foolishly bestowed you upon these impotent men. What will you gain by serving them? Abandon them and select a worthy husband from among the Kauravas."

Bhima suddenly started toward Dushasana, as a mountain lion might rush upon a deer. Seeing Yudhishthira's frown, he checked himself with difficulty and loudly rebuked the Kaurava prince. "Crooked-minded wretch! Thanks to Shakuni's skill at dice, you arrogantly blather on. Know for certain that I will pierce your heart in battle, just as you now pierce our hearts with arrow-like words."

Dushasana burst out laughing. He again danced around and pointed at Bhima, calling out insults. Bhima, his mind fixed in virtue, restrained himself from killing the prince on the spot.

Having put on the deerskins, the Pandavas began to walk slowly out of the hall. Duryodhana walked behind them, caricaturing Bhima's powerful gait. Seeing this, Bhima coldly said, "I shall be Duryodhana's slayer. Felling him in a mace fight, I will place my foot on his head. Arjuna will slay Karna, and Sahadeva will kill the gambler, Shakuni."

Arjuna fixed his gaze on Karna and said, "O Bhima, all this will surely come to pass. The promises of powerful men are not mere words. This malicious, vain, and envious wretch will die at my hand, along with anyone who is foolish enough to support him."

Sahadeva then confirmed that he would kill Shakuni, and Nakula also uttered a vow to kill many of Duryodhana's followers.

After offering his respects to Dhritarashtra and the other senior Kurus, Yudhishthira turned to leave. Vidura then came up to him and spoke consolingly. "O Yudhishthira, best of the Bharatas, do not feel any shame or guilt, for you have been defeated by sinful means. This has all been arranged by destiny for your ultimate welfare. In the forest, you will be instructed by the rishis and will also develop detachment from worldly affairs. Your power will thus greatly increase. O son of Kunti, be blessed. You have never committed any sin. We hope to see you return soon, crowned with success."

Before leaving, Draupadi went to see Kunti. Bowing at her feet, she wept for some time and Kunti wept with her. At last, in a choked voice, Kunti said, "O child, be strong. You have adorned the Kurus with your shining qualities. It is fortunate for them that they were not burned to ashes by your wrath. Go now with my blessings. Protected by your own great virtue, you will surely obtain good fortune before long."

The Kuru queen embraced Draupadi, who then joined her husbands. Kunti followed her out of the palace and, when she saw her sons clad in deerskins, surrounded by grieving friends and rejoicing foes, she cried out in sorrow. She ran over and embraced them, one after another, and began to lament. "O my sons, how could such reverses happen to virtuous men like yourselves? Oh, why did I bring you here from the mountains? Why did I not ascend your father's fire, like Madri? Surely, that princess saw this disaster looming, and thus, she chose to follow our lord."

Kunti raised her arms to the sky and cried out to Krishna. "O dweller of Dwaraka, where are you? Why do you not save my sons and me? The wise say that you are without beginning or end, and that you always save those who seek you. Has that now proved false?"

Kunti wept uncontrollably. She berated the Kuru elders and called out to Pandu. Inconsolable, she shook with sorrow. Vidura took her arm and spoke soothingly. He led her away, as her sons made their way along the street toward the city gate. The news of their exile had quickly spread, and the roads were crowded with grieving citizens. Shocked at the sudden turn of events, they shouted out blessings and good wishes to the five brothers, who slowly walked out of the city, unable to say anything to anyone.

*   *   *

After the Pandavas had gone, Dhritarashtra fell prey to great anxiety. Clearly an injustice had been perpetrated. He could have intervened at any time but had remained silent as his brother's children were robbed and insulted. Abashed, the blind king called for Vidura and timidly asked, "Did you see how the Pandavas left the city? Please describe everything to me."

Vidura replied, "From the signs present when those heroes and their wife left Hastinapura, it is plain that we face great peril. Arjuna was scattering sands that represented the innumerable arrows he will fire in battle against your sons; Bhima was slapping his powerful arms, no doubt thinking of how, in due course, he will crush the Kauravas. Yudhishthira himself kept his eyes down, knowing that his anger alone might consume those upon whom his gaze fell."

Vidura described how various threatening omens had been seen: lightning in a cloudless sky, the earth trembling, and jackals, vultures, and ravens all uttering harsh cries. "All these signs portend a fearful destruction, O king, as a result of your acts."

As Vidura spoke with Dhritarashtra, the sage Narada suddenly appeared in the hall, surrounded by other great rishis. Looking at the king, he said, "In fourteen years from now, due to Duryodhana's fault, the Kurus will be destroyed."

As the alarmed Kauravas looked on, the sages disappeared. Duryodhana and his brothers, as well as Karna and Shakuni, then went before Drona, considering him their best shelter. Folding his palms and speaking humbly, Duryodhana said, "O brahmin, a great danger has arisen from the Pandavas. Tell us what we should do now. You are our guru and a peerless warrior. Please guide us across the terrible Pandava ocean."

Drona made a wry smile. Duryodhana had not cared for his advice when it was to give the Pandavas their rightful share of the kingdom. Nevertheless, Drona felt it was still his duty to give protection to the Kurus, who, after all, had maintained him for many years. He said, "I will do whatever I can, although the rishis have said that the Pandavas, being of celestial origin, cannot be slain. When their exile is over, they will return in anger, more powerful than ever, to seek redress. With them will be

Dhrishtadyumna, who is destined to be my slayer. I see little hope. You should spend the next thirteen years performing sacrifice and enjoying life, for at the end of that period a great calamity will overwhelm you."

Hearing Drona's words, Dhritarashtra felt even more anxious. He said to Vidura, "Dear brother, the Pandavas have gone and will not return until the agreed period is over. Yudhishthira will never break his word. However, you should arrange that they have every desirable thing—soldiers, chariots, servants, and whatever else they need."

Vidura shook his head at the blind king's empty gesture. The Pandavas would not accept anything now. Dhritarashtra was trying to build a dam after he had already let all the water run away.

As the king sat sighing, his charioteer and secretary, Sanjaya, came to him. Sanjaya was Vyasadeva's spiritual disciple and, despite his low social status, was noted for his wisdom. Seeing his master sunk in worry, he said to him, "O lord of the world, you have now obtained the entire earth and all its wealth. Why, then, do you grieve?"

"What worries are not theirs who have the Pandavas as their enemies?" answered Dhritarashtra.

"O king, this is due to your own great folly." Having long served the king with affection, Sanjaya had his full trust, and he spoke frankly. "Allowed by you, your wicked-minded and shameless son had the virtuous wife of the Pandavas dragged into the assembly and grievously abused. This act will destroy the world. A great hostility will arise to annihilate all the earth's monarchs. The gods deprive a man of his senses when his defeat is ordained. He thus sees evil as good and good as evil. How, otherwise, could such a heinous act of sin have been allowed in this very assembly?"

Dhritarashtra hung his head in shame. " I greatly fear Draupadi's wrath. Her afflicted glances could consume the world. When she was insulted, everything became inauspicious. Gandhari and the palace ladies wailed loudly and are still weeping now. The brahmins refused to light the sacred fires that day. Terrible omens were witnessed in all directions. Therefore did I grant her boons. Still, my affection for Duryodhana made me deprive the Pandavas of everything and send them into the wilderness."

The blind king lamented for some time. He told Sanjaya that he felt certain that the Pandavas would wreak an awful vengeance. All his counselors were now warning him to prepare for that time. Vidura in particular was full of foreboding. Turning to him then, Dhritarashtra asked, "O Vidura, tell me what I should now do. What will be best for the Kurus? How can we avoid total extermination?"

Vidura replied, "O king, the sages say that all good fortune ensues when one adheres strictly to virtue. Headed by Shakuni, your evil-hearted sons destroyed virtue when they cheated Yudhishthira at dice. The only way to make amends is to restore the Pandavas to their rightful position. Give them back their kingdom."

Dhritarashtra did not like this advice. He had hoped Vidura would offer some counsel as to how the Kurus could secure their position. Although he knew his sons' acts were questionable, the outcome had been that they, and indeed he, had achieved unrivaled prosperity. The blind king was already becoming attached to the idea of being the emperor. It had always pained him that, even though he was older than Pandu, he had been denied the throne due to his disability. Although he had only assumed the throne due to Pandu's premature retirement, it seemed that destiny had conferred upon him supreme rulership of the earth. How could he simply give it away?

Vidura saw Dhritarashtra's disappointed expression, and he spoke strongly. "O king, if you do not follow my advice, you will be destroyed. Neither Bhima nor Arjuna will leave any of their enemies unslain. You must act quickly. Abandon the wretch Duryodhana, send Shakuni away in disgrace, and embrace the virtuous Pandavas. Have Dushasana beg for Draupadi's forgiveness in the open court. Then, install Yudhishthira on the throne with all due ceremony. What else can I advise? This is the only proper course for you now."

Dhritarashtra felt his anger rise. Yet again Vidura was telling him to reject his own sons in favor of the Pandavas. How could such advice be followed? Duryodhana was always saying that Vidura was really an enemy in the guise of a friend. Was there some truth in that? The king replied harshly to his brother. "Vidura, your words are not meant for my good. Why do you always favor the Pandavas? Do you expect me to abandon my own flesh and blood for their sake? Although I hold you in high esteem, I feel your advice is crooked. I cannot accept it. You may do as you please. Stay here or go, I do not care. However well an unchaste wife is treated, she still forsakes her husband."

Dhritarashtra rose suddenly and called for his servants. Waving his hand to dismiss his counselors, he went to his inner chambers. Vidura watched in dismay. This was the worst possible outcome. Saying, "The Kurus are doomed," he went out of the hall and prepared to follow the Pandavas into the forest.

Fourteen

HEROES IN EXILE

AFTER LEAVING HASTINAPURA, the Pandavas were followed for some distance by crowds of citizens, who loudly criticized the Kuru leaders. They pleaded with the Pandavas not to go, praising the brothers' many virtues. All of them appeared greatly distressed. Yudhishthira, feeling compassion, turned to address them. "O pious citizens of Hastinapura, we feel blessed that you feel so much affection for us, crediting us with merits we do not possess. But we cannot return. For the sake of the love you bear for us, I ask that you go back and serve King Dhritarashtra. All our friends and relatives in Hastinapura are filled with grief to see us leave. Do not abandon them now."

Seeing that Yudhishthira was determined, the citizens resigned themselves to returning to the city without him. They shed tears and cried loudly. Reluctantly, they began to head back to the city.

The Pandavas then ascended chariots and went quickly away from Hastinapura. By evening they reached the edge of the forest and stopped for the night under a great banyan tree. Hundreds of ascetic brahmins came to see them, and they lit fires that cast an orange glow into the black night. They chanted hymns and prayers, and these comforted the grief-stricken Pandavas and their wife. Sitting around those sacred fires with the brahmins, the brothers appeared like resplendent gods surrounded by a concourse of celestial beings.

When morning came, the Pandavas prepared to enter into the forest. The brahmins began to follow them, but Yudhishthira checked them. Looking into the dense woodlands, he said, "O ever truthful men, how will we maintain you in this terrible place? The forest is full of dangers. Please stay near the city, where you will easily find your sustenance."

The brahmins were reluctant to let the Pandavas go without them. They told Yudhishthira that they would procure their own food without difficulty. "We are used to an ascetic life," said their leader, Shaunaka. "Allow us to accompany you, and we will benefit you by our prayers and readings of holy scripture."

"Then let it be as you say," replied Yudhishthira reluctantly. As he looked at the effulgent rishis who stood around him, he was seized with sorrow. In Indraprastha he had maintained hundreds of thousands of brahmins, and now he could hardly look after a few. He sat down on the ground and wept. "Alas! Fie on Dhritarashtra's sons. We are overwhelmed by destitution. How shall I look upon you all, my well-wishers and gurus, who deserve no suffering, scrounging for food in the forest?"

Shaunaka looked compassionately at the distraught Pandava. "O king, hundreds of fears and thousands of causes for grief overwhelm the ignorant, day after day, but never the wise. Suffering and pain are afflictions of the body only. A learned man knows that his true identity is different from the body and that misery is an illusion. O great hero, men like you are never subject to illusion. They are detached from the body and, indeed, from all material circumstances. Attachment is the root cause of suffering, dear child. This is well known to you. Fix yourself in that knowledge now and take heart."

The rishi thus instructed Yudhishthira for some time, gradually relieving his mind of its affliction. Yudhishthira listened with rapt attention. He always relished the rishis' words. This, at least, would be one consolation for him while he dwelt in the forest—he would get many opportunities to hear such instructions.

Shaunaka concluded, "You have achieved success in your householder life, O king, culminating in the great Rajasuya sacrifice. Now you should cultivate detachment. Practice yoga and meditation, and you will achieve all spiritual success."

His grief assuaged, Yudhishthira got to his feet again and thanked Shaunaka. The Pandavas then set off into the forest, with Draupadi in their midst. Behind them walked the brahmins, continuously chanting auspicious Vedic hymns. Traveling in a northwesterly direction, they crossed over the great field of Kurukshetra. When they reached the banks of the river Sarasvati, they saw ahead of them the Kamyaka forest. Numerous hermitages lined the riverbank, and the travelers saw many rishis standing in the gently flowing river, deep in meditation. The late afternoon sun reflected off the water, making the river appear like a long sheet of gold.

Yudhishthira decided they should stay in that beautiful and mind-soothing region, and they constructed several cottages for their residence. They dwelt there peacefully, hunting by day and spending their evenings hearing spiritual wisdom from the sages. Although, the pain of what had happened in Hastinapura was still fresh, the association of the rishis relieved them. They wondered if they would ever again see their friends and relatives back home. To their surprise, only a few days after they had arrived at Kamyaka, they saw Vidura approaching.

Yudhishthira jumped up and said to Bhima, "There is Vidura. What brings him here, I wonder? Does the mean-minded Shakuni desire to win from us even our weapons? O Bhima, if challenged, I will be unable to refuse, but without Arjuna's Gandiva, the recovery of our kingdom is unlikely."

The Pandavas greeted their uncle with love and respect. They sat him down and asked him why he had come. Vidura explained what had happened in Hastinapura, and the Pandavas shook their heads in despair. Dhritarashtra's behavior did not bode well for the future. Vidura then said, "As the king will not heed my advice, I have left him and come here to offer you whatever counsel I can. O rulers of men, be patient. Tolerate silently the wrongs you have suffered. Increase your strength by spiritual practices and bide your time. Soon you will win back your wealth, without doubt."

The Pandavas were delighted to have Vidura with them. Yudhishthira replied, "I will be entirely guided by you, O uncle."

Vidura had spent some time in discussion with the Pandavas when they noticed another chariot approaching. They saw that it was Sanjaya. Rising to greet him, they brought him into their midst and listened as he described what had happened in Hastinapura after Vidura's departure. "When the old king heard that Vidura had left, he fell down in a faint. When he recovered, he said to me, 'My wise brother is equal to the god of justice, Yamaraja himself. Alas, I have cruelly offended him. My heart burns in grief. Please go and bring him back.'"

Sanjaya turned to Vidura, "O descendant of Kuru, your brother, the king, is consumed with repentance. Please return to Hastinapura and relieve his sorrow."

Vidura immediately agreed. Although Dhritarashtra was loath to accept his advice, it would be better if he were near him. At least then there would be a chance that the blind monarch might come to his senses. Offering his blessings to the Pandavas, Vidura mounted his chariot and went back to Hastinapura with Sanjaya. When he arrived there, the king rose from his throne to embrace him, saying, "Please forgive me. When you left, I felt like one lost. Surely you are sinless and have never done me the slightest harm. How could I have been so cruel?"

Vidura spoke affectionately to the king. "Dear brother, I forgive you. My favoring the Pandavas is natural, for one feels more for those in distress than he does for others. Both your sons and the Pandavas are equally dear to me, but the Pandavas are now in despair and greatly suffering."

Speaking apologetic words to each other, the brothers spent some time together, then retired for the night.

*   *   *

When Vidura left Hastinapura, Duryodhana had been delighted. Hearing that he had again returned and was reconciled with the king, he became depressed. He spoke with Shakuni, Karna, and Dushasana. "I fear that sooner or later the intelligent Vidura will convince the king to bring back the Pandavas. If that happens, I shall certainly die. I cannot tolerate seeing them in prosperity."

Duryodhana pressed his bejeweled fingers together. He stood up and paced around the beautifully furnished chamber, pausing to look absently out of the window at the expansive palace gardens. Thinking only of the Pandavas, his eyes moved about restlessly. "They cannot be allowed to return. If the king brings them back, I will drink poison, or throw myself into blazing fire, or fall upon my sword."

Shakuni came over to him and placed an arm around his shoulders. "O king, ruler of the world, what has come over you? How will the Pandavas return? They have agreed to spend thirteen years away. Yudhishthira will never break his word. And even if he does, why should we be worried? I still have my dice."

Duryodhana turned away from Shakuni and walked toward the table where his wine stood. He picked up the flagon and then put it down again. It seemed that the Pandavas had taken possession of him. How could he enjoy life as long as they were alive?

Karna could understand his friend's mind. He stood up suddenly and drew his sword. Raising it high, he said loudly, "Here is my opinion, O rulers of the land. Let us go now in a body and fall upon the Pandavas. They are weakened, devoid of allies and in distress. We will soon crush them. Let us do it quickly, before they again become powerful. Ridding the earth of our enemies, we shall live in undisturbed peace."

Hearing Karna's bold words, everyone cheered. They all agreed with him. Duryodhana wanted to leave immediately, and they went out of the palace and mounted their great war chariots. The prince quickly assembled a phalanx of troops and was about to leave the city when he saw Vyasadeva ahead of him. The sage held up his hand and commanded him to stop.

Duryodhana felt unable to defy the rishi, fearing the power of his curse. Reluctantly he turned around and headed back for the palace.

Vyasadeva then went to Dhritarashtra and said, "O king, I have not been pleased by your treatment of the Pandavas. You will face the consequences thirteen years from now, when they return to shower deadly arrows on the Kurus. Your wicked son seems bent on suicide, for he has rushed out to confront the Pandavas. Why do you not check him? You possess great intelligence. Surely you can see what will shortly ensue."

Dhritarashtra listened meekly as his father spoke. Vyasadeva suggested that he send Duryodhana alone into the forest to serve the Pandavas. Maybe then the prince would lose his envy for them, and they in turn may develop an attachment for him.

The king replied, "Without doubt I was deluded by ignorance when I allowed the gambling match. Everyone warned me against it, but out of too much affection for my son, I would not listen."

"This is the truth, O king. You have excessively favored your sons over those of Pandu. This is not surprising, as one's son is the dearmost object of a man's affection. Indeed, you are also dear to me. Out of affection only do I tell you that your best course of action is to have Duryodhana make peace with the Pandavas."

In the presence of Vyasadeva, Dhritarashtra could understand everything clearly. Pressing his fingers against his blind eyes, he said, "O greatly intelligent rishi, it is exactly as you say. Vidura, Bhishma, and Drona have also pointed this out to me. Still, I seem unable to do what is necessary. Please, therefore, teach my son for me. Set him on the right path."

Vyasadeva stood up and everyone present also rose in respect. He pulled his shawl around his shoulders, which were thin due to extended fasting and austerity, and said, "I shall now depart, but the illustrious rishi Maitreya will soon come here. He will admonish your son for the Kurus' sake. O king, ensure that his advice is followed without delay. If it is not, he will curse your son in anger."

The sage left and, as he had predicted, Maitreya soon arrived. He was brought into the Kuru assembly and given a seat of honor. The rishi looked around the great hall, lit by shafts of sunlight that shone through the high windows. The light was reflected from the jewels and ornaments of the Kurus, who resembled an assembly of celestials.

Informed that Maitreya was present, Dhritarashtra asked after his welfare and then inquired, "Have you seen the Pandavas on your travels? Are they well? Will the brotherly affection between them and us remain unimpaired?"

Maitreya replied that he had seen the Pandavas not long ago in the forest. They were attired in deerskins and surrounded by rishis. "I learned from them of the danger that has arisen for the Kurus due to gambling." Maitreya spoke gently and with obvious concern. He said he had come to Hastinapura for the welfare of the Kurus. Chiding Dhritarashtra, he said, "Why, O king, did you allow such sins to be perpetrated in this assembly? You are in full control here and must therefore take the blame."

Maitreya turned toward Duryodhana, who was frowning and looking away from him. "O mighty-armed Duryodhana, listen to the words I shall speak for your good. Do not quarrel with the Pandavas. Those heroes are possessed of godly power. Bhima alone has already slain Hidimba, Baka, and Kirmira—Rakshasas of immeasurable strength—as well as the mighty Jarasandha. Who is there who can face him and his brothers, especially when they have Krishna as their friend and relation? O prince, make peace with them. Do not place yourself in unnecessary danger."

Duryodhana made no reply, still not looking at Maitreya. Stretching out his leg, he slapped his thigh and scratched the floor with his foot, showing complete disinterest and offering insult to the rishi.

Maitreya's eyes turned red with anger. As if impelled by fate, he immediately uttered a curse, his angry voice resounding through the hall. "O insolent one, you shall soon reap the consequences of your acts. In the great war that will arise due to your sinful acts, Bhima will smash your thigh with his mace."

Dhritarashtra became alarmed. He tried to pacify the rishi, asking him to be merciful, but Maitreya said, "This will surely come to pass unless your son makes peace with the Pandavas."

Hearing the curse mitigated, Dhritarashtra felt some relief and said, "O great sage, please tell us more about how Bhima killed Kirmira. We have only heard about the other two Rakshasas."

Maitreya shook his head and rose to leave. "I shall not say anything more in the presence of your son. Vidura also knows about this; ask him to describe the incident."

The sage strode out of the hall, and Dhritarashtra then asked Vidura to tell him about Kirmira. Vidura replied that he had heard the story from Yudhishthira when he visited him in the forest. "He told me how they had encountered the Rakshasa one night as they were traveling through the forest. The demon came before the brothers, holding a blazing torch and obstructing their way like a mountain. By his roars alone, he made birds and other forest animals drop down in terror. Draupadi practically fainted in fear and had to be held up by the twins."

Vidura then described how Bhima had attacked and killed the demon, smashing him on the ground and breaking his back in two. "I saw for myself the Rakshasa's colossal and bloodied corpse as I came back to Hastinapura."

As Vidura finished his account, Duryodhana rose and walked out of the hall. He tried to appear unconcerned, but his mind was filled with alarm. Dhritarashtra sat absorbed in thought, remembering again his omission during the gambling match.

Fifteen

MORAL INSTRUCTIONS
IN THE FOREST

WHEN NEWS REACHED Dwaraka of the Pandavas' exile, Krishna went with Balarama and other leading Yadus to visit them in the forest. Seeing the Pandavas attired in deerskins and seated on the bare ground, he cried out in anger. "The earth will drink the blood of Duryodhana, Karna, Shakuni, and Dushasana! Slaying them and all their followers, we shall install the virtuous Yudhishthira on the throne. This is eternal morality."

Krishna was aflame with anger. His eyes glowed red. Knowing him to be capable of consuming all created things, Arjuna quickly sought to placate him. He praised Krishna's inconceivable power and recounted his many incarnations in former ages, describing the wonderful feats they had all achieved. "Rishi Vyasadeva has told me that you are the cause of creation and the beginning and end of all things. O Krishna, whatever you desire is immediately brought into being."

Arjuna spoke at length about Krishna, finally becoming overwhelmed with transcendental emotion. Unable to speak further, he simply gazed at Krishna with tear-filled eyes.

Krishna was pleased by Arjuna's words and became pacified. He replied to him in an affectionate voice. "You are mine, and I am yours. What is mine is also yours. Whoever hates you, hates me, and whoever follows you is also my follower. O hero, you are Nara and I am Narayana. We are born in this world of men for a special purpose. No one can understand us."

Draupadi was sitting amidst her husbands. Folding her palms, she also began to praise Krishna as the Lord of all the worlds. She then said, "O Lord, I am the wife of the Pandavas, Dhrishtadyumna's sister, and above all, your friend. How is it, then, that I was so grievously insulted?"

Draupadi buried her face in her hands and wept. She had taken a vow not to dress her hair again until Dushasana was slain, and it hung loosely around her shoulders, which shook as she softly cried. She lifted her tear-streaked face and said in a trembling voice, "It seems I have no one to protect me. Not husbands, brothers, friends, or anyone, for you all sit here and do nothing. Who will assuage the grief that has arisen from Karna's insult and ridicule in the assembly? O Krishna, I seek your shelter."

Krishna gently consoled her. "O fair lady, the wives of those who insulted you will soon weep even as you do now. They will see their husbands lying dead on the ground, covered with arrows and weltering in blood. Do not grieve. I will do everything in my power to help the Pandavas. Your husbands will be kings and you will be queen. Know that the heavens may fall or the Himalayas split, but my words will never prove false."

Draupadi felt reassured. She glanced across at Arjuna, seeking his confirmation of Krishna's words. Catching her glance, Arjuna said, "O beautiful lady, do not weep. What Krishna has said will come to pass. It cannot be otherwise."

Krishna then said, "O Yudhishthira, when the gambling match was announced, I was indisposed and could not attend. Otherwise, even if not invited, I would have gone there and saved you from this calamity. By pointing out the many evils inherent in gambling, I would have stopped the game."

Still angry, Krishna declared that if Dhritarashtra had not accepted his advice, he would have compelled him by force. "And if anyone, passing as Dhritarashtra's friend, had tried to prevent me and offer contrary advice, they would have been destroyed."

Yudhishthira asked Krishna where he had been when the match took place. Krishna replied that he had been engaged in combat with a demonic king named Shalva, who had attacked Dwaraka during Krishna's absence. "When I returned from the Rajasuya I saw the damage he had caused, and I learned that my son Pradyumna had pursued him with a number of Yadu fighters. Thus, I went to give them my assistance."

At Yudhishthira's request, Krishna described in detail his battle with Shalva, which culminated in that king's death. He described how the evil-minded monarch had obtained a wonderful airship from Shiva and had used it to oppress Dwaraka. When Krishna found him, he had smashed the ship to pieces and then killed Shalva with the Sudarshan chakra.

The Pandavas applauded Krishna, who concluded, "It was for this reason I could not attend the gambling match. Otherwise, I think Duryodhana would not be alive today. But what can I do now? It is difficult to stop the water once the dam has broken."

Krishna knew that Yudhishthira would certainly remain in the forest until the full thirteen years had expired. Only then would it be possible to assist him, should it be necessary, in recovering his kingdom. After spending some hours with the brothers, Krishna finally mounted his splendid chariot again.

When Krishna and his party had departed, Yudhishthira decided to move more deeply into the forest. Still accompanied by numerous brahmins, the brothers set off into the thick woods, traveling until they arrived at a great lake known as Dwaitavana. It was crowded with swans and surrounded by rishis who sat rapt in meditation, Yudhishthira decided to stay there. The region around the lake resembled heaven, with countless blossoming trees that filled the air with a sweet fragrance. Golden fruits hung from those trees, and peacocks, cuckoos, and many other birds played in their foliage, singing delightful songs.

Dhaumya performed various rituals to sanctify the area where the brothers constructed their residences. They began to live there peacefully, serving the rishis by offering them food gleaned from the forest. During the day, they practiced their martial skills by hunting. According to scriptural direction, they controlled the population of wild beasts in the forest, thus protecting the rishis from disturbance. The rishis reciprocated by reciting to them many Vedic histories that were replete with spiritual instructions.

Finding forest life a welcome interlude from the onerous and often harsh duties of a king, Yudhishthira did not lament for the loss of his wealth or kingdom. The gentle son of Dharma found the association of the rishis enjoyable. However, he knew that his God-given duty was to rule over the people, and he kept his mind fixed on the time when his period of exile would be over.

Draupadi, though, was not enjoying her time in the forest. Her heart burned with the memory of the dice game. It seemed to her that Yudhishthira had taken everything far too easily. The Kauravas had clearly acted sinfully. Surely, any virtuous monarch should see it as his duty to immediately punish them. Why had Yudhishthira simply gone meekly into exile?

One evening when the Pandavas were seated together, Draupadi began to question Yudhishthira. "My lord, when I think of Duryodhana living happily in Hastinapura while we reside in this lonely forest, I am seized with anger. Does it not anger you? Does the fact that you have been consigned to obscurity by sinful men through a sinful act not move you? Look at you now, clad in barks and deerskins when formerly you wore the finest silk robes. You sit on a grass mat instead of your jeweled throne. Your body is daubed with mud from the riverbank, when before it would be smeared with the costliest unguents. How do you tolerate all this in silent acquiescence?"

Draupadi found herself crying again. She felt frustrated. Yudhishthira seemed gentle to a fault, although she knew his grasp of morality was without equal. Still, his present mood was hard to understand. Looking across at Bhima, she continued to speak. "Just see your powerful brother Bhima, glancing at you again and again. It is only his love for you that prevents him from rising up at once and annihilating the Kauravas. Arjuna, grief-stricken himself by your plight, is always trying to pacify him. The twins are similarly afflicted. Why, then, do you do nothing? There is a time for forgiveness and a time for anger, especially for powerful rulers. I feel you have confused the two. Surely, now is the appropriate time for you to display fierce anger and punish Duryodhana."

Yudhishthira looked compassionately at Draupadi. She had suffered much and he knew she was still feeling great pain. He felt her pain as his own. The moment when she had been dragged into the hall was still vivid in his mind. He would never forget it. It had only been due to his own avidity that she and his brothers had been put through such misery. But anger was not the proper response—yet.

Yudhishthira's golden features reflected the light of the fire around which they sat. Lifting his hand, he calmly replied, "O most intelligent lady, you advocate anger as the right course for me now, but I am doubtful. Although through anger one may sometimes achieve some immediate gains, ultimately it always leads to destruction. Anger clouds one's discrimination and impels one to act in ways he would never otherwise consider. For this reason, the wise keep anger at a distance."

Yudhishthira went on to praise the virtue of forgiveness. "In my view, forgiveness is best. It always behooves a man of character to exercise forgiveness, for if there were no forgiving men, chaos would soon prevail throughout the world. If kings give way to anger, the people will soon meet with destruction. If inferiors do not tolerate their superior's admonishments, sin will quickly take root and destroy mankind. In ancient times the great rishi Kashyapa said, 'Forgiveness is virtue, sacrifice, purity, penance, truth, piety, and religion. By practicing forgiveness a man can achieve everlasting regions of happiness.'"

Yudhishthira made it clear that he would not renounce forgiveness. Any other course would lead to certain conflict. "Bhishma, Drona, Vidura, and Kripa will all counsel Dhritarashtra to peacefully resolve this matter. If he does not take their advice and give back our kingdom, he will be destroyed, but let me not be the cause. Forgiveness and humility, both unknown to Duryodhana, are attributes of the self-controlled, and they always lead to victory. I shall therefore adopt them, O gentle lady."

Draupadi seemed confused. "How can virtue lead to success when we see you in such adversity? Who is more virtuous than you? Who is more self-controlled and, indeed, more humble? Even when you assumed control of the earth, we did not see in you even the slightest amount of pride. You could abandon your brothers and me before giving up virtue. And yet, O king, destiny caused your mind to become confused and you gambled away everything. It is quite incredible."

Draupadi went on revealing her mind. It seemed to her that the only explanation for Yudhishthira's having acted so much out of character was that he was moved by the Lord's supreme will. After all, God was in ultimate control of everything. But how could he have ordained something so contrary to virtue? How had he allowed the sinful Duryodhana to prosper and Yudhishthira to suffer? It made no sense to her at all.

Yudhishthira could see that his wife was bewildered by her grief and anger. He replied to her in an affectionate voice. "O divine lady, surely you are afflicted by atheistic doubts. Virtue should never be performed with a desire for its fruits. Such a sinful mentality deprives one of the results, as does doubting the efficacy of virtue. There is no question that true virtue always has a glorious result. You have seen for yourself the limitless powers of great rishis like Narada and Vyasadeva, which have been acquired through virtue. These rishis declare piety and virtue to be the foremost duty."

Yudhishthira instructed Draupadi at length. He explained that although it sometimes appears that sinful men flourish, in the end they are always destroyed. Becoming degraded, they descend into lower and lower states of life. "The fruits of both sin and virtue are not immediately seen, gentle lady, but they manifest in due course. This is a highly mysterious subject, bewildering to even the gods. The results of work, known as karma, are controlled by Supreme Providence, and he alone understands its mysteries. Never speak ill of him, O Draupadi, for he is never partial or vicious toward anyone."

Night fell as Yudhishthira spoke, and the rishis lit many fires, thus illuminating the lakeshore where they sat. The crackling of the fires mingled with the chirping of crickets and the murmur of rishis chanting their evening prayers. Many of them sat around the Pandavas, listening to Yudhishthira. They nodded in agreement as he concluded his speech.

Draupadi, however, was still doubtful. "I accept all you have said, O foremost of the Bharatas. God is certainly giving us the results of our own acts. But we are still free to make further acts. We must still endeavor to achieve virtue, as you have said. Why, then, do you not act now to recover your kingdom? Is this not the right thing to do?"

Bhima had been listening carefully. Draupadi's words resonated with him and when she stopped speaking, he immediately said, "O king, this life of an ascetic is not meant for you. How can you acquire virtue in this lonely wood? You are a king, meant to possess wealth, give charity, and protect the people, not live like a yogi. What trifling virtue will you gain by keeping a promise made to sinful men?"

Bhima spoke with passion. Like Draupadi, he could not bear the thought of the Kauravas living in opulence, while Yudhishthira languished in the forest. His angry voice echoed across the lake as he went on. "O lord of the Bharatas, have you lost sight of your duty? Has despair deprived you of your manliness? Why do you weakly allow Duryodhana to enjoy your wealth? He is exactly like an offal-eating jackal stealing a lion's prey. To him, your forgiveness and virtue is nothing more than weakness. It was folly alone that made us desist from killing him when we had the chance. Let us no longer fall victim to that folly. We should rise up at once and kill the Kauravas to a man."

Yudhishthira summoned patience as he listened to Bhima venting his long-pent-up anger. The Pandava king felt chastised by his brother, but he made no attempt to defend himself. When Bhima had at last finished speaking, Yudhishthira sat silent for some moments, then finally said, "O Bhima, I cannot reproach you for lancing me with your sharp words, for it was truly my mistake that has brought about our present condition. I should have exercised more self-control during the dice game. It was always clear that Shakuni could not be defeated. And yet, even though my mind was overcome by pride and foolishness, I still believe that everything was preordained."

Yudhishthira fell silent again, thinking back to the day of the match. What had come over him? He had felt that he was acting only for virtue, but the result had been misery for everyone he loved. Something must have moved him to act so contrary to his nature. But what could he do now? An agreement had been made. It could not be broken, especially when it would almost surely lead to wholesale carnage.

"O Bhima, I cannot falsify my words. Truth is certainly the highest virtue and duty of all. We shall remain here for thirteen years, in pursuance of truth. Without doubt, better times will come, for virtue always has its rewards."

Seeing that Bhima was still seething with frustration, Yudhishthira continued, his tone becoming more grave. "O mighty-armed hero, we should not be rash. Acts performed out of pride or passion will end in grief. Let me tell you what I feel will be the result of your suggestion, born as it is from mental agitation."

Yudhishthira listed the many kings and warriors who would support the Kauravas. As well as all the mighty Kurus themselves, who included Bhishma, Drona, Kripa, and dozens of other fighters who could all contend single-handedly with great divisions of warriors, there were also numerous monarchs who had been subjugated by the Pandavas during the Rajasuya. Those kings would take Duryodhana's side without any doubt.

"Since our departure you can be sure that Duryodhana's main business will have been to build his military strength. He now has control of tremendous wealth and can amass an immense and unassailable army. We, however, are without anything, alone in the forest and unable to put together even a small force."

Yudhishthira spoke about Karna, whom he especially feared. Remembering how Karna had matched every martial feat displayed by Arjuna during the exhibition, Yudhishthira felt highly anxious. "I consider the impetuous and ever-angry Karna our greatest danger. Encased in his natural armor and accomplished in every weapon, he will be difficult to overcome. Thus do I feel that victory is far from assured should we join in battle now with the Kurus."

Bhima became pensive and said nothing, squeezing his hands together. Reflecting upon Yudhishthira's words, all his brothers began to feel almost hopeless about recovering their kingdom. How could men like Bhishma, Drona, Kripa, and Karna ever be overpowered—even by the celestials?

As the brothers sat in thought, Vyasadeva appeared in their midst. He took his seat by their side and told them that he had understood their anxiety. "O Yudhishthira, I saw what was in your mind, and thus did I speedily come here. Listen now as I tell you how you will be able to defeat your foes."

Vyasadeva said that he would impart to Yudhishthira the knowledge of a particular mystic power called pratismriti, which enabled its user to achieve success in any endeavor. "Give this power to Arjuna. With it, he will be able to approach the gods and learn from them the secrets of their celestial weapons. In due course of time, he will achieve great deeds with these mighty missiles."

After teaching Yudhishthira the pratismriti mantras, Vyasadeva left. Yudhishthira consulted with the rishis and, on an auspicious day marked by favorable constellations, he passed the knowledge on to Arjuna, instructing him to begin his quest for the celestial weapons. Arjuna then clad himself from head to toe in armor and took up his Gandiva bow and inexhaustible quivers. Blessed by the brahmins and bid a fond farewell by his brothers and Draupadi, he set off toward the north. His aim was to reach the celestial Mandara Mountain, the gateway to the gods' abode that lay amid the Himalayas.

Sixteen

ARJUNA MEETS THE GODS

ARJUNA MOVED SWIFTLY along the forest paths. As a result of chanting the pratismriti mantras, he found himself traveling at tremendous speeds. The forest creatures ran away in all directions as he raced by, his bow held at the ready. At the end of one day he reached the Mandara and began to ascend its heights. As he climbed toward the bluish peak, he saw varieties of brightly-colored flowers and trees, as well as crystal clear waterfalls falling onto sparkling rocks. Siddhas, Charanas, Gandharvas, and other celestial beings sported in delightful wooded groves. The air was heavy with fragrance and resonant with the sound of countless exotic birds.

Reaching a broad plateau halfway up the mountain, Arjuna stopped and looked around, considering that he might remain there and practice asceticism. He knew he would only be able to see the gods if they revealed themselves to him, and for that to happen, he would need to perform yoga and meditation. As he gazed around at the heavenly landscape, he heard a voice that seemed to come from the sky. "Stop!" it commanded.

Startled, Arjuna suddenly noticed a brahmin seated at the foot of a tree. He seemed ablaze with spiritual effulgence. Matted locks hung around his powerful shoulders, and he was clad in simple tree bark garments. He said, "O child, who are you who have come here bearing weapons and wearing armor? This is the abode of peaceful brahmins. There is no need for any aggression here; throw away your bow."

Arjuna bowed to the brahmin and introduced himself, but he made it clear he would not part with his weapons. The brahmin then smiled and revealed himself to be Indra. "My child, I am pleased to see you," he said. "Ask from me a boon."

Arjuna was overjoyed. If the great Indra had come to see him, then surely his mission would soon be successful. He folded his palms and replied,

"O exalted one, I desire to learn from you all the divine weapons of the gods."

Indra continued to smile. "Why do you want weapons? You are virtually in heaven now. What do you have to achieve by fighting? You have only to ask me and I shall raise you to regions of bliss."

Arjuna was respectful but firm. "My lord, I have no desire for celestial pleasures. My brothers await me in a lonely forest, and they are depending upon me. How can I desert them for my own happiness?"

Seeing Arjuna's distress as he remembered his brothers, Indra consoled him and said, "O child, try to see the great god Shiva. By gaining his audience you will have all your desires fulfilled."

Indra then disappeared, leaving Arjuna standing under the tree where he had been seated. Arjuna began at once to practice asceticism. He leaned his bow against the tree and took off his armor. After bathing in a nearby mountain stream, he fashioned himself a crude garment from the long grasses growing all around. Tying it around his waist, he spread blades of kusha grass on the ground and sat down to meditate. He focused his mind on Shiva and began to intone the sacred syllable Om. Days became weeks as he sat in the same spot, eating very sparsely and keeping his mind and passions fully in check. After a full month, he assumed a standing posture with his arms raised above his head. He bathed three times daily and ate only once a week. After another month, he began to stand on one leg. Eating only dry leaves, he controlled his breathing to the point where he inhaled and exhaled only once every hour. Eventually, he suspended his breathing entirely by the technique of kumbhaka.

The great rishis living in that region soon noticed Arjuna's austerities. By the force of his fierce asceticism, he generated such spiritual power that the very order of the universe appeared threatened. Understanding Arjuna's desire, the rishis went in a body to Shiva and said, "O Maheshvara, almighty one, see how Arjuna is engaged in rigid asceticism on the breast of Mount Mandara. If he is not soon stopped, we fear he will destroy the world. O lord, we seek your refuge. Please try to check him."

Shiva raised a hand in blessing and replied, "Fear not; I will fulfill Arjuna's desire even today."

The relieved sages then left, and Shiva immediately assumed the form of a hunter. Tall and golden-hued, he seemed like a shining mountain. He descended to earth accompanied by his consort, Uma, as well as many of his female goblin followers, who all assumed attractive forms. As they came to the region where Arjuna stood, it seemed to glow with radiant beauty. A strange quiet fell over the whole area; the birds stopped singing and even the flowing streams ran silent.

At that moment, a powerful celestial demon was passing that region. Seeing Arjuna meditating, he decided to attack him. He assumed the form of a huge boar and charged at Arjuna with a loud bellow. Arjuna fully opened his eyes, which had been half closed in meditation, and glared angrily at the fast-approaching beast. Within seconds, he took up his bow and drew back an arrow. He shouted out, "O wicked one, I do not know who you are, but as you seek to injure one who has done you no harm, I shall send you to Death's abode."

But just as he was about to fire his arrow, Arjuna heard a voice behind him. "Stop! Leave this one to me. I saw him first and have already aimed my arrow."

Ignoring that voice, Arjuna released his shaft. At the same time, Shiva fired an arrow. The shafts simultaneously struck the charging demon with a crack like thunder. Screaming in pain, the demon resumed his natural form and fell dead.

Arjuna looked around and saw the hunter. He smiled at him, but spoke strongly. "Who are you? Why do you wander here surrounded by women? And why did you shoot this Rakshasa who was first targeted by me? I cannot brook such an insult. You will pay with your life."

Shiva took a few steps closer and replied, "Do not worry about us. We are hunters and the forest is our residence. But who are you? You look like royalty and hardly belong in such a place."

Arjuna kept his bow at the ready. "Depending upon my Gandiva, I live here without any fear. See how I slew this mighty demon."

Shiva laughed. "This one was killed by me, not you. I saw him first and it was my arrow that struck him down. You should not boast so much. Indeed, it is I who have received insult here. Stand ready, for I shall shoot my thunder-like arrows at you. Resist them if you can."

Before Shiva could even raise his bow, Arjuna shot a volley of arrows at him that whistled through the air, but all of them seemed to disappear into Shiva's body. The god replied with his own arrows, and Arjuna expertly countered the attack. The Pandava fired countless arrows at his adversary, but they had no effect on the unusual hunter. Arjuna gazed at him in surprise and awe. "Well done! Excellent!" he called out in admiration. There were few men who could withstand arrows shot from the Gandiva with such impunity.

Arjuna began to wonder who his foe might be. Surely he was a celestial, perhaps even Shiva himself. Maybe that god had come to him in disguise. But whoever this hunter was, he had come as an aggressor and therefore had to be fought. Arjuna concluded that if this person was anyone other than Shiva, he would soon be killed. He raised his bow again and fired another cluster of deadly arrows at him. Again, the hunter's body absorbed them. Arjuna fired hundreds and thousands of shafts, but they had no effect whatsoever on his opponent. Then,to his amazement, Arjuna saw that his previously inexhaustible quivers had become empty.

Filled with wonder, Arjuna surveyed his imperturbable foe. The hunter stood smiling at him, with no sign of any wounds. Arjuna then rushed at him and began smashing him with the Gandiva. Still the hunter was unmoved. He snatched Arjuna's bow and drew it into his body. Arjuna quickly took up his sword and brought it down on Shiva's head, but it simply smashed to pieces.

Arjuna tried everything to overcome the hunter. He tore up trees to strike him with and hurled great rocks at him. When this failed, he pummeled him with his bare fists. The hunter fought back, catching Arjuna with blows that felt like thunderbolts. Arjuna seized him in his powerful arms and tried to crush the life out of him. Shiva, in turn, grasped hold of Arjuna, and the two fighters stood locked together. Their bodies emitted smoke and sparks as they exerted immense pressure on each other.

Pressed with such force by the god of gods, Arjuna became practically senseless. He turned blue and fell to his knees in a swoon. Observing the rules of combat, Shiva stood back. Arjuna soon came around and he looked up at the still unharmed hunter. There was no doubt that he must be the exalted Shiva.

Covered in blood and exhausted, Arjuna bowed before his opponent. He fashioned an image of Shiva from the earth and worshipped it with flower petals, and as he did so, he saw that the hunter was also covered with flowers. Arjuna was filled with joy. This was indeed the great deity!

Shiva then spoke to Arjuna in a powerful voice that filled the plateau where they stood. "I am pleased with you, Arjuna. No other warrior has your courage or determination. Your strength is practically equal to mine. Soon you shall acquire all the weapons you need to vanquish your enemies. Now behold me as I am."

Arjuna folded his palms and bowed in respect as Shiva exhibited his actual form. Seeing the effulgent god, with his three eyes and great trident, a divine serpent draped around his bluish neck, Arjuna offered prayers. He begged forgiveness for attacking him. Shiva replied that he had already pardoned him. He gave back to Arjuna the Gandiva bow and said that his quivers would again be inexhaustible. "Now ask from me a boon," said Shiva, holding up his hand, which was adorned with every auspicious mark.

Arjuna said, "Please give to me the knowledge of your personal weapon, the Pashupata."

Shiva agreed, and he then taught Arjuna the mantras for summoning the weapon. As soon as he chanted these mantras, the Pashupata appeared in his personal form and stood by Arjuna's side, saying he would be at the Pandava's service. Shiva then said, "Go to heaven now and receive the other divine weapons. I shall depart."

Before Arjuna's astonished eyes, Shiva rose up to the skies, along with all his followers. He stood gazing up at the sky for some minutes, wondering at his good fortune. As he watched, he saw a blazing circle of light appearing in the heavens. Gradually it assumed a form, and Arjuna saw that it was Indra, seated on the back of his celestial elephant, Airavata. He descended onto a nearby mountain ledge. Arjuna then saw that all the other principal gods had also appeared there. They shone like so many suns and lit up the whole region.

In a voice that rang out like thunderclaps, Indra said, "O Arjuna, sinless one, you shall soon accomplish a great work for the gods. All the deities will bestow upon you their own weapons. You should now come to the heavens, where I shall teach you all of my martial skills."

At Indra's command, the gods approached Arjuna one by one and gave him their weapons. They then went away with Indra, leaving Arjuna standing alone on the plateau. Suddenly he heard a tremendous sound in the sky. Looking up, he saw a huge chariot coming down, pulled by many hundreds of golden-hued steeds. It seemed to divide the heavens as it raced toward him. Furnished with canon, swords, missiles, thunderbolts, maces, and blazing lightning flashes, it came to a halt by Arjuna's side. The charioteer got down and said, "I am Matali, Indra's driver, sent here to fetch you to his abode."

After paying his respects to the Mandara Mountain, Arjuna climbed aboard the wonderful chariot and it rose up into the sky. It soon reached the heavenly paths that led to the higher worlds. Arjuna saw thousands of other celestial vehicles coursing in all directions. He saw countless brilliant planets, shining rishis, and warriors slain in battle who had attained heavenly forms. Matali told him that, from the earth, they were visible as stars.

Gradually the chariot approached Indra's planet, which shone like a second sun. Fanned by fragrant breezes, it was covered with celestial trees and flowers. Many Siddhas and other perfected beings moved gracefully across the beautiful landscape as the chariot passed overhead.

Seeing Arjuna open-mouthed in amazement at the planet's spectacular opulence, Matali said, "This region cannot be reached by anyone of atheistic temperament. Only those who have practiced sacrifice and penance can come here. Heroes who never turn their backs in battle, as well as rishis of rigid vows, ascend to this planet, O pure-minded one. The sinful can never see this abode, even in their dreams. Behold now Amaravati, Indra's capital."

The chariot passed through a golden gate studded with brilliant and many-hued celestial gems. It entered the famed Nandana pleasure gardens, filled with charming groves where the gods sported with beautiful Apsaras. Passing mansions of diverse and exquisite design, they came at last to Indra's immense palace. Arjuna was then greeted by Gandharvas, who eulogized him with captivating songs. While brahmins and bards chanted Vedic hymns, he was led to Indra, who immediately got down from his throne and tightly embraced him. The king of the gods then brought Arjuna up onto his expansive gold seat and sat next to him. Indra spoke consoling words to his son, telling him that he and his brothers would soon be restored to their rightful position.

After he had been refreshed with varieties of ambrosial food and drink, and entertained with song and dance by the Gandharvas and Apsaras, Arjuna was taken to his quarters in Indra's palace.

Arjuna began to live amid the splendid affluence of Indra's abode. Indra taught him the science of arms known only to the gods, in particular instructing him in the use of his own weapon, the Vajra thunderbolt. At Indra's command, Arjuna also studied under Chitrasena, king of the Gandharvas, who taught him the skills of celestial music and dance. Indra told him that these skills would prove useful in the future.

Five years passed, during which Arjuna thought always of his brothers in the forest and of the dice game and the insulting of Draupadi. Although surrounded by every conceivable kind of enjoyment, his mind could not be peaceful, and he longed to rejoin his brothers. As the time for his departure drew close, he received a visit one evening from Urvashi, one of Indra's Apsara consorts. Seeing the bewilderingly beautiful maiden at his door, Arjuna bowed and closed his eyes out of modesty. "Please come in and take a seat," he said, nervously. "Pray tell me why you have come here at this late hour."

Urvashi had been asked by Indra to go to Arjuna. The god had seen him casting glances at her in his assembly. Smiling demurely, she explained this to Arjuna and said, "I am thus here to wait upon you. O hero, seeing

you and knowing of your many virtues, I am held under Cupid's sway. Give
yourself to me and satisfy my desire."

Arjuna felt almost intoxicated by her fragrance, but he controlled his
mind and averted her gaze. Covering his ears as she spoke, he replied, "O
blessed lady, I could never accept you as a wife. Indeed, you are exactly like
my mother."

Arjuna explained that he had only been looking at her out of wonder,
thinking of how, thousands of years previously, she had married one of his
great ancestors. She was the mother of a famous forefather of Arjuna's
dynasty. "How, then, could I possibly enter into a conjugal relationship with
you?" he asked.

Urvashi's smile seemed to light up Arjuna's room. She replied in a
voice that resembled the tinkling of golden bells. "You need not fear incurring any sin. Apsaras are not bound by worldly morality. We are free to consort with all who reside here. Indeed, other descendants of your dynasty
have sported with us, and you may also do so."

Urvashi implored Arjuna to accept her, but he could not agree. He
made it clear that he was unable to see her as anything but a mother.
Urvashi felt insulted by his refusal. She began to tremble in anger.
Contracting her delicate eyebrows, she said, "As you refuse a woman who
has come here on the order of your father, a woman pierced by love's arrows,
so you shall have to lose your manhood and live among women."

The indignant Apsara then rose up and left the room, leaving Arjuna
in a state of consternation. He went at once to Indra and told him what had
happened. Laughing, Indra said, "My child, your patience and self-control is
surely without comparison. Do not worry about this curse. It will serve you
well during the thirteenth year of your exile. After passing one year as a
eunuch, you will regain your power."

Indra then informed Arjuna that he would arrange for his return to
earth the next day. Greatly relieved, Arjuna thanked Indra and went back
to his room, no longer worrying about the curse.

Seventeen

HEAVEN ON EARTH

FTER ARJUNA HAD departed for the Himalayas, the other Pandavas continued to live in the Kamyaka forest. They missed their brother and prayed for his swift return. Spending their time hunting, gathering food, and hearing from the brahmins, they fell into a routine that made the days pass quickly. Among the many rishis who lived there, one named Vrihadashwa came one evening to their ashram. He was fully acquainted with the mystical secrets of dice playing. After Bhima revealed to the *rishi* his fear that Shakuni might challenge Yudhisthira to yet another game of dice, even after the Pandavas had left the forest, Vrihadashwa taught Yudhishthira the science of gambling. He said, "Not even Shakuni will be able to defeat you at dice now."

Soon after Vrihadashwa left, Narada visited the Pandavas. He suggested that while they waited for Arjuna's return they should visit the many holy tirthas or pilgrimage sites that were situated in that Himalayan region. He described the merits that one accrued from going to each of dozens of different tirthas. When he had finished, he told the brothers that Lomasha Rishi would soon arrive. "He will lead you to these tirthas," said Narada, as he departed from their ashram.

A few days later, as Narada had predicted, the famous *rishi* Lomasha came to the Pandavas. He told them that he had been traveling in the higher planets and had seen Arjuna. "Your brother is sharing Indra's throne. He has already received Shiva's mighty weapon and is now being instructed by Indra."

Lomasha said that Indra had sent a message confirming Narada's suggestion that they visit the Himalayan tirthas. "By going to these sacred sites you will meet many highly exalted sages and gain great spiritual power," Lomasha said. "I have already traveled to these sites and know the way to all of them."

Overjoyed to hear of Arjuna's success, Yudhishthira replied, "What great good fortune is ours that the king of the gods thinks of our welfare. That fortune is made complete by your presence, O sage. Pray lead us to the tirthas."

Yudhishthira then addressed the many brahmins who were living with them. He knew that the journey into the high Himalayas, where many of the tirthas lay, would be difficult. He did not want to expose the brahmins to unnecessary suffering, and he warned them that food and drink might be hard to obtain. "The climate will be severe and the way fraught with danger. If you wish, you may now go to Hastinapura, where King Dhritarashtra will provide your maintenance."

Many of the brahmins decided to go to Hastinapura, and they sorrowfully took their leave from the Pandavas. Accompanied by only a few dozen brahmins and a number of servants, the brothers set off with Lomasha and Dhaumya leading the way. As they began their journey, Yudhishthira, within the hearing of his brothers and Draupadi, asked Lomasha, "O foremost of rishis, I do not think I am without any virtue, and yet, I am afflicted with so much sorrow. On the other hand, I feel my enemies have very little virtue. Why, then, do they prosper?"

Lomasha nodded in understanding. "It seems contradictory, dear child, but you should not grieve. Any success obtained as a consequence of sin is soon lost. It may be seen that wicked men prosper for a while, but eventually they are destroyed to the root."

The party walked single file along a narrow forest path. Bhima carried Draupadi and all four brothers kept their weapons at the ready. The twins went ahead with the rishis, alertly watching all sides, with their swords drawn. Rakshasas were known to frequent the mountain passes, and the Pandavas did not want to take any chances.

Lomasha went on speaking. "In a previous age, I saw how the Daityas and Danavas, the powerful demon races, once gained ascendancy over the gods by virtue of penance. They took possession of great wealth and became filled with pride. Shunning all virtuous acts, they engaged in nothing but licentious and sinful behavior. The goddess of prosperity, Lakshmi, soon forsook them and they were afflicted by adversity. Anger then overtook them, and they were quickly ruined."

Lomasha described how, on the other hand, the gods had practiced asceticism and virtue. Visiting holy places and serving the brahmins, they entirely eschewed sin. Thus, Lakshmi sought them and they again flourished. "In the same way, O Yudhishthira, you brothers should adhere to virtue and you will soon see your good fortune returning. Dhritarashtra's sons are exactly like the demons and will surely meet with the same end."

Reassured by Lomasha's words, the Pandavas made their way through the forest. Gradually they visited the many tirthas, bathing in the sacred lakes and hearing spiritual instruction from the rishis residing in those places. The rishis recited to them the fascinating histories of their forefathers and other great kings, which they heard with rapt attention. They offered oblations to their ancestors and worshipped the ascetic rishis. Dhritarashtra had sent some wealth to the forest, and Yudhishthira had his servants carry this with them to give in charity to those sages.

After traveling for a long time, they came to Mount Mandara. As they gazed at the splendid mountain with its peak shrouded in clouds, Lomasha said, "Behold the holy abode of Kuvera and his many Yaksha followers. It rises fifty miles into the heavens and cannot be accessed by the sinful. Concentrate your mind and proceed with caution. On account of your virtue and asceticism, you will be able to enter this region and mix with the celestials."

Lomasha said that Arjuna would soon be descending from heaven onto the summit of the Mandara. "Let us therefore ascend the mountain and wait for him there. We shall meet with Kuvera and receive his blessings also."

Close to the foot of the mountain was the kingdom of Suvaka. The party rested there for a night before beginning their ascent. They were well received by the king, who offered them all hospitality. Leaving all their servants and possessions with him, they departed in the morning and made their way to Mandara Mountain. Lomasha began offering prayers to the Goddess Ganga, who, as the Ganges River, had her source somewhere in its heights. He spent some time praying for her protection before they made their way up the mountain.

Yudhishthira said to his brothers, "Keep your thoughts pure and guard Draupadi carefully. Lomasha's apprehension is astonishing. The way ahead must surely be precarious."

Bhima placed Draupadi on his shoulders as they began their climb. The terrain was rugged and nearly inaccessible. Thick with trees and creepers, there were no paths, and the ground was strewn with rocks. They could hear the roars of fierce beasts, and a strong wind blew in their faces. After climbing throughout the day they reached a plateau, where they rested, exhausted from their toil. As they looked around them, it seemed they had arrived in heaven. The ground was carpeted with soft bluish grasses and expanses of wild flowers. Trees filled with brightly-colored blossoms stood around lakes of clear water that were covered with lotuses and crowded with swans, cranes, and storks. The whole region seemed to be illuminated by its own effulgence.

In the distance they saw what appeared to be a number of massive white rocks. Lomasha told them they were the bones of Naraka, a great demon slain in ancient times by Vishnu. He related the story to them as they continued on their way.

Leaving behind the heavenly region, they began climbing snow-bound and treacherous paths. Thinking only of Arjuna, the brothers slowly made their arduous ascent toward the distant summit of the mountain. But gradually the climb became so perilous and the wind so fierce that they felt they could not continue. Their limbs were frozen and, with the exception of Bhima, they felt utterly exhausted.

Bhima placed Draupadi on the ground, and she lay there, barely conscious. Yudhishthira slumped onto a rock and said, "Alas for our lot. We have become rangers of the wilderness. The beautiful Draupadi is close to fainting. Her lotus-like hands and feet are blue with cold. Oh, I am the most wretched man! My addiction to dice has caused immense suffering for this innocent princess. Her noble father has vainly bestowed her upon the Pandavas in the hope of her happiness. Now she lies here on the bare ground, overcome by hardship and sorrow."

Lomasha and Dhaumya consoled Yudhishthira with gentle words. They uttered mantras that gave strength to Draupadi. The twins then laid out a deerskin, and the princess lay on it to rest as they massaged her feet.

Yudhishthira looked up at the great mountain. It seemed impossible to go any further. He turned to Bhima and said, "How shall we carry on?"

Bhima suggested that they summon his son, Ghatotkacha. "Surely he will be able to carry us up this steep mountain pass."

Yudhishthira agreed and Bhima concentrated his mind upon his son. Within moments, Ghatotkacha appeared before them. He prostrated himself before the Pandavas and the rishis, touching their feet and saying, "I am your servant. Command me what I should do."

Bhima embraced his son, and Yudhishthira said, "O Bhima, let your heroic and powerful son carry Draupadi, who is like his own mother. With his help, I think we shall be able to reach our destination."

Ghatotkacha smiled, his huge mouth opening to reveal rows of sharp fangs. "I will carry the queen, and my Rakshasa followers will carry the others. Tell us where we should go."

A number of powerful-looking Rakshasas appeared in the sky and, on Ghatotkacha's order, they came before the Pandavas with folded palms. They took the brothers up onto their shoulders, while Ghatotkacha respectfully carried Draupadi. Lomasha, by virtue of his own mystic power, rose unaided into the sky alongside the Rakshasas, blazing like the sun. Travelling swiftly, they coursed over the mountain, seeing beneath them many wondrous regions inhabited by the celestials. Passing over the country of the Uttara Kurus, they came at last to the great peak known as Gandhamadana. On Lomasha's order, the Rakshasas alighted close to a huge *badari* tree.

"Here is Badarika Ashram," said the sage. "This is the ancient hermitage of Nara and Narayana Rishis."

The brothers gazed around in awe. The badari tree spread out its limbs like a vast green umbrella of lush foliage. It exuded freshness and calm, inviting shelter beneath its boughs. Ripe fruits hung down, and all kinds of birds, maddened by the honey falling from the fruits, played in its branches. Nearby they saw the crystal waters of the Ganges where she descended from the heavens onto the earth. Crowded with sages' hermitages, the entire region resounded with the sacred chanting of those rishis. It was lit by its own mystical effulgence and, untouched by the rays of the sun or moon, seemed to exist in a separate and transcendent dimension of space. Having arrived there, the Pandavas immediately felt all their bodily and mental pains assuaged. Even hunger and thirst left them, and their minds became profoundly peaceful.

Some of the rishis, who, through their own inner vision, had already understood their visitors' identities, came forward to greet them. The Pandavas lay flat on the ground in obeisance and were blessed by the sages. After being honored with offerings of celestial fruits and flowers, the brothers took up residence in a spacious cottage near the river. Yudhishthira asked Ghatotkacha to remain with them until after Arjuna's arrival, when they would return to the Kamyaka. They then began to spend their time hearing discourses and instructions from the rishis.

* * *

In Hastinapura, Dhritarashtra had learned from Vyasadeva of Arjuna's ascent to heaven. He heard how the Pandava had performed severe austerities and gained the favor of all the gods. Dhritarashtra was already experiencing acute anxiety, and when he heard this news it grew even more intense. The period of exile was quickly passing, and the Pandavas would be back before he realized it. What would be their mood? Yudhishthira was peacefully inclined, but Bhima would never renounce his fury. Nor would Draupadi let her husbands forget the events in the assembly. And now

Arjuna was acquiring the gods' own weapons. There could only be one reason for that, and it was something Dhritarashtra could hardly bear to consider. In search of solace, he called for Sanjaya.

When his secretary was present, the king said, "O Sanjaya, have you
heard about Arjuna's activities? That foe-slaying hero has gone to heaven
in his mortal body. He has received the Pashupata as a gift from Shiva, and
he has also received all the other celestial weapons of the gods. How can
there be any hope for my wicked sons? Soon they and all who follow them
will lie prostrate on the battlefield."

Tears fell from Dhritarashtra's eyes. He foresaw disaster. Duryodhana's
intractable attitude toward the Pandavas made war seem inevitable.

Tapping his fingers against his forehead, the blind king continued,
"Reflecting day and night, I do not see a single warrior who can stand
against Arjuna. He is wrathful, unrelenting, proud, and greatly powerful. O
Sanjaya, even the thunderbolt falling on a mountain peak may leave some
portion unburnt, but Arjuna's arrows leave absolutely nothing standing. It
seems to me that our armies have already fled in all directions, terrified by
the clatter of his chariot wheels."

Sanjaya listened in silence. Many times since the Pandavas' departure
his master had bewailed along similar lines. Yet he was still not making any
move to control Duryodhana. There had been no chastisement for his
heinous behavior during the gambling match. Nor had Karna received any
punishment for ordering Draupadi to be stripped. Indeed, with Karna's assistance, Duryodhana was now ruling the kingdom. Dhritarashtra was given to
extended periods of depression, sitting alone for hours on end, fearing the
future.

Sanjaya looked up at the king. "Your words are true, O great monarch.
The immeasurably powerful Pandavas were consumed by anger when they
saw their chaste wife insulted. I do not think they will forgive the Kauravas.
Your sons have brought upon themselves a fearful calamity. The Pandavas
will surely kill them all."

Dhritarashtra winced at his secretary's strong words and replied in
doleful tones, "O charioteer, seeing me blind and inactive, Duryodhana considers me a fool. He does whatever he likes. Counseled by avaricious
wretches, he fails to properly understand anything. Even the arrows shot by
Arjuna in sport can consume all my sons, what to speak of those fired in
anger. He has already defeated the gods at Khandava, and now he has also
gratified the immortal Shiva. United with his brothers and Krishna, he will
finish our armies to a man."

Sanjaya spoke consolingly to his old master. He seemed to understand the situation well enough. It now remained for him to take the right action when the Pandavas returned from the forest. But there was little cause for optimism. Despite his censures of Duryodhana, the king seemed as attached to him as ever.

*   *   *

The Pandavas lived peacefully on the Gandhamadana mountain for some time, enjoying their heavenly surroundings, but they thought continuously of Arjuna. Then one day, shortly after their morning prayers and meal, they saw a brilliant light in the sky. It grew in size as it approached the mountain, and the brothers saw that it was a celestial chariot. To their overwhelming joy, they saw Arjuna seated on that chariot, dressed in radiant silk robes and adorned with jewels, a brilliant coronet on his head. As the chariot reached the ground, Arjuna dismounted and bowed before Dhaumya and Yudhishthira. He touched Bhima's feet and received his embrace, and the twins offered him their obeisances. Arjuna then affectionately greeted Draupadi, who appeared like a lotus flower opening to greet the morning sun. He presented her with many celestial gems as splendorous as the sun, which Indra had given him.

Yudhishthira greeted and worshipped Indra's charioteer, Matali, as if he were Indra himself. He inquired after the gods, and Matali spoke to him in gentle words, conveying Indra's good wishes. He then ascended the chariot and drove away, back to the heavens.

The brothers all crowded around Arjuna, eager to hear of his adventures. Arjuna told them everything, from his arrival at the Gandhamadana and meeting there with Indra and Shiva, right up to the moment of his departure from heaven. He described how, just before it was time to leave, Indra had asked him to do something for him, by way of *dakshina*, in return for the weapons he had received. Indra had requested him to fight with a race of fierce demons, known as the Nivata-kavachas, who had been disturbing the gods for a long time. "Indra gave me a suit of impenetrable armor and placed this coronet on my head, saying, 'Go out and win victory over all your enemies.' I then proceeded for battle on his chariot."

As his brothers listened in awestruck silence, Arjuna described in detail the cosmic battle that had ensued. Using all the celestial weapons he had acquired, Arjuna had eventually overpowered the demons, after a terrible fight.

When Arjuna finished his narration, his brothers cheered him. Yudhishthira said, "O Dhananjaya, we are fortunate indeed to have you back. Great, too, is our fortune that you have received these incredible weapons. I consider the earth conquered and the Kauravas already subdued."

Yudhishthira asked Arjuna to display the weapons. Arjuna stood up and began to fix his mind in order to invoke them. Suddenly, however, the brothers began to see all kinds of natural disturbances. The ground trembled and the sky became covered with dark clouds. The brahmins found themselves unable to recite the Vedas, and all creatures felt oppressed. As the Pandavas looked around in surprise, they saw Narada Rishi coming toward them. He said, "I have been sent here by the gods. O Arjuna, do not invoke the weapons without good reason, or their divine power may destroy the world."

The sage turned to Yudhishthira. "O king, you will see Arjuna's prowess with the weapons in the war with the Kauravas."

The Pandavas bowed to Narada and he disappeared, leaving them to discuss their plans now that Arjuna had returned. Consulting with Dhaumya and Lomasha, they decided to stay at Badarika ashram. Five years of their exile remained before they needed to enter some inhabited region. That time would be best spent in the association of the great rishis in Badarika.

Four years thus passed, and the brothers increased their spiritual knowledge by hearing from the sages, as well as their personal power born of asceticism. At the end of this period, Arjuna and Bhima approached Yudhishthira to suggest that they begin their descent back to the Kamyaka forest. Bhima said, "O king, eleven years have now gone by with us living in the forest. Out of our love for you, and restrained by morality, we have not killed Dhritarashtra's sons. But the time for our return is coming close. Let us therefore leave this heavenly region and think about finding some place to spend our final year."

Yudhishthira agreed and, after discussing with the rishis, he decided to leave at once. As it was summer, he decided to go on foot, and he dismissed Ghatotkacha and his followers, bidding a fond farewell to Bhima's son and asking that he come again to assist them if a war with the Kauravas ensued. Then they slowly made their way back to Kamyaka, arriving just before the start of the monsoon season. They set up camp on high ground near the Dwaitavana Lake and watched as the rains fell, flooding the earth and sending bubbling streams surging through the forest.

Eighteen

DEMONIC INFLUENCES

A S THE PANDAVAS' exile wore on, Duryodhana grew increasingly confident. For eleven years he had enjoyed his position as virtual emperor. His father had left the affairs of state to him, and he had steadily increased his strength and influence by forming alliances all around the world. If and when the Pandavas ever came back, he felt more than ready for them. The impoverished brothers would no doubt have become emaciated and weak from their long sojourn in the wild. It should not prove too difficult to deal with them. As the Kaurava prince sat on his splendid throne, looking supremely satisfied, Shakuni began to address him.

"O ruler of men, you now have no rivals on earth. The Pandavas are gone and no longer pose any threat. Their wealth, which formerly gave you grief, is now the source of your pleasure. The world's kings are subservient to you, and you are adored by countless brahmins. All this has been achieved by the force of intellect alone."

Duryodhana folded his hands together and smiled, looking around the great hall where the gambling match had taken place. Now it was frequently visited by state leaders offering the same respect and tribute as they'd once given to Yudhishthira.

Shakuni went on, "Now that your position is secure, why not pay a visit to the Pandavas? The wise say that wealth that is seen by both friends and foes alike is truly wealth. As you once suffered, let Yudhishthira and his brothers now suffer, seeing you possessed of all grandeur and surrounded by the Kurus, while they rot in the forest."

Duryodhana looked at his uncle's sinisterly smiling face. His idea was appealing, but Duryodhana was not sure. "I think my father would object to this suggestion," he said, remembering how Dhritarashtra was always consumed with anxiety about the Pandavas. "He would immediately understand my motives and would be fearful of the consequences. The old man seems to think they have grown more powerful during their exile."

"Do not worry about the king," Karna interjected. He, too, found Shakuni's proposal attractive. It would be good to see the Pandavas and their haughty wife clad in barks. "I am sure we can find a good pretext for our excursion."

Duryodhana did not take much convincing. He got up from his throne and put an arm around Karna's shoulders. "Yes, let us think of a reason that will convince the king. What greater delight could there be for us than to see Yudhishthira, Arjuna, and especially Bhima sunk in misery? If those proud men see me graced with all wealth, then the goal of my life is attained."

The three men then conferred together for some time. Finally, they hit upon an idea that they felt sure would work. They had heard that the Pandavas were living in the Dwaitavana region, which was exactly where the Kurus were presently grazing their cattle herds. And it was not uncommon for members of the royal order to personally go and check on their cattle.

Having made their plan, they went the next morning, as usual, to see Dhritarashtra. While they were talking with him, a cowherd arrived. Having been previously instructed by Duryodhana, he began to speak about the cows at Dwaitavana, saying that it was time to mark the calves. Karna at once took the opportunity and said, "O king, why not let us go to Dwaitavana to take care of the cows? It would be a pleasant break. We can also enjoy some hunting in that charming region."

Dhritarashtra was doubtful. "I have heard that the Pandavas are there. If they see you, there will surely be problems. Arjuna has been to heaven and acquired the gods' divine weapons. Why, then, will he not kill you all? Remembering the insulting of Draupadi and their own abuse, both he and Bhima will instantly scorch you with their fury should you appear before them."

Shakuni dismissed the king's doubts. "There is no possibility that Yudhishthira will be unfaithful to his vow. He will not permit his brothers to fight the Kauravas now. Anyway, we will keep clear of them; you need have no fear."

Dhritarashtra was still uncertain, but upon seeing his son's eagerness, he finally relented. Duryodhana immediately assembled a large force of troops and, taking all his brothers and their wives, he soon set off for the forest. Thousands of chariots, elephants, horses, and infantry made up the procession as it left the city. Dressed in their most elegant clothes and richly ornamented, the women traveled in fine carriages drawn by tall white steeds.

When he arrived at the Dwaitavana Lake, Duryodhana learned that Yudhishthira was engaged in performing a sacrifice on its opposite shore. He decided to set up camp nearby so the Pandavas could see him in all his opulence. His men went ahead to search out a suitable site, but when they came near the lake, they were accosted by a voice from the waters. "Stop! Who goes there? Know me to be Chitrasena, king of the Gandharvas. This lake and its surrounding woodlands are mine. Leave at once, if you value your lives."

Duryodhana's soldiers looked down into the lake, where they saw the radiant Gandharva, surrounded by Apsaras and other celestials. They quickly returned to Duryodhana and informed him, but the Kaurava prince was not inclined to submit to Chitrasena. He ordered his men to confront the Gandharvas, and they returned to the lake in force. They rushed forward, roaring and sending up a huge clatter with their chariot wheels. Thousands of Gandharvas rose from the waters and stood on the lakeside to meet the attack.

A fierce battle ensued. The Gandharvas quickly killed hundreds of Duryodhana's soldiers. With a mighty roar, Karna then entered the fray and began to display his dazzling prowess with a bow. Hundreds of Gandharvas fell as his mantra-charged arrows flashed toward them by the thousands. Duryodhana also joined the battle, and the two friends fought side by side. They soon put the Gandharvas to flight. Seeing this, Chitrasena himself entered the fight. He appeared to be dancing on the battlefield as he released countless deadly arrows. Conversant with all mystical forms of warfare, he bewildered his opponents. It seemed as if a hundred Chitrasenas assailed them from all sides. Arrows flew at them from every direction, while huge maces and battle-axes fell from the sky.

Encouraged by their leader, the other Gandharvas rallied and fought with renewed energy. They surrounded Karna, raining down showers of weapons. Slaying his horses and charioteer, they smashed his chariot apart. Feeling hopelessly outnumbered, Karna leapt from his broken chariot and fled. Jumping aboard another chariot, he raced away into the forest.

As the Gandharvas gained the upper hand, only Duryodhana and his brothers remained facing them. But gradually they were overpowered by the many thousands of celestial fighters bearing down on them. Chitrasena personally targeted Duryodhana. He shattered his chariot and struck him with a hundred blazing arrows. Duryodhana fell, stunned, to the ground and Chitrasena quickly seized him by the hair. While other Gandharvas took hold of his brothers, Duryodhana was bound and taken prisoner. The Gandharvas then ran to the Kaurava camp, where they also took the Kuru wives captive.

Some of the fleeing Kuru soldiers ran around the lake and fell before Yudhishthira, begging him to come to their aid. Yudhishthira felt compassion toward the wretched-looking soldiers, but Bhima laughed when he heard their pleas. "It seems the Gandharvas have already achieved our ends for us, saving us so much effort. Obviously, Duryodhana came here to gloat in front of us. Why should we save him? He is getting exactly what he deserves."

But Yudhishthira did not agree. He held up a hand to silence Bhima. "Where is your honor, dear brother? These men are afraid and have sought our protection. Furthermore, we are Kurus, and thus it is our own family who is being attacked. Amongst ourselves, we may be five and they a hundred, but when an enemy of the Kurus approaches, we are a hundred and five brothers. Therefore, we must act. As well as capturing our cousins, the wicked Gandharvas have insulted the Kuru ladies in our presence."

Yudhishthira instructed his brothers to go at once to rescue the Kauravas. He smiled at Bhima. "Your sworn enemy now depends on you. What could give you more happiness than this opportunity to protect him?"

Arjuna rose up at once and took hold of his weapons. "Either the Gandharvas shall release the Kauravas or the earth shall drink their blood."

Accepting Yudhishthira's words, Bhima also got up and went with Arjuna. The twins followed, leaving Yudhishthira to continue with the sacrifice. All four brothers mounted chariots provided by the Kuru soldiers and pursued the Gandharvas. Seeing them rushing for battle with raised weapons, looking like four blazing fires, the Kuru soldiers shouted for joy.

The Gandharvas quickly assumed their battle formation again, preparing to face the Pandavas. Arjuna tried to reason with them before fighting. He called out, "O celestials, it is not right for you to fight with ordinary men, nor, indeed, to seize their wives. We are here on Yudhishthira's order to ask for their release. Please comply, and we shall avoid unnecessary bloodshed."

The Gandharvas only laughed and said they would not release their prisoners. "Chitrasena is our leader, and it his command alone which we obey."

Angered, Arjuna immediately fired a volley of gold-winged arrows at them. The Gandharvas responded with their own shafts. They surrounded the four brothers and hurled every kind of weapon at them. Undaunted, the Pandavas expertly countered the assault and continued attacking their foes. An extraordinary battle ensued, with the four humans standing against thousands of Gandharvas. Becoming enraged with his celestial opponents, Arjuna invoked mystical weapons, slaying hundreds of them.

Oppressed by the brothers' forceful attack, the Gandharvas rose into the sky, but Arjuna checked them with a network of arrows shot from the Gandiva. Chitrasena then joined the fight. After only a brief skirmish with Arjuna, he shouted out, "Hey Partha! Behold, I am your friend Chitrasena."

Seeing the Gandharva king approaching them in peace, the Pandavas withdrew their weapons. Arjuna asked him why he and his followers were persecuting the Kurus, and Chitrasena replied, "They came here only to gloat before you, O heroes. Indra understood this and he ordered me to capture them. Allow me to carry them away. They have grievously wronged you and your wife. Imprisonment is therefore only right for them."

Arjuna replied that, despite their numerous sins and offenses, they were still family members, and therefore Yudhishthira had asked for their release.

"I think your brother did not know why the evil-minded Kauravas came here," answered Chitrasena. "Let us take them before him and hear his judgment."

Agreeing to this, the Pandavas went with Chitrasena and his followers to Yudhishthira, bringing Duryodhana and his brothers bound with chains. Yudhishthira thanked Chitrasena for not slaying the Kauravas. "You have thus saved our family honor, and it will be further saved if you release them," he said, folding his hands in respect.

Delighted to see Yudhishthira's tolerance, humility, and compassion, Chitrasena at once agreed. He had the bedraggled Kauravas released in Yudhishthira's presence and their women taken back to their camp. Indra then appeared and revived the slain Gandharvas by sprinkling them with amrita, heavenly nectar. All of the celestials then rose into the sky and vanished.

Yudhishthira turned to Duryodhana and spoke in a gentle voice. "O child, do not again be so reckless. A rash and thoughtless man never achieves happiness. O Kuru prince, go home now, in peace, with all your brothers. Do not be despondent."

Duryodhana was devastated. He could make no reply, nor even look at Yudhishthira. Turning away, he walked off like a wooden doll, hardly even conscious of his own movements. He and his brothers mounted their chariots and slowly made their way back to their camp, leaving the Pandavas to continue with their sacrifice.

The Kauravas decided to leave immediately for Hastinapura. They set off, a sorry-looking train of travelers compared to the pompous procession that had left Hastinapura. After they had covered about ten miles, Karna caught up to them. Covered with wounds, he went straight to Duryodhana and said, "O king, regretfully, I had to abandon the fight for fear of my life. Hard pressed by hordes of Gandharvas, I fled into the forest. But still I see you here, safe and well. Surely you have achieved a great feat today, defeating those superhuman beings. Tell me how you did it."

Duryodhana sighed and looked at his friend. Tears fell from his eyes as he replied, "You do not know the truth. Alas, I am ruined. O friend, life has lost all its luster for me now."

Karna listened in dismay as Duryodhana described what had happened. At the end of his account, the crestfallen prince said, "Having become a source of joy for my enemies and grief for my friends, I cannot continue to live. How can I return to Hastinapura? What would the Kuru chiefs say to me? Alas, I am a wretch who deserves only to die."

In his misery, Duryodhana realized his foolishness. It was madness only that had made him come to the forest. Why had he not heeded Vidura's often-given advice? Now he was receiving the bitter consequences of that mistake.

Weeping, the prince turned to Dushasana and said, "Vain and insolent men like me cannot achieve happiness for long, even when they attain prosperity. I cannot drag on my miserable existence any longer. O brother, here and now do I hand over the kingdom to you. Take my place and rule this earth. I shall stay on this very spot and give up my life."

Before the eyes of his shocked brothers and friends, Duryodhana cast off his armor and royal robes. Tying on a waistcloth, he sat on the ground in a yogic posture, determined to fast till death. Dushasana fell at his feet and cried out, "Relent! Dear brother, do not do this. How can I rule without you?"

Karna also tried to dissuade Duryodhana, imploring him in many ways and reassuring him that there was no shame in his defeat at the hands of the celestials. "Do not make yourself the butt of ridicule by this act. O hero, rise up. The Pandavas only did their duty by protecting you, who are their king. There is nothing to be lamented in that."

Shakuni also tried to stop Duryodhana, but the prince would not be diverted from his purpose. He had made up his mind to die. As everyone gradually stopped speaking, he began to enter a trance of meditation, intending to observe the praya vow of fasting until death.

In the nether regions, the demons became aware of Duryodhana's resolve. Having been defeated in a war with the gods, the races of Daityas and Danavas had been planning their revenge. Many of them had taken birth on earth as kings and warriors, with the hope of overthrowing the pious kings who made sacrifices to the gods. Fearing their party would not succeed without Duryodhana to lead them, they began a ritual to invoke a powerful demoness who would be capable of bringing Duryodhana into their presence. Through her mystic powers, the Kaurava was brought to their planet in his subtle body.

As if in a dream, Duryodhana found himself standing in an assembly of Danavas. Their leader addressed him in respectful tones. "O king of kings, great hero, why have you undertaken such a rash vow? Suicide always leads to hell. He who takes his own life is reviled on earth and gains no auspicious destination. Your resolve is thus contrary to your own best interests. Nor is it necessary. Listen now as I describe how all success will soon be yours."

The Danava told Duryodhana how there were many thousands of mighty demons incarnated on earth. They would join his army to fight against the Pandavas. Other celestial demons would also possess the hearts of Bhishma, Drona, Kripa, and all the principal Kuru warriors. They would thus lose all restraint in battle and mercilessly slay anyone and everyone who came before them.

"You need not fear Arjuna, O king, for your friend Karna is the very powerful Naraka, a demon formerly slain by Vishnu himself. He has reincarnated to assist you on earth, and even if he does not kill Arjuna, there are hundreds of thousands of Daityas who have become the Samshapatakas, an invincible army that will challenge him again and again. Thus, your success is certain, and all your enemies will be annihilated. Be in good cheer and await your time. It will soon come."

Duryodhana was then returned to his gross body, which still sat in meditation. He opened his eyes and looked around in amazement, vividly recalling his meeting. Had it been a dream? It had certainly seemed real, and the promise it held out was too good to pass up. The prince decided to get up and go back to Hastinapura. He would not reveal his mystical experience, in case it proved to be nothing more than a hallucination, but he had a strong feeling it had actually happened. He got to his feet with a smile.

Seeing him abandoning his determination to die, his brothers joyfully surrounded him. Karna embraced him with tears in his eyes and said, "By good fortune you have regained your senses. O king, a dead man cannot conquer his enemies. Do not die so ignominiously. Go out and attain victory and immortal fame. With me as your friend, why do you grieve? As soon as the Pandavas emerge from exile, I swear I shall crush them. Have no doubt."

Duryodhana returned Karna's embrace. "So be it," he replied, giving the order to return to Hastinapura. His mind was now set on amassing an army for war.

Nineteen

THE GODS TAKE A HAND

S OME TIME AFTER the fight with the Gandharvas, the Pandavas went out hunting together. Dhaumya remained at the hermitage, along with Draupadi. While the brothers were gone, the king of the Sindhu province, Jayadratha, on his way to another kingdom, passed their ashram. Seated on a great chariot and surrounded by numerous troops, he happened to see Draupadi as she was out gathering flowers. He was struck by her beauty and practically lost his senses with desire. Stopping his party, he gazed at her for some time. Draupadi saw him looking at her and pulled her cloth over her head. Picking up her basket of flowers, she hurried back to her cottage.

As he stared at Draupadi's faultless body, covered only by a light summer sari, Jayadratha was entranced. He had to have her. Accompanied by a few of his followers, he jumped down from his chariot and walked over to the cottage. He called in, "O most beautiful maiden, are you there? Who and whose are you? Are you an Apsara? Why do you live in this lonely wood? Know me to be Jayadratha, lord of the Sindhus."

Draupadi was immediately apprehensive. She could sense the king's lusty intentions, but she replied respectfully, "You are welcome here, O king. I am Draupadi, wife of the Pandavas. They will soon be here. If you wait for a while, I am sure Yudhishthira will receive you with all hospitality."

Jayadratha, his mind overpowered by desire, took a step closer. "I am surprised that you remain with the Pandavas. O lady of beautiful hips, you deserve better. Your husbands are fallen from their position and have lost everything. Renounce them and become my wife. Give up this wretched forest life and share with me the opulent Sindhu kingdom."

Draupadi frowned and retreated from Jayadratha. It was just as she suspected. She was immediately angered to hear her husbands defamed. Her face flushed a deep red as she rebuked the king. "How dare you speak in such a way! Are you not ashamed? Only dogs would make such a suggestion. The wise never criticize men who practice devout penance, even if they are impoverished."

Jayadratha laughed, becoming even more enchanted by the furious Draupadi, who was trying to move away from him. He stood squarely between her and the door to the cottage. She reproached him even more fiercely. "Fool! Your destruction is close. You are rousing a sleeping lion by plucking a hair from his face. When Arjuna and Bhima return, you will not know which way to run."

Bewildered by passion, Jayadratha cared nothing for Draupadi's warning. Laughing all the more, he stepped forward and tried to seize her arm. Draupadi cried out and swung around with clenched hands. She caught him on the side of the head, sending him sprawling to the ground. But as she lunged toward the door, he jumped up and grasped her in his powerful arms. He then began to drag the squirming princess toward his chariot.

Dhaumya heard the commotion and ran out of his hut. Seeing Jayadratha with the weeping Draupadi, he called out, "Stop! O king, you cannot take this lady without first defeating the Pandavas. This is the kshatriya code. Truly, you will soon reap the result of this wicked act."

Jayadratha ignored Dhaumya. He pulled Draupadi onto his chariot and urged on his horses. As his chariot picked up speed, Dhaumya ran after him, constantly reprimanding him with strong words. Although able, the *rishi* did not curse Jayadratha, for he knew that the Pandavas were close by. They would deal with the sinful king soon enough.

Jayadratha and his followers had not been gone for long when the Pandavas returned. Yudhishthira had perceived some evil omens, and he raced anxiously toward the ashram. His fears were confirmed when he saw Draupadi's servant, Dhatreyika, lying on the ground, sobbing. She told Yudhishthira what had happened. "The wretched Jayadratha has snatched away Draupadi, disregarding her Indra-like husbands. O heroes, give chase and you will soon catch him. He left here not so long ago."

Dhatreyika pointed in the direction that Jayadratha had taken, and the five brothers immediately went after him. Twanging their bows and breathing hot and heavy sighs, they careered along the forest paths. Before long, they saw ahead of them the dust raised by Jayadratha's party. As they drew closer, they saw Dhaumya still running after them and loudly wailing. Yudhishthira consoled the *rishi* and told him to return to the ashram. "O sage, be assured that this low-minded sinner will soon be punished."

Bhima bellowed out his terrifying war cry, and the soldiers froze with fear, then turned to face the Pandavas. Bhima began to release his deadly shafts at them, but Arjuna checked him, saying, "What will you gain by killing these poor soldiers? It is Jayadratha we want."

Bhima lowered his bow. He and Arjuna then charged through the ranks of soldiers, scattering them as they made their way toward Jayadratha. They saw that he was surrounded and protected by many hundreds of chariot warriors. Those fighters released showers of arrows at the advancing Pandavas. Raising their maces and swords, they rushed into battle.

Infuriated, Arjuna raised the Gandiva and began picking off his foes. Arrows flew from his bow in hundreds. Before long, the ground was covered with severed heads and arms. Shattered armors and gleaming helmets dropped to the earth. Chariots were smashed and their riders cut to pieces before Arjuna's relentless onslaught. Ravens, vultures, and jackals cried out in delight and came to feast on the mangled bodies that littered the earth.

Seeing his men being massacred, Jayadratha was terrified. He quickly put Draupadi off his chariot and fled into the woods. Bhima grasped hold of his mace and began to give chase, but Yudhishthira called out, "O hero, remember that this one is the husband of Gandhari's daughter, Dushala. He should not be slain."

Draupadi, who had been taken onto Sahadeva's chariot, found it hard to accept Yudhishthira's words. "Why should he be spared?" she exclaimed. "An enemy who carries off one's wife should be immediately killed."

Yudhishthira consoled Draupadi and returned with her to the hermitage. Bhima and Arjuna pursued Jayadratha, as the twins put to flight his remaining followers. The Sindhu king had already gone some distance when Arjuna fired four arrows from his bow. Charged with mantras, those shafts flew a full two miles and slew Jayadratha's four horses. The king leapt from his chariot shaking in fear. Leaving the path, he began to stumble through the bushes. The Pandavas soon caught up with him, and Arjuna called out, "O king, with what prowess did you dare to steal our wife? Stand and fight now. How can you flee, leaving your followers to fight?"

Jayadratha did not look back. He crashed through the woods in terror. Bhima jumped down and ran after him. Catching hold of him, the Pandava delivered to him a number of powerful blows. He seized him by the hair and dragged him about. Arjuna reminded him of Yudhishthira's command. "Do not slay him," he shouted.

Bhima restrained himself with difficulty. He kicked the half-conscious king and threw him to the ground. "Yudhishthira is always merciful," he said, through clenched teeth. "I will not kill him, but according to the accepted custom, he is now our slave." Bhima took out a razor-headed arrow and shaved off Jayadratha's hair, indicating that he had been defeated in battle and made into a slave. He then said, "Let us take this wretch to Yudhishthira for his decision."

The brothers brought Jayadratha back to their ashram. By this time, Draupadi had calmed down. She felt compassion for the humiliated king, and especially for his wife Dushala, with whom she was friendly. She said, "Yudhishthira is right. Let him be spared. He has already become our slave; that is punishment enough."

Yudhishthira went over to Jayadratha, who knelt on the ground, trembling, "Because you are weak, you should not provoke others. You may go now, but do not commit such a vile act again. Be blessed. May your heart grow in virtue."

Jayadratha got up and silently slunk away, thinking only of revenge. Realizing that he would never be able to overcome the Pandavas in battle, he decided to seek a boon from Shiva. Perhaps, by the grace of that powerful god, he would be able to defeat them. Going deep into the forest, he began to practice severe asceticism, his mind bent upon harming the Pandavas. For many months he ate sparsely and constantly prayed to Shiva. Eventually the god appeared to him and asked, "What do you desire?"

The delighted king replied, "O almighty one, let me conquer the Pandavas."

Shiva laughed. "This can never be. They are protected by Krishna and cannot, therefore, be conquered, even by me. I will, however, grant you one thing. With the exception of Arjuna, who is the immortal sage Nara incarnate, you will be able hold off all the brothers once only in battle."

Shiva then vanished, leaving Jayadratha to return to his kingdom, wondering when the day would come when he could use the boon.

*   *   *

Filled with new hope after his meeting with the Danavas, Duryodhana entered Hastinapura. He began to see the kings and warriors who supported him in a different light, realizing that many of them must be incarnations of celestial demons. Surely, when they all came together, there would be little the Pandavas could do to avoid defeat.

Bhishma, however, saw the events at Dwaitavana as an opportunity to make Duryodhana see sense. Soon after Duryodhana's return from the forest, Bhishma said to him, "You have now seen for yourself the Pandavas' power and, indeed, Karna's inferiority. Your hopes for defeating Arjuna rest largely on the suta's son, but know for certain that he is not even a fourth

part of Arjuna. My dear child, make peace with the Pandavas now, before it
is too late."

Duryodhana only smiled and said nothing. What did old Bhishma
know? Even he would soon be playing his part in crushing the Pandavas
when the demons possessed him. Thinking of this, Duryodhana suddenly
laughed. He stood up and left the room, leaving Bhishma sadly shaking his
head.

Duryodhana went straight to Karna and told him what Bhishma had
said. Karna felt pained because Bhishma was always berating him with harsh
words. It was hard to understand. Karna felt he had shown his loyalty to the
Kurus beyond any doubt. He wished only for Duryodhana's success and was
prepared to lay down his life for the Kuru prince. Why, then, did Bhishma
always deride him?

Karna asked Duryodhana if he could do something that would prove
his power. "Formerly the Pandavas conquered the earth, and you are now
enjoying the result. But if you permit, I will go out and conquer the whole
world on your behalf. The senile and crooked-minded Bhishma will be consumed with regret when he sees my prowess and my allegiance to the
Kurus."

Duryodhana's eyes expanded with delight. He embraced his friend and
agreed to arrange for a vast army to accompany him. Within a short time,
Karna was on his way, surrounded by the powerful Kuru forces. Ranging to
all quarters of the globe, he again established the Kuru empire, just as the
Pandavas had done before him. He took the opportunity to solidify existing
alliances and to make new friendships through diplomatic negotiations. Any
king who opposed him in battle was soon subdued by the unstoppable power
of the Kuru army, with Karna himself fighting at their head. At the end of
his expedition he returned victorious, offering to Duryodhana the immense
amount of tribute and booty he had collected.

Seeing him marching back into Hastinapura with an almost endless
line of asses, camels, and elephants bearing wealth, Duryodhana laughed
with joy. With the mighty Karna by his side, the world under his control,
and the Danavas backing him, his position was surely unassailable. The
prince considered the Pandavas as already defeated. Walking in his spacious
palace garden with Karna, he said, "Dear friend, my desire now is to perform
the Rajasuya, even more opulently than Yudhishthira."

Duryodhana told his friend that, despite his desire, the brahmins had
said he could only perform the Rajasuya after Yudhishthira's death. Lifting
his manicured and sandal-clad foot, the prince kicked out at a flower.

"Unfortunately, that greatest of all sacrifices cannot be performed by two different kings co-existing on the earth."

Karna stopped walking and, looking toward Duryodhana, he spoke solemnly. "O king, know for certain that I will do everything in my power to bring about the Pandavas' destruction. Here and now do I make a vow. As long as I have not slain Arjuna, I will not taste meat nor accept any luxuries. When asked for anything in charity, I will not refuse."

Duryodhana embraced Karna with a smile. Feeling even more confident of his ultimate success, he entered his palace for the evening.

After Karna had made his vow, Indra decided to help the Pandavas. He knew that Yudhishthira's greatest fear came from Karna. Although Arjuna had so far shown greater prowess than he, Karna, Yudhishthira felt, still posed a real threat due his natural bodily armor. The Pandava king knew it would be difficult to kill him. Indra, therefore, disguised himself as a brahmin and went one morning to see Karna.

Karna had just come out of the Ganges after performing his daily worship of the sun god. At that time he always gave charity, and on this particular day he saw an effulgent brahmin approach him. He welcomed him and asked what he would like. Indra then said, "I wish to have your bodily armor."

Karna at once realized the brahmin's identity. In a dream, he had already been warned by the sun god that Indra would try to take his armor. The sun god had advised him not to give it, but Karna knew he could not refuse. Still, he tried to change the brahmin's mind. "I will give you anything you desire. Why take my armor? I can give you enough wealth to maintain you for your whole life."

Indra insisted that he only wanted the armor, and Karna said, "Very well, it must be so. O brahmin, I know you are Indra. Surya has already informed me that you would be coming. O lord of the gods, you may take my armor, but I ask that you grant me something in exchange."

Indra agreed. "With the exception of my thunderbolt, you may ask for anything you like."

Surya had told Karna that if he were to surrender his armor to Indra, he should ask the deity for his Shakti weapon, a great dart that could not be resisted even by the gods. Karna therefore asked Indra for that weapon, and the god replied, "I will give this infallible missile to you, but with one condition. You may release it only once. It will certainly slay your opponent, but it will then return to me."

Karna said, "I agree. There is only one mighty foe whose death I desire."

With a razor-edged dagger, Karna then slit off his natural armor. With his mind fixed on his vow and his desire to adhere to virtue, he smiled through the pain as the golden armor came away from his body. He then handed it, wet with blood, to Indra. The god thanked him and gave him the Shakti. Then he soared into the heavens, feeling that the Pandavas' purpose had been accomplished.

*   *   *

In the forest, the Pandavas knew they would soon have to find a town or city in which to spend their final year. They did not know where to go. How could they possibly remain incognito without separating? That was a painful prospect—especially for Draupadi. And even then there would be no guarantee that no one would recognize them. The brothers were world famous, and it was well known that they would soon be emerging from the forest. Duryodhana would certainly have his spies everywhere. Their discovery seemed inevitable. Then there would be another thirteen years of exile, for Yudhishthira would never break his word.

One day, as the brothers sat discussing their situation, a brahmin in obvious distress ran up to them. Pointing in the direction of the thick forest, he said, "O heroes, help me. It is time for my daily sacrifice, but all my paraphernalia, tied into a bundle, has been snagged on a deer's horns. The animal has gone deep into the woods, carrying the bundle."

Yudhishthira jumped up at once. It was always a kshatriya's duty to protect the brahmins. He took hold of his bow. With his brothers right behind him, he ran into the forest. Before long, they saw the deer ahead of them, but somehow, despite their best efforts, they could not capture it nor strike it with their arrows. The animal bounded away, deeper and deeper into the forest, with the five brothers in hot pursuit.

After some time, it seemed that the deer had disappeared. The Pandavas came together and sat down on a fallen tree branch, exhausted and perspiring. Distraught at their failure to rescue the brahmin's paraphernalia, they looked around at the dense foliage, wondering which way the deer had gone. Yudhishthira said to Nakula, "Dear brother, see if you can find us some water. Let us refresh ourselves and then resume our search.

Nakula put down his bow and quickly shinned up a tree. Not far off, he saw waterfowl circling around. Realizing that there must be a lake nearby, he took an empty quiver and set off to fetch water. He soon came to a large, clear lake covered with lotuses and lilies. Dropping to his knees on the shore, he was about to drink the water when he heard a stern voice. "Stop!"

it commanded. "O child, this lake is mine. You must first answer my questions before you may drink."

Nakula looked around, but could not see anyone. Feeling intensely thirst, he decided to drink the inviting water and then search for the source of the voice. He cupped his hands and drew the water toward his mouth. As soon as it passed his lips, he fell dead.

After some time, Yudhishthira became anxious. He told Sahadeva to go after his brother. Sahadeva soon found Nakula lying on the lakeshore. Shocked, he fell by his side and cried out in anguish. Although Nakula's bodily luster had not left him, he appeared to be dead, with no sign of any heartbeat or breathing. Sahadeva was perplexed. He, too, was burning with thirst, and he leaned over the water's edge to take a drink. Again the voice commanded that he stop, telling him that he must first answer some questions.

Even more perplexed at this, Sahadeva looked all around but saw no one. His hands were already in the water. Oppressed with thirst, he brought a palmful to his mouth. Suddenly he, too, fell dead, next to his brother.

When neither of the twins returned after almost an hour, Yudhishthira told Arjuna to follow them. Arjuna took his bow and proceeded cautiously through the forest. Before long he found the twins by the lake, apparently dead. He cried out in grief. Setting an arrow on his bowstring, he looked around carefully. There was no sign of any struggle. Who could have killed the twins without a fight? Everything seemed peaceful; the broad lake was calm and the surrounding trees swayed gently in the breeze. Only a few waterfowl disturbed the tranquil atmosphere as they flapped across the lake.

Like his brothers before him, Arjuna desperately needed a drink. He knelt at the water's edge and reached down with cupped palms. Once more, the voice rang out. "Do not drink the water. First, answer my questions."

Arjuna leapt to his feet and raised his bow. Unable to see anyone, he began firing mantra-charged arrows capable of striking invisible targets. They flew in all directions. Arjuna filled the sky with shafts, but no foe became visible. The voice spoke again. "Do not waste your time, Arjuna. Answer my questions or, if you drink the water, you will die."

Infuriated, Arjuna cared nothing for the warning. If he drank the water, perhaps the speaker would come out. Then he would see about his questions. He began to drink, but within moments he, too, had fallen to the ground next to his brothers.

Back in the woods, Yudhishthira felt increasing anxiety. He said to Bhima, "What can our brothers be doing? O tormentor of foes, I think you should find them and bring them back."

Bhima got up and ran through the woods. Finding his three brothers lying prostrate by the lake, he was astonished. Were they dead? The horrified Bhima could see no signs of life. What mighty being could have slain them? It was unimaginable! Bhima considered that he would soon have to face some tremendous enemy in battle. He had best slake his thirst and overcome his fatigue. But as he was about to drink, the voice commanded him to stop.

Bhima thought the voice must belong to whoever had killed his brothers. He would soon deal with him. First, though, he would take a drink; then the fight could commence. He leaned down to the water. As soon as it passed his lips, however, he fell dead alongside his three brothers.

Left alone, Yudhishthira was filled with foreboding. As the time went by and still his brothers did not return, he decided to go after them. He pushed his way through the bushes, going quickly toward the sound of cranes in the distance. Suddenly he came into a clearing and saw the lake. Seeing his brothers lying on the shore, he wailed in grief. Completely baffled at that seemingly impossible sight, he ran to them and fell to the ground. There were no signs of life. Yudhishthira looked around with tear-filled eyes. The tranquil lake appeared as if transported from heaven. A sweet fragrance filled the air, and the trees nearby were covered with red, blue, and yellow blossoms. But surely some sinister danger must lurk behind the apparently peaceful exterior.

Yudhishthira thought carefully. Although his brothers appeared dead, their bodies were lustrous. It seemed their souls were still present, though their life energy was gone. Who could have done such a thing? It did not seem as if they had been slain in any normal fight. Perhaps the god of death himself had taken their lives. But why? Yudhishthira looked down at the lake. The answer must be there. This lake was somehow the cause of their deaths. Yudhishthira plunged into the water. As he surfaced, the voice called out, "O child, do not drink. This lake is mine. Answer my questions first or die like your brothers."

Yudhishthira gazed searchingly around the lake. "Who are you?" he shouted.

"I am a crane who lives in these waters. Your brothers disregarded my warning and have thus been brought under death's control. Do not suffer the same fate."

To his amazement, Yudhishthira saw a large crane sitting on a tree bough close to him. "Are you a god?" he asked. "Surely no mere bird could have killed my brothers."

Suddenly the crane transformed into a huge, frightening-looking being. With large red eyes and long, pointed ears, he blazed with effulgence. He roared like a thundercloud and said, "Know me to be a Yaksha. Your brothers died for their own faults. I forbade them to drink, but they ignored me. This water is mine; anyone wishing to drink it must first answer my questions."

Fearful and apprehensive, Yudhishthira replied, "O Yaksha, I do not wish to take what is yours. Ask me your questions. If it is in my power, I shall answer them."

"Very well then. Tell me, how does the soul rise out of his entanglement in matter? Who keeps him company, who is his guide, and on what is he established?"

"Knowledge of God makes the soul rise. Godly qualities are his companions, eternal religion is his guide, and he is established on truth."

The Yaksha smiled and began to place more questions. One after another, Yudhishthira answered them all. For half an hour the questioning went on. At last, the Yaksha said, "O son of Pandu, here are my final questions: What is the most wonderful thing? What are the tidings of this world, and how can one find the path of eternal religion?"

Yudhishthira, who was kneeling on the lakeshore before the Yaksha, replied, "The most wonderful thing is that although every day countless creatures go to Death's abode, still a man thinks he will not die. The tidings of this world are that all beings here are being destroyed by time, and the eternal religious path is found in the hearts of great saints."

The Yaksha appeared pleased. He congratulated Yudhishthira. "You have answered my questions correctly. Which of your brothers would you like revived?"

Yudhishthira thought for a moment, then replied, "Let Nakula be brought to life."

"I am surprised," said the Yaksha. "I expected you to choose either Bhima or Arjuna."

Yudhishthira explained that he chose Nakula because he wanted to act equally toward both his mothers. If he did not select one of the twins, then Madri would be left with no surviving sons. "I will not abandon virtue for my own sake," he said.

"Excellent!" Expressing his satisfaction, the Yaksha said, "Since you are always so virtuous, never harming any creature, I shall restore all your brothers to life."

As the Yaksha spoke, Yudhishthira saw his four brothers begin to stir. Rubbing their eyes, they sat up and looked around, as if waking from a deep sleep. Yudhishthira was overjoyed. He thanked the Yaksha and then asked,

"O great being, who are you? Are you a god? Perhaps you are my father, the lord of religion." Yudhishthira knew that no ordinary Yaksha could have brought about his brothers' deaths—and then revived them again.

The Yaksha replied, "I am indeed your father, O best of the Bharatas. Know me to be Dharma. I came here to meet you and to test you. My dear son, every godly quality rests in you, and your great fame has been expanded today. Ask me for a boon."

Bowing low before the god, Yudhishthira asked that the brahmin's paraphernalia be restored to him. Dharma then told him that it was he who had assumed the form of a deer to take away the paraphernalia. "It is here. Take it, but ask from me some other boon."

"O mighty deity, we shall soon commence our final year of exile and must remain incognito. Please grant that wherever we stay, even if we are our actual selves, no one will recognize us."

"It shall be so. Through my favor, you shall remain unrecognized for the whole year. Dear Yudhishthira, you are a part of me. So, too, is your friend and well-wisher Vidura. Let me grant you one further boon before I depart."

"O lord, I am satisfied simply by seeing you, but as you wish to benedict me, I ask only that my mind always be inclined to charity, asceticism, and truth."

In a voice that resembled rolling thunder, Dharma said, "You are the very embodiment of virtue already. It shall surely be as you desire."

The god then vanished. Yudhishthira and his brothers got to their feet and collected the brahmin's paraphernalia that lay nearby. In complete wonder, they returned to their hermitage.

Twenty

A Lesson Not Learned

IT WAS THE end of the rainy season. According to Dhaumya's astrological calculations, the time for the Pandavas to enter a city had arrived. After some discussion, they decided to go to Virata. It was not far away, and the king there, himself named Virata, was a friend of the Pandavas. Feeling assured by Dharma's boon, the brothers decided it would be safe for them to remain together. But, because they did not want to take any unnecessary chances, they thought carefully about the guises they should assume. Knowing of Virata's affinity for dice, Yudhishthira said he would present himself to the king as an expert at the game. "I shall say that I was formerly Yudhishthira's personal servant. Entertaining Virata with my skills, I shall become his friend and minister."

Bhima decided that he would offer his services as a cook, at which he was highly skilled. Nakula, a past master at handling horses, said he would find engagement in the king's stables. For his part, Sahadeva said he would utilize his considerable talents as a cowherd and work with the king's cattle.

Arjuna remembered Urvashi's curse and Indra's words thereafter. "It is already destined that I should become a member of the third sex. Calling myself Brihannala, I shall offer to instruct the young girls of the royal house in the arts of singing and dancing, which I learned from the Gandharvas."

Arjuna's brothers looked at him in wonder. It was hard to imagine the mighty hero as a eunuch. The ways of destiny were certainly unfathomable.

Draupadi then said she would enter the city as a serving maid, seeking engagement in the king's palace. When everything had been decided, Yudhishthira told Dhaumya to go to Drupada's city, Kampilya, and wait there for the final year. He also sent all the servants with him. The brothers then set off for the city of Virata, in the kingdom of the Matsyas.

When they reached the outskirts of Virata, they decided to leave their weapons in a safe place outside the city. They bundled them into a cloth and then tied them high upon a tree, announcing to the local people that it was their deceased mother. Then, one by one, on successive days, they entered the city. When the king saw each of them approaching him, he was amazed. They appeared like mighty lords of men, regal in bearing and striding with the gait of lions. The king was especially astonished at the sight of Arjuna dressed in a sari, his powerful bowstring-scarred arms completely covered with bangles and bracelets. Virata listened to the brothers introduce themselves in the way they had agreed. Accepting their stories and feeling highly fortunate that such obviously qualified men should have come to him, he immediately engaged them in his service. By the gods' arrangement, he did not at any time suspect them to be the Pandavas.

Draupadi caused a considerable stir when she entered the city dressed as a serving maid. Her transcendent beauty bewildered the mind of every man who saw her. She went to the queen, asking to be accepted as a maidservant. The queen, fearing that her husband would become besotted with this beautiful new arrival, was at first reluctant, but Draupadi assured her, "I have five powerful Gandharva husbands. They will always protect me, and I will never even cast a glance upon another man."

The Pandavas and Draupadi began to live peacefully in Virata. Carefully applying themselves to the duties given by the king, they kept a low profile and rarely came together. It was a difficult year, especially for Draupadi, who had to remain in the servants' quarters and could not associate with her husbands. But the time passed quickly, and soon only a few weeks of exile remained. No one had any inkling of their real identities, and they began to think of coming out of exile and reclaiming their kingdom.

In the final weeks, however, Draupadi was again assaulted. The king had a powerful brother-in-law named Kichaka, who became enchanted by the Pandavas' wife. Despite her warnings about her five husbands, he tried to forcibly win her over. In desperation, she went in secret to Bhima. "Save me from this depraved beast," she pleaded. "I will give up my life before allowing him to possess me." Bhima was apprehensive, worried about giving away his identity, but Draupadi finally convinced him. She then agreed to meet Kichaka late one night, arranging for Bhima to be present. When Kichaka came for the meeting, the furious Bhima pounced upon him and pounded him to death.

The king was amazed that his mighty brother had been killed, but he accepted Draupadi's story that it was her Gandharva husbands who were responsible. He became highly fearful of the Panchala princess, but upon hearing that she would soon be leaving the city, he agreed to let her stay until that time.

News of Kichaka's death also reached Hastinapura. During the final year of the Pandavas' exile, the Kauravas had dispatched thousands of spies around the world to search them out. None of them had reported any sightings of the brothers, and Duryodhana was growing increasingly concerned. Although confident that he could win a war with the Pandavas, he would prefer to avoid it. It would certainly be very costly and result in a wholesale loss of life. And no one could absolutely guarantee the result.

Duryodhana's anxiety was stoked by the repeated cautions of his elders. Bhishma, Drona, Kripa, and Vidura were particularly worried about what would happen when the Pandavas emerged from exile. All of them warned that a war would be catastrophic for the Kurus. In their opinions, the Pandavas were invincible. Realizing that Duryodhana was loath to hand them back their kingdom, the Kuru elders tried by every means to change his mind. "You will rue the day that you ever joined battle with the Pandavas," they counseled.

As usual, Duryodhana cared little for his elders' advice. He had already been making arrangements for the war by securing whatever alliances he could. It would definitely be a brutal battle; far better if the Pandavas could somehow be discovered. Hearing the news about Kichaka, he thought carefully. It was not bad news—Virata's mighty brother had been a constant thorn in the Kurus' side; many times they had been approached by tributary kings seeking protection from the bellicose Kichaka. But he had been difficult to overpower. Duryodhana had been considering for some time how to deal with him. Now it had been done—but by whom? Who could possibly be powerful enough? There were only a few men who could have beaten Kichaka to death, and Bhima was one of them. It was especially suspicious because Kichaka had been killed secretly, in the dead of night. Due to their circumstances, Bhima would have had to do it that way.

After giving the matter some thought, Duryodhana stood up in the Kuru assembly and said, "Now that Kichaka is dead, the Matsyas have lost their protector. We can now exact revenge from them for Kichaka's long aggression. I propose that we go there immediately and recover the wealth he has seized. We can also gain their acquiescence to our rule."

Duryodhana's suggestion met with strong approval, and an army was assembled for the expedition. Before long, they were on their way to the Matsya kingdom.

*   *   *

In Virata, the king was considering who he could find to replace Kichaka. He thought about the new arrivals to his kingdom, each of whom appeared able to lead his entire army. It was not long before an opportunity to test this idea arrived. As he sat in his court one day, a cowherd ran in, exclaiming, "O king, come quickly! An army is carrying away your cattle out in the fields."

The king at once gave orders for his army to assemble. He also asked that the Pandavas, except for Arjuna, be given armor and weapons. "I do not see how men with bodies like mountains and arms like elephant trunks cannot fight."

Charging out at the head of his army, Virata led them toward the cow pastures. In his burnished gold armor, decorated with the motifs of a hundred suns and a hundred eyes, the king shone brilliantly as he stood aboard his great chariot. A force of sixty thousand warriors followed him, with the four Pandavas in their midst.

The Kurus had deployed their troops in two forces. They had sent one force, headed by the Trigarta king Susharma, to take the cattle, while the Kurus themselves attacked the city from elsewhere. Virata and his army came upon the Trigartas and shouted out their war cries, immediately launching volleys of arrows at them.

Hearing those cries, the Trigartas turned and met the Matsyas. The two armies closed and began to engage in fierce combat. A huge cloud of dust rose up as the warriors tore into each other. The clash of weapons and the screams of men and animals were deafening. Bodies began to fall in hundreds. Severed arms and legs dropped to the ground, which was muddied with blood. Many heads, adorned with helmets and gleaming earrings, rolled about.

While this battle raged, Duryodhana and the Kurus reached the other side of the city. Finding more cattle grazing there, they began to herd them away. The terrified cowherds raced into the city and went before Bhuminjaya, Virata's son, who was left to administrate in the king's absence. They found the prince surrounded by the palace ladies, and when he heard that the Kurus were stealing Virata's cows, he boldly declared, "Watch today as I exhibit my prowess in battle. The haughty Kurus will soon regret their folly. I shall put them to flight and recover the cows. Indeed, they will wonder if it is Arjuna himself come to fight with them."

The prince, who knew he had no chance of single-handedly overpowering the Kuru army, then said, "Alas, I have no charioteer. All the best men have gone out with my father to the other side of the city. I cannot fight unless a suitable man be found to govern my horses."

The prince carried on boasting about his strength and how he was Arjuna's equal. Draupadi heard this and, finding his references to Arjuna intolerable, she said, "O prince, there is one present who can drive your chariot. Brihannala was formerly Arjuna's charioteer. He is a matchless driver."

Bhuminjaya looked at her in disbelief. "Brihannala? How can I ask a eunuch to be my charioteer?" he asked with a laugh.

Draupadi reassured him that she was speaking the truth. "With Brihannala as your driver, you will doubtlessly vanquish the Kurus."

Everyone looked at the bemused prince. It was time for him to make good his boasts. He swallowed nervously. "All right, I shall try him." He had Brihannala fetched from the ladies' quarters. Equipping him with armor, he led him to his chariot, and they were soon charging out of the city to confront the Kurus. But when Bhuminjaya saw them in the distance, his heart sank. The vast Kuru army resembled an ocean. Their many tall standards were like a forest moving through the sky.

Ordering Brihannala to stop his chariot, the prince said, "This is madness! How can I face such an army? In their midst are Bhishma, Drona, Kripa, Karna and the heroic king Duryodhana. The gods themselves would find it hard to overpower them."

Throwing back his long braid of hair, Arjuna glowered at the terrified prince. "You are a warrior and it behooves you to fight. Having vaunted of your prowess, how can you turn back, like a coward? As for myself, I will certainly not run from this army."

But Bhuminjaya had lost all his courage. Shaking with fear, he declared that even if he became the butt of jokes and ridicule, he had no intention of fighting.

Arjuna stretched his fingers and looked around for the tree where his weapons lay. "Very well then, O prince, if you permit me, I shall fight in your place. You take the reins."

Bhuminjaya stared at the Kurus. How could anyone face them and live? Brihannala must surely have lost his mind. But he seemed extremely confident. Reassured by Brihannala's fearlessness, the prince said, "How do you propose to challenge this tremendous army?"

Arjuna pointed across to the great tree with the bundle still high in its branches. "Drive the chariot to that tree and you shall see."

Taking the reins, the prince drove the chariot to the tree, and Arjuna had him bring down the weapons. When the deerskin covering was cut open, the prince gasped. Seeing the array of mighty weapons, he was astonished. "Whose are these? They look like so many sighing serpents, ready to leap up of their own accord."

Arjuna realized it was time to tell Bhuminjaya the truth. "These are the Pandavas' weapons. Indeed, I am Arjuna, and my four brothers reside with me in Virata. The bow you see there, shining like a brilliant rainbow, is the famous Gandiva."

The prince's mouth fell open. He looked from Arjuna to the bow, and then back to Arjuna. "Is this true? How have you managed to remain concealed for so long? Can you prove that you are Arjuna? He has ten names. Tell them to me and I shall believe you."

"The gods have protected us," Arjuna replied. He then told the prince all his ten names. Bhuminjaya's eyes opened wide. Thinking of how Arjuna and four other mysterious men had entered his city a year ago, as well as a beautiful woman, the truth dawned on him. He fell prostrate before Arjuna. "I had no idea of your true identity. Please forgive me if I have offended you in any way."

Arjuna reassured the prince and then said, "Let us go now and face the Kurus. I have been waiting a long time for this opportunity."

Arjuna removed his bangles and pulled on a pair of gloves. He sat on the chariot and thought of his celestial weapons. They appeared within his mind and said, "We are here, O son of Pandu, ready to do your bidding."

"Dwell within my memory," Arjuna replied. He looked across the field toward the Kurus. They would soon realize his identity, but it did not matter. The period of exile was now over, and this certainly seemed like a good way to end it. Arjuna strung the Gandiva and gave it a mighty twang. The bow produced a sound like that of two mountains colliding, causing the earth to vibrate and the trees to shake.

Hearing that terrific sound, the Kurus paused in their theft of the cows and looked around in surprise. Bhishma and Drona both knew at once that it was Arjuna with the Gandiva. They felt joy, realizing that the Pandavas were well, but apprehension at the prospect of an encounter with Arjuna.

Drona said to Duryodhana, "O king, from the sound of his bow, from the way in which the earth shakes, and from numerous portents, I am sure that Arjuna is approaching."

Duryodhana looked across at the solitary chariot racing across the field in the distance. Arjuna? That would certainly be fortuitous. The Pandavas' exile was surely not yet over. If Arjuna showed himself, then another thirteen years in the wilderness awaited them.

Drona described the evil omens he was seeing, indicating great danger to the Kuru army. "The troops appear cheerless and bereft of energy. A pall of gloom hangs over them, and crows swoop down upon them with harsh sounds. Make ready for battle. When Arjuna confronts us, you will have to repent for your actions."

Duryodhana scowled. Maybe it would be Arjuna who would soon be repenting. The Kaurava went over to Bhishma and said, "O grandfather, it seems that Arjuna approaches. Have you calculated the time? Is the exile complete?"

"This is certainly Partha coming upon us," Bhishma replied. Like Duryodhana, he had carefully considered the report about Kichaka, concluding that the Pandavas must be in Virata. He had already calculated the period they had been away. It was now more than thirteen years.

As Bhishma spoke, Karna began to laugh. "Whether or not the exile is complete is of no consequence. Arjuna will meet his end today at my hands. By killing him, I will repay my debt to Duryodhana. All of you may stand down. Even if all five brothers come onto the field, you will see them crushed by me."

Kripa threw a contemptuous glance at the bragging Karna. "It seems you have quickly forgotten the incident with the Gandharvas. Where was this mighty prowess of yours then? Who was it who came to Duryodhana's rescue then?"

Bhishma and Drona shouted out their agreement with Kripa and looked over at Karna. Fuming, he raised his bow and gazed across at Arjuna. He said nothing in reply to the Kurus. They would soon be silenced when he felled Arjuna. Karna felt he had been caught by surprise by the Gandharvas. But he was ready now.

Bhishma spoke again. "The virtuous sons of Pandu have fulfilled the terms of their agreement. Their time is complete. We need not fear them, for they will never do anything sinful. We should now receive them with affection. O Duryodhana, give them back their kingdom and avoid unnecessary slaughter."

Duryodhana smoldered with anger. "I will never give them anything," he snarled. "Our reunion will take place on the battlefield."

Bhishma drew a deep and sorrowful breath. He recalled the time long ago when he had made his vow of celibacy, renouncing the throne. His father had then blessed him that he would only die when he willed it himself. In return, Bhishma had sworn that, even though he would never occupy Hastinapura's throne, he would nevertheless always protect it. He had to stand by Dhritarashtra's side—and that meant supporting Duryodhana. Duty was surely a difficult path.

Drona began issuing orders for battle. As he spoke, a couple of arrows fell from the sky, landing at his feet. Arrows also fell at Bhishma's and Kripa's feet. "Seeing his elders after a long time, Arjuna is offering his respects," said Drona. "Stand firm. His next arrows will not be carrying respects."

Arjuna gave orders to Bhuminjaya. "Approach this army with caution. Karna should be carefully watched, for he always desires my death. So, too, does Duryodhana. But the others, headed by Bhishma, Drona, and Kripa, never wish me any harm."

The Matsya prince began to drive toward the Kurus. Arjuna held the Gandiva at the ready. He had no wish to hurt any of his elders, nor even Duryodhana and his brothers, if it could be avoided. Now that the exile was over, there should first be some attempt at a peaceful settlement. Yudhishthira definitely wanted that. Perhaps, though, this encounter would help Duryodhana see sense. When he realized the power of Arjuna's weapons—weapons that had overcome hordes of celestial demons—he might be more inclined to peace.

"Take me straight toward Duryodhana." Arjuna fixed his gaze on the Kaurava prince. He began to release arrows in thousands. They sped toward Duryodhana like swarms of locusts. The Kurus raced to his assistance. Drona and Kripa countered Arjuna's attack by striking down his arrows with their own. Smiling, Arjuna stepped up his assault. His mantra-charged shafts filled the sky. Holding off his two teachers, who were fighting only half-heartedly, he pressed on toward Duryodhana.

Struck all over by Arjuna's steel shafts, which seemed to come from every direction, Duryodhana reeled. He was hardly able to raise his own bow to defend himself. Arrows embedded themselves in his chariot, cut down his standard, pierced his horses, and glanced off his armor. "Get away from here fast!" he yelled to his sorely oppressed charioteer. The charioteer urged on his steeds and the chariot raced away.

"Let us leave this coward for now," said Arjuna. "Make your way to Karna, who stands roaring over there in his chariot marked with the emblem of an elephant rope."

Bhuminjaya veered his golden chariot around to face Karna. As he closed on him, Karna's brother came between them. He attacked Arjuna with a fierce cluster of razor-faced arrows. The Pandava expertly warded off those shafts. Smiling tautly, he fired four arrows in swift succession, which slew his opponent's horses. He then shot a single crescent-headed arrow that beheaded Karna's brother right before his eyes.

Screaming in fury, Karna attacked Arjuna with lightning-fast shafts. Arjuna responded in kind, and the two warriors traded thousands of arrows. They appeared like the sun and moon meeting for a contest in the heavens. Both invoked celestial weapons that lit up the sky. Skillfully countering each other's attacks, they both fervently sought the advantage. Their chariots wheeled and zigzagged from side to side. The other warriors on the field watched in amazement as the two mighty heroes battled each other. Their hands were hardly visible as they fired their arrows with blinding speed.

Gradually, Arjuna gained the edge over his foe. His arrows penetrated Karna's defenses and began piercing through his armor. Karna's arms, thighs, and breast were badly lacerated. Stunned by the incessant ferocity of Arjuna's attack, he fell back, shouting in pain. Ordering his charioteer to retreat, he fled from the fight.

Arjuna then turned his attention to Duryodhana's army. He rushed into their midst with the Gandiva constantly twanging, firing off countless deadly shafts. Warriors fell on all sides. Arjuna seemed hardly approachable. From whichever angle he was attacked, he was ready, creating carnage among the Kuru forces.

Bhishma and the other Kuru elders watched in admiration. They had no desire for a serious fight with their beloved Arjuna. Like Yudhishthira, they also hoped for a peaceful settlement to the dispute between the Kauravas and Pandavas.

Seeing his troops being overpowered by the rampant Arjuna and realizing that his elders were not fighting to their full power, Duryodhana decided to desist from fighting. The time to defeat the Pandavas had not yet arrived. First, he needed to assemble all his allies into an unconquerable army. He needed to secure the commitment of Bhishma, Drona, and Kripa for the fight. And when the time came, he would have the support of his celestial allies, the Danavas and Daityas. It would be a different story then.

The prince issued the order to withdraw. The Kurus turned and began pulling away from Virata. They headed straight back to Hastinapura, with Duryodhana thinking of how he could best prepare himself for war, while his elders considered how it could now be avoided.

*　　*　　*

On the other side of the city, King Virata had watched with amazement as his four newest fighters had shown their power. Who were these men? Just one of them—his cook—had almost single-handedly routed the enemy army. Whirling around the battlefield with his mace, he had sent horsemen, chariots, and even elephants crashing to the ground. The other three had also exhibited unparalleled prowess. Between the four of them, they had forced the terrified Trigartas to flee in all directions. As the Matsyas made their way back to the city, Virata looked in awe at the three men. With them on his side, he need not fear even the gods and demons combined!

When the king reached his city, he was informed that his son had gone out to confront the Kurus, with Brihannala as his charioteer. Shocked, he turned to Yudhishthira and said, "My son is in dire danger. What chance does he stand against the Kurus?"

Yudhishthira smiled. "Have no fear; with Brihannala on his chariot, he could face even the celestials."

Virata looked incredulously at his minister. Was he serious? A single eunuch against the Kuru army? The king began ordering his generals to have his army march out again, but suddenly a breathless messenger ran up to him and reported, "The Kurus have been routed and are withdrawing! Your son is on his way back."

The king threw up his arms in delight. "Amazing! I never knew my son had such power. Decorate the city with festoons and garlands. This is a cause for celebration!"

As the prince entered the city, his father ran up to him and tightly embraced him. "Well done, my son! Well done! Tell me how you overcame the Kurus."

The prince shook his head. "No, Father. It was not I who defeated them." He pointed to Arjuna. "This man here is no eunuch. Know him to be Arjuna, the famous son of Pandu. It was he who scattered the Kuru forces."

The king stared in disbelief at Brihannala. He turned toward Yudhishthira, who was now surrounded by his other three brothers. How did he know?

"Your son speaks the truth," said Arjuna. "And the man who has been your minister this past year is no mere courtier. Worthy of sharing a seat with even Indra, always engaged in sacrifice and the practice of virtue, know him to be the far-sighted, truthful, and ever forgiving Yudhishthira."

Virata looked carefully at Yudhishthira. Was it true? How had he not recognized him? He looked back at Arjuna. "Then these other three must be. . . ."

"Yes, O king, you are right. That mighty-armed mountain of a man who has been preparing your meals is none other than Bhima. By his side are the twins, Nakula and Sahadeva. And in your inner chambers lives Draupadi, spending her days in menial service to your queen. We are all in your debt.

For the last year we have lived safely in your city, like creatures in the womb."

Virata's eyes flooded with tears. Of course! Why had he not realized earlier? Who else could have shown such power on the battlefield?

Exclaiming, "What good fortune!" the king folded his hands and bowed to Yudhishthira. "Take my entire kingdom, O sinless man, with all its lands, treasury, and army."

"I am already in your debt, O king," Yudhishthira replied. "By God's grace, I am sure my own kingdom will soon be restored to me."

"Then permit Arjuna to accept my daughter's hand in marriage," Virata said. "What else can I offer?"

"It would be better if she became my daughter-in-law," answered Arjuna. "Since I have been her dancing instructor, I have dealt with her like a father with his daughter. I could not change that relationship, but she will make an excellent bride for my son Abhimanyu."

Virata happily agreed. A marriage alliance with the Pandavas was more than he might ever have hoped for. After arranging for the brothers to be accommodated in his palace, the king sent out messengers to announce that they were now out of exile and living in his kingdom. He invited their friends and allies to come to his city, and before long they began to arrive. Krishna and Balarama came from Dwaraka, bringing Abhimanyu and many other members of their family. Drupada arrived, accompanied by his sons, as well as a huge army, and in the next few weeks, many other kings also came to Virata.

The wedding between Abhimanyu and Virata's daughter, Uttara, duly took place. Arjuna's son resembled a god and, with the beautiful Uttara by his side, he appeared like Vishnu accompanied by the goddess of fortune. The city was filled with celebration and great amounts of charity were distributed to brahmins and other citizens.

Twenty-one

PREPARING FOR WAR

SOON AFTER ABHIMANYU'S wedding, the Pandavas discussed their next move with Krishna. No word had been received from Hastinapura. It seemed that the Kauravas were not about to honor the agreement made at the gambling match. According to this agreement, the Pandavas should now have their kingdom returned to them. Krishna suggested that an assembly be called for a general discussion among all the kings present. Agreeing to this, Virata arranged for the monarchs to be brought into his hall the next day, and the conference began.

Krishna spoke first. Rising up from his gem-studded seat, he seemed like the moon rising from the ocean. His voice resounded throughout the great chamber like the melodic beat of a deep-toned drum. "It is well known that Yudhishthira was unfairly deprived of his wealth and kingdom by Shakuni. Nevertheless, he has fulfilled the terms of the agreement made with the Kauravas. Thirteen years have passed with the Pandavas dwelling in exile. The designated period of time is now complete, and they seek to again possess their rightful kingdom."

All five Pandavas fixed their eyes upon Krishna as he spoke. They were ready to accept whatever he decided. Pleasing him meant more to them than even possessing the entire earth. However, it was clear that he wanted them to recover their kingdom. It seemed that the vows they had made at the time of the gambling match would soon have to be fulfilled.

Krishna looked around the assembly as he continued. "Yudhishthira will never renounce virtue, and his brothers are always obedient to him. Despite everything that has happened, he still wishes Duryodhana well. Perhaps this matter can be settled peacefully. Let us send a messenger to Hastinapura to establish the Kauravas' intentions. But if they refuse to return the kingdom, I see war as the only recourse, and the Kauravas will be slain, with all their followers. If, O kings, war should ensue and you feel the

Pandavas' cause is just, then I urge you to unite with them and march out for battle. What do you all say?"

A murmur of approval went through the hall. The kings looked at each other and nodded in agreement with Krishna's words. As they again fell silent, Balarama got to his feet and raised a hand to speak. Everyone turned towards him. Krishna's brother appeared extraordinarily beautiful, with his pure white complexion, jeweled helmet on his head, and a garland of white lotuses around his neck. Resting a hand on his golden plough weapon, he said, "Krishna has spoken well. The Kuru kingdom should be shared between the Pandavas and the Kauravas. Send a man to Hastinapura to address the Kauravas, but ensure that due deference is shown to them. After all, it was Yudhishthira's fault that he gambled and lost the kingdom. Although unskilled, he accepted Shakuni's challenge. Therefore, we should approach the Kauravas in a conciliatory mood. War should be avoided by any means."

Yudhishthira again felt remorse. Balarama was right. The whole awkward situation had come about only due to his foolishness. He looked down and said nothing, but Bhima and Arjuna looked querulously at Balarama. They knew Krishna's brother had a soft spot for Duryodhana, who was his student at mace fighting, but when he had last seen the Pandavas in the forest, he had expressed anger at the Kauravas. His present mood was difficult to understand.

As Balarama stopped speaking, a powerful Yadu warrior named Satyaki stood up. He was a great friend and student of Arjuna, and he found Balarama's words hard to tolerate. His angry voice echoed throughout the hall. "How can anyone listen to such suggestions without objecting? How can you say that Yudhishthira was at fault? How were the Kauravas not guilty of trickery and deceit? They induced Yudhishthira to play against a man who knows every facet of dice play and gambling. Yudhishthira had no desire for the game, nor did he wish to stake his kingdom. He was drawn into it by the wicked-minded Kauravas, who had but one intention—to divest him of everything by whatever means possible."

Satyaki stood with his hand on the hilt of his sword. He strode into the center of the hall, where he looked around at the assembled kings. "Whatever may have happened in the past, there can be no doubt that Yudhishthira should now be given back his kingdom. It is his by birthright and also by virtue of his undeniable qualifications. He is fit to rule the entire earth. If the Kauravas will not agree, then I, for one, am ready for a fight. By means of cold steel, I shall change their minds. O heroes, take up your arms and join me. After killing all the usurpers, let us install Yudhishthira as emperor."

Red-faced with fury, Satyaki glared at Balarama once more and marched back to his seat. Balarama simply smiled. He knew how much the hot-blooded Satyaki loved the Pandavas. Drupada then rose from his seat to speak. The old king was respected by all for his wisdom and maturity, and everyone in the hall listened attentively. Looking directly at Krishna, he said, "In my view, we need to prepare for battle. I will send my priest to Hastinapura, but I do not expect a peaceful settlement. War seems inevitable. We must therefore send out messages to all our friends and allies, for we shall soon need their help. Duryodhana will certainly be doing the same, even as we speak. There are many noble kings who will assist who-ever first comes to them with a plea."

Drupada named over fifty monarchs who he felt they should immedi-ately approach. When he had finished, Krishna applauded him, recom-mending that his suggestion be taken seriously. Everyone in the assembly agreed. Krishna then said, "I shall now depart for Dwaraka. O kings, do all that you can to bring about peace. If, however, the attempt fails, then sum-mon me again. I shall do all in my power to resolve the situation."

The assembly withdrew, and Virata, after worshipping both Krishna and Balarama with all respect, sent them on their way back to Dwaraka. Then he began making preparations for war. Swift messengers were dis-patched to all parts of the world. Soon, large armies began arriving in Virata. Troops poured in from all directions and set up camp around the city. Crowded with men and animals, the earth seemed covered with dark clouds. Their clamor resembled the roar of the sea. Virata made arrange-ments to ensure that all of them had everything they needed.

When at last a huge force had assembled, Drupada requested his priest to leave for Hastinapura. He asked him to speak reasonably and gently to the Kurus, trying to convince them of the justness of Yudhishthira's claim. "Although I am sure you will not be able to change Duryodhana's mind, you may still win the hearts of the other Kuru elders. At least, you may be able to sow the seeds of dissension among them. That will give us more time to make ready for the inevitable war. And who knows, perhaps Dhritarashtra may yet accept our plea and do the proper thing."

The priest then left for Hastinapura, leaving Virata to continue with preparations for battle.

*　　*　　*

After returning from Virata, Duryodhana had thought only of amassing his forces. Smarting from yet another humiliation at the Pandavas' hands, he simmered with anger as he went about preparing for war. The thought of returning his cousins' kingdom never crossed his mind. He dispatched emissaries to all his allies. In his mind, there was only one way to end this dispute, and all advice to the contrary fell on deaf ears.

When news of Krishna's return to Dwaraka reached Duryodhana, he decided to go personally to ask for his assistance. Krishna and his Yadu forces were unconquerable. Duryodhana knew that Krishna would hardly be able to refuse his request if he got there first. The Yadu chief had always made it clear that he was equally disposed to both the Kauravas and the Pandavas. Till now Duryodhana felt he had not had any cause to seek Krishna's assistance. It had always been the Pandavas who had turned to him for help—which he had never refused. Now it was time to redress the balance.

Mounting a swift horse, Duryodhana raced toward Dwaraka. At the same time, Arjuna left Virata with the same idea in mind. Having accepted the inevitability of war, Yudhishthira decided that Krishna's dear friend, Arjuna, should ask for his personal assistance. Arjuna reached Krishna's palace in Dwaraka just after Duryodhana. He saw him being shown into Krishna's chamber. Walking in right after Duryodhana, Arjuna saw that Krishna was asleep on his bed. Duryodhana had taken a seat by his head. He smiled smugly at Arjuna. The Pandava had arrived too late. Arjuna simply stood at Krishna's feet, gazing at him with tears of affection in his eyes.

After some time Krishna awoke. As he opened his eyes, he saw Arjuna, who bowed to him in love. Sitting up, he saw Duryodhana by his side. Krishna welcomed both of his visitors and ordered a servant to bring them some refreshment. After politely inquiring after their welfare, he asked what had brought them there.

Arjuna raised his hand toward Duryodhana, allowing him to speak first. The prince said, "O Keshava, it is well known that you are equally disposed toward the Kauravas and Pandavas. I have thus come here to ask your assistance in the war which will soon be fought between us."

Krishna had seated his two visitors together on a large white couch. Duryodhana turned to Arjuna as he went on, "Arjuna will confirm that I arrived here before him. I therefore have first claim for your help. This is the practice of good men, and you, O Krishna, are the best of men."

Krishna looked thoughtful. He nodded slowly and replied, "I accept that you arrived first, O king, but I first saw Arjuna. I will therefore help you both. Scripture ordains that the youngest should be helped first, which means I must give Arjuna first choice. I offer either my army, consisting of a million highly powerful warriors known as the Narayanas, or myself alone. However, I shall not fight. My weapons will be laid aside and not lifted for the entire duration of the battle."

Krishna turned his lotus-petal eyes toward Arjuna. "What do you choose then, O son of Kunti?"

Without the slightest hesitation, Arjuna replied, "I select you, O Krishna. With you by my side, what more could I want?"

Duryodhana, who had become apprehensive as he listened to Krishna's words, smiled broadly. Arjuna had surely let his sentiment overcome his reason. "Fair enough, then, I shall take the army," he said, getting to his feet. "I will not take any more of your time, Krishna. Please permit me to leave."

Duryodhana went out of Krishna's room, almost laughing. A million-man army! And the Narayanas were famous as ferocious and implacable warriors. What would the Pandavas do now? The prince then thought of Balarama, his friend and well-wisher. Surely, he would also help. Duryodhana quickly made his way to Balarama's palace and was shown into his room.

After hearing Duryodhana's request, Balarama said, "O hero, for your sake I spoke out in Virata's assembly. However, Krishna did not accept my words. You should know that I cannot exist for a moment separated from him. My decision, therefore, is to help neither side. I will not take part in this war. Go forth and fight to the best of your ability, O king. May good fortune be yours."

Balarama stood up and embraced Duryodhana. Knowing that Krishna was assisting the Pandavas, he considered the Kauravas as already defeated. Disappointed, Duryodhana left his palace and went to see Kritavarman, the commander of the Narayana army. The Yadu general, although unhappy to be opposing Krishna, felt duty-bound, and he soon gathered his army and left Dwaraka, accompanied by Duryodhana.

Arjuna and Krishna traveled together to Virata. When they arrived at the great city, they saw men streaming in from all directions. Satyaki had followed them from Dwaraka, bringing a large force of men with him. Drupada arrived with his two sons and another great platoon of warriors. Virata himself had provided a division, and numerous other kings came with their armies. Eventually, seven enormous divisions of warriors, on foot, horseback, chariots, and elephants, were assembled—over two million in total.

In Hastinapura, an even larger force had amassed, totaling eleven great divisions. They crowded the city and its surrounding regions so that there was hardly any free space anywhere. Bearing their polished swords and maces, as well as axes, lances, spears, mallets, and bows of every type, the armies appeared like dark clouds adorned with countless lightning flashes. The earth trembled under their weight. Their shouts, the clash of their weapons, and the cries of their animals combined to create a tremendous roar that filled the whole city.

* * *

Soon after the troops had assembled on both sides, Drupada's priest arrived at Hastinapura. He made his way through the crowded streets and was received by Dhritarashtra, Bhishma, and Vidura. They brought him to the royal court, where an assembly had been called. After worshipping him with various respectful offerings, they asked him to address the assembly.

Standing before Dhritarashtra's throne, the priest said, "I come in peace and desiring peace. As you all know, both Dhritarashtra's sons and those of Pandu are equally entitled to the Kuru kingdom. Yet, somehow the Kauravas have wrested the Pandavas' share away from them. They have persecuted their cousins in many ways, even trying to take their lives, but, by God's grace, the Pandavas have survived. Despite everything Yudhishthira bears the Kauravas no ill will. He only wishes to have his kingdom returned. Let war be avoided—this is his desire."

The priest paused. He slowly surveyed the hall. By the king's side sat Bhishma, Drona, Kripa, Vidura, and other senior Kuru ministers. Duryodhana and all his brothers sat opposite them, with Karna and Shakuni. Many other kings filled up the surrounding seats in the great chamber. Everyone remained silent and the priest continued. Realizing that appeals to reason were likely to fail, he began describing the Pandavas' military might. "They have amassed seven great divisions of men. Besides this, they have the inconceivably powerful Krishna on their side. Many kings are with them, and each of the brothers is himself a mighty *maharatha*, capable of contending single-handedly with thousands of other warriors. Arjuna alone exceeds the strength of your entire army. Therefore, give them back their kingdom. Do not ruin yourselves and destroy the world for nothing."

Duryodhana drummed his fingers on his knee and said nothing. He knew his own army was almost twice the size of the Pandavas' forces. He recalled the Danavas' words. This war would no doubt see their fulfillment. What was there to fear?

Bhishma then spoke, thanking the priest for coming to Hastinapura and praising him with kind words. He concurred with him, agreeing that even Arjuna alone could defeat the Kuru army. They had already seen enough evidence of that.

Galled as ever by Bhishma's speech, Karna jumped up and interrupted him, glaring at the messenger. "O brahmin, do not waste your breath trying to scare us. The Kauravas have done nothing wrong. Yudhishthira was fairly defeated and went to the forest in accordance with our agreement. Indeed, I, for one, do not believe his prescribed term of exile has even ended. Why, then, is he demanding the kingdom? Duryodhana will not yield to any threats. He will, however, always act in accordance with virtue. Let the Pandavas complete their term of exile and then come humbly before Duryodhana. He will surely afford them refuge."

Duryodhana would not accept any calculations that concluded that the Pandavas had been away for their full term. Brahmins faithful to him had told him otherwise, and that was good enough for him. In any event, whether or not the time was up did not matter. It was all going to end in war, without a doubt.

Bhishma rebuked Karna, reminding him again of occasions when he had seen Arjuna's superiority in battle. The hall became agitated, some kings agreeing with Bhishma and others supporting Duryodhana. A clamor of voices rose up, and Dhritarashtra raised his hand for silence. He addressed the assembly. "Bhishma has spoken well. He has only our interests in mind. I need time now to deliberate. Let us adjourn this assembly. O brahmin, return to the Pandavas and tell them that I shall soon send Sanjaya with my reply."

The brahmin then left the assembly and it broke up, leaving the king sitting alone. He thought for some time before calling for Sanjaya. Bhishma's assessment of the situation was accurate. The Pandavas, and especially Arjuna, were powerful beyond measure. Wisdom therefore dictated that their demands be met, but Duryodhana would never agree. The prince had been almost peaceful these last thirteen years, with his cousins out of the way and the world under his control. He would certainly not relinquish his position without a fight.

The old king loosened his silk tunic. As usual, he felt torn. He had lost many a night's sleep worrying about a fight with the Pandavas. Maybe there was some way he could persuade the ever-virtuous Yudhishthira to avoid war, while at the same time keeping Duryodhana happy. Surely Pandu's pious son would not be attached to worldly wealth and opulence. Without doubt, he would go a long way to avoid fighting.

Making up his mind, Dhritarashtra summoned Sanjaya and said, "O wise man, I wish for you to go to the Pandavas. They are affectionate toward you and will receive you well. Those heroes are devoted to virtue, and I cannot think of a single fault in any of them. It is only my weak-brained son and his wicked followers who wish them ill. Duryodhana thinks that his greater-sized army will assure him of success, but he has not thought deeply enough. In my view, the five brothers, with Krishna as their support, are unconquerable."

Dhritarashtra had heard the rishis describe Krishna's power many times. They said he was the origin of everything, including even the immortal lord of the gods, Vishnu. It hardly mattered that he was not fighting. If he really was God, then his will alone would be sufficient to destroy any enemy.

Sanjaya murmured in agreement as the king spoke, listing the numerous demons who had already been slain by Krishna. The old charioteer was himself a believer in Krishna, having heard much about him from the sage Vyasadeva.

The king went on, "O Sanjaya, I also greatly fear Yudhishthira. He has practiced long asceticism and is dedicated to virtue. His spiritual power is immense. If we incur his wrath, we will be burned to ashes like reeds falling into a fire."

The king instructed Sanjaya to leave at once. "Say whatever you can to pacify and please the Pandavas. Give them every assurance that I am their well-wisher. Here is my suggestion for Yudhishthira."

Sanjaya listened carefully as the king spoke, memorizing every detail. Then he immediately left for Virata.

Twenty-two

KRISHNA'S PEACE MISSION

A S SOON AS the Pandavas heard of Sanjaya's arrival, they called him in and greeted him warmly. Asking after everyone's welfare, Yudhishthira said, "Although we desire peace, I do not think we will ever win Duryodhana's friendship. Alas, Sanjaya, war now seems unavoidable."

"It is as you say," the charioteer replied, standing before Yudhishthira with his hands folded in respect. "The prince is guided only by fools and seems incorrigible. The way he has treated you is unforgivable. His father sincerely regrets it. Desirous of forging a lasting peace with you, he has sent me here with his message."

Yudhishthira asked that Sanjaya relay his message in the assembly, where all the kings could hear it. He escorted the charioteer into the hall, and everyone was soon assembled. Standing in their midst, Sanjaya said, "Here are Dhritarashtra's own words. Pandu's sons are all virtuous men who could never perform a vicious act. Yudhishthira himself is mild, generous, and always forgiving. How, then, could he ever do anything which would destroy us all? Surely, those men are blessed who can sacrifice their own interests for the welfare of others."

Dhritarashtra's message was immediately clear. Sanjaya made it even clearer. "O king, O sons of Pandu, do not begin a war that will end in the deaths of all your relatives. This is Dhritarashtra's request. Even if you thus regain your kingdom, what pleasure will it give you? "

Sanjaya looked around the hall, supplicating all the kings not to engage in battle. He spoke for some time, but without making any suggestion that the Pandavas would have their kingdom returned.

When Sanjaya finished, Yudhishthira glanced over at the smiling Krishna and calmly replied, "What have I ever said that indicated that I desire war, O Sanjaya? Only a cursed man would seek through war that which can be had by peaceful means. But, in fact, peace can only be had when we control our senses. One who acts only for the pleasure of his senses soon encounters misery. Dhritarashtra and his sons plainly do not see this truth. Thus, they act in ways that can never bring about peace and happiness."

The Pandava monarch rose from his seat, looking, in his robes and ornaments, like a jewel-studded banner raised in honor of Indra. "It seems that the king will not check his avaricious and lustful son. He has had ample opportunity and enough advice from the wise Vidura, but still he does nothing. He and his son desire to rule the earth undisputed, enjoying another's property, which they have gained through deceit. Obviously, they have not carefully considered the consequences of such a sinful desire."

Yudhishthira looked around at the many kings in the hall. They sat in silence, listening as the Pandava spoke. "All of these kings here know well the actual situation. They are ready for battle. Make no mistake, Sanjaya; if Indraprastha is not given back to us, war will surely ensue. But it need not happen. The Kauravas can keep Hastinapura and be happy with that prosperous realm. We only ask that they give us what is rightfully ours."

Yudhishthira looked again at Krishna and said, "Here is Krishna. He knows every facet of morality and religion. Let him say what is right. I will do whatever he decides. Indeed, he is everyone's greatest well-wisher, and we should follow his advice without any hesitation."

Krishna rose from his seat. He seemed to illuminate the hall with his bodily luster. Dressed in brilliant yellow silks and decorated with many jeweled ornaments, he appeared like a blackish cloud framed by sunlight and adorned with lightning flashes. Raising a graceful hand, he said," No fault can be found in Yudhishthira. He desires to do his God-given duty as a king. Indraprastha should be given back. If it is not, Yudhishthira will perform his duty by fighting."

Krishna spoke firmly. In his view, the Kauravas were acting sinfully. He reminded Sanjaya of the awful incidents that had occurred thirteen years ago in the Kuru assembly. By tolerating all those acts of aggression, Yudhishthira had already demonstrated his great commitment to peace. Now, it was Dhritarashtra's turn. "Everything depends upon the Kuru monarch. Let him do what is right and war will be averted. Otherwise, a great destruction is imminent. I shall personally go to Hastinapura to negotiate with him. Either he peacefully restores to the Pandavas their property, or he loses everything on the battlefield."

The assembly voiced its approval of Krishna's speech. Arjuna, knowing that the Kauravas would not honor their agreement, had already requested him to go to Hastinapura and try to persuade them. Out of his love for Arjuna and his brothers, Krishna had readily agreed.

Yudhishthira had nothing further to add. He told Sanjaya to deliver his and Krishna's words to Dhritarashtra. After asking each of his brothers to add their own personal messages, he bade Sanjaya farewell and sent him back to Hastinapura.

Sanjaya arrived home to find Dhritarashtra waiting anxiously. The blind king had sought Vidura's counsel and been told in no uncertain terms that he faced ruin. Vidura had tried to make his brother see sense, warning him that he had no chance of denying the Pandavas their rights. Now that Krishna had taken their side, Dhritarashtra should give up any hope that they might be overpowered in battle.

Dhritarashtra was still not sure. His mind went one way and then the other. Would Krishna really make such a big difference? He had not done anything to prevent the Pandavas from losing everything and being exiled. Now, he had promised that he would not even fight. He had given his personal army to Duryodhana. Surely, he was an enigma. But no matter what Krishna decided to do, it still appeared that the Kauravas' position was stronger. Their army far outnumbered the Pandavas', and on their side they had an array of invincible heroes, like Bhishma, Drona, Kripa, and so many others. For that reason alone, Yudhishthira might finally decide that war was not a wise choice.

Dhritarashtra's hopes that war might be avoided were soon dashed when Sanjaya delivered the messages of Yudhishthira, his brothers, and Krishna. Standing before the Kuru assembly, he said, "The Pandavas desire their ancestral lands. If these are not returned, battle will be joined without delay."

Sanjaya repeated Arjuna's message word for word, which was full of heroic assertion and deadly threats. Arjuna restated the vows he and his brothers had made during the gambling match. Summoning the full fury with which Arjuna had spoken, Sanjaya said, "The Kauravas will pay for their many sins. They will be consumed like a field of dry grass in a fire. With Krishna as my charioteer, none will be able to stand before me. Anyone desiring to overcome Krishna wishes to extinguish a blazing fire with his bare hands, or to swim the ocean with a stone slab secured to his neck."

Sanjaya delivered similar messages from the other Pandavas. There was no question of peace without their kingdom being returned. Hearing this, Duryodhana simply sneered and said nothing. He looked toward Karna and smiled. Seeing his indifference, Bhishma stood up and said, "There is no doubt it will be as Arjuna has said. He and Krishna are the two immortal sages Nara and Narayana—indeed, they are much more. No one can know them, and no one can overpower them at any time. Duryodhana's hope that Karna will overcome Arjuna is vain and useless. Karna does not possess even a fraction of Arjuna's power."

Karna leapt to his feet. "Again you criticize me! Why? You will soon see my power, when I slay the Pandavas."

Bhishma looked at Karna with a mixture of sadness and annoyance. "Do not waste your breath, foolish man. You give Duryodhana false hopes. It is largely your fault that we face such a calamity now. We have already seen your power. Should I remind you of the incidents at Dwaitavana and Virata? Surely, you have not forgotten already?"

Karna snorted. Things would be different next time. He would make no mistake. Indra's Shakti weapon would take care of Arjuna. It was a shame he had not thought to bring it when he went to Virata.

Understanding Karna's mind, Bhishma said, "You will see your cherished Shakti missile smashed and rendered useless when you direct it at Arjuna and Krishna. Cursed by your own guru, as well as by the brahmins, your position is hopeless."

Hearing Bhishma remind him of those two unfortunate incidents in his life, Karna winced. He recalled how he had offended a brahmin by accidentally slaying his cow when hunting one day. In grief and anger, the brahmin had said, "When you face your deadliest enemy in battle, the earth will swallow your chariot wheel." Still reeling from that curse, Karna had not long after upset his martial teacher, the sage Parashurama. Karna had lied to him, saying that he was a brahmin in order to receive the sage's instructions. Discovering the deceit, Parashurama had cursed Karna, saying, "When you most need it, you will forget how to invoke the most powerful Brahma weapon."

Karna writhed as Bhishma rebuked him. He felt he could take no more. When the Kuru grandfather stopped speaking, he rose up and said, "Since, you deride me and consider me without prowess, O Bhishma, I will not fight with you as my commander. Since you will lead the Kuru army, I will only come out for the fight when you are laid low. Then the world will see my actual power."

Karna then stormed out of the hall. Bhishma laughed. "The suta's son is rash and given to passion. He says whatever comes to his mind without ever weighing its worth or truth. At the very moment when he cheated the holy sage Parashurama, he lost all virtue and merit."

The discord between two of his most powerful warriors made Dhritarashtra even more anxious. He spoke out in apprehension. "Surely our party now faces a dire danger. I do not see how we will ever overcome those divinely born sons of Kunti. Hearing about Arjuna and Krishna's actual identities completely convinces me of this fact. O Duryodhana, be peaceful. Give up all thought of war. Live happily with your cousins. Even half of this wide and prosperous kingdom is more than enough for anybody."

Duryodhana was losing patience. He stood up from his great gilded throne and gazed around the hall. Karna's sudden exit had disturbed him, and he spoke out angrily. "All I ever hear is how the Pandavas are so powerful. Are they not mortals like us? They can be defeated, without doubt. Just see how we have already obliged them to go like hermits into the forest. What use then was Arjuna's much-vaunted prowess? Where was Krishna's help then? We have nothing to fear. You have yet to see my prowess. Why, with my mystic powers I can hold back blazing fire, break apart mountains, and solidify great lakes so that armies can march over them."

Becoming enlivened, Duryodhana went on praising himself for some time. He asserted that, if necessary, he alone would crush the Pandavas. When he was finished, his brothers applauded him, but Bhishma, Vidura, and Drona sadly shook their heads. They looked toward the blind king. His admonitions of Duryodhana were empty words if he did not back them up with stern action. But there was no sign of that. It was plain that Dhritarashtra had more or less abdicated his power to the prince.

Once again, Dhritarashtra asked for time to think, dismissing the assembly. Days passed, during which time the king was visited by Vidura and Sanjaya, who both tried hard to sway his mind. Sanjaya even called for Vyasadeva to speak with him, and the sage clearly described how events were being arranged by Krishna. "He desires to lift the earth's burden, O king," the *rishi* solemnly said. "Many demonic elements will be destroyed, and your sons will be among them."

But Dhritarashtra found this hard to accept. His attachment for his sons kept alive in him the hope that they still might succeed. Anyway, thought the king, everything depends upon destiny. If it is God's will that the Kurus be destroyed, then what could anyone do?

* * *

In Virata, the Pandavas consulted with Krishna. After hearing Sanjaya's message, there seemed little doubt that Dhritarashtra would not give them back their kingdom. It had been over a month since Sanjaya had gone back with their reply, but they had heard nothing more. All that remained now was for Krishna to go to Hastinapura, as he had promised. Sitting with him in Virata's palace, Yudhishthira said, "O Krishna, we have no better friend than you. Your willingness to carry our petition to the Kauravas proves it beyond doubt. But I fear they will not receive you well. O Lord, they will laugh away your respectful submissions. Duryodhana, especially, will never respond to sweet speech. He will see it as a sign of our weakness. All he understands is the language of force."

Krishna was seated amid the Pandavas on a golden throne. Curling black hair fell around his face and a brilliant diamond-encrusted crown shone from his head. His shark-shaped earrings flashed as he turned toward Yudhishthira and said, "You are right, O Pandava, but still I must go. Every chance must be given to the Kauravas before war begins."

The prospect of a war with his relatives depressed Yudhishthira. He was tempted to forget the whole thing, but he knew it was not Krishna's desire. Nor was it his prescribed duty as a kshatriya. Sighing, he said, "I cannot see any way of recovering our kingdom other than war. When the times comes, fighting even with loved ones is the hard duty of kings. But how can I challenge respectable elders like Bhishma and Drona? Would it not be more virtuous to humbly stand down and let them keep the kingdom? O Krishna, please guide me."

"You are not challenging anyone, O king," Krishna replied. "The choice of whether or not to fight lies with Dhritarashtra. If he will not act virtuously, he must face the consequences, along with all those who side with him. An elder, teacher, or superior is fit to be rejected when he abandons virtue. No sin will attach to you for killing the Kurus under such circumstances."

Krishna said he would try his best, by every diplomatic means, to avoid war and thereby save the Kurus from destruction. "No one will be able to criticize you, O Yudhishthira, for you seek peace. It is the war-like Duryodhana and his small-minded followers who desire to fight. I think their wish will soon be fulfilled."

Yudhishthira told Krishna that even if the Kurus will not give back the kingdom, he should ask them for just five villages. "I and my brothers will each rule one. Thus, we will accomplish our duty as kshatriyas. We are not greedy for vast provinces."

Krishna smiled and stood up to leave. Accompanied by Satyaki, he went out and mounted his shining chariot. The Pandavas followed him and circumambulated the chariot in respect before bidding him farewell. Urged on by Krishna's charioteer, Daruka, the four tall steeds moved off, and soon the chariot was speeding toward Hastinapura. Traveling throughout the day, they reached the outskirts of the city by evening. As they approached the main road that led into Hastinapura, they saw thousands of citizens lining it to greet them. Cheered by those people, who threw flower petals and rice grains onto the road, they entered the city, where the Kuru elders met them.

After formal greetings had been exchanged, Krishna went to visit Kunti, who was living in Vidura's house. The noble Kuru queen wept with joy when she saw Krishna, and he spent some time giving her news of her sons and consoling her. Kunti then gave a message to him for Yudhishthira, exhorting him not to be hesitant about fighting. "The time for which a kshatriya woman bears sons has arrived," she exclaimed, expressing her anger against the Kauravas. Kunti had been distraught when she heard what had happened to Draupadi in the Kuru assembly. Now, at last, the Kauravas would receive justice.

"O Krishna, I understand your actual position," Kunti said, as he stood up to leave. "You are the all-powerful Supreme Person. Your will is truth. Please bless me that I always act only for your pleasure. This is my deepest desire."

Assuring Kunti that she was dear to him and that all her desires would be fulfilled, Krishna returned to Dhritarashtra's palace. The king had called for a full assembly, and it rose in respect as Krishna entered the hall. He was led to a fine seat close to the king, and as he walked toward it, a large number of rishis entered the hall, headed by Narada. They appeared like a line of glowing planets, descended from the heavens. All of them took their seats at the front of the hall, and the assembly then settled down to hear Krishna speak.

When the hall became silent, Krishna looked at Dhritarashtra and said, "O Bharata chief, let there be peace between the Kauravas and Pandavas. May no heroes be slain on either side. For this reason I have come, O king. That is the sum and substance of my message."

Krishna praised the Kuru line, pointing out how it was famous for its virtue, its good behavior, kindness, compassion, and truthfulness. He told Dhritarashtra that, as the incumbent Kuru monarch, he had a great responsibility to maintain the noble Kuru traditions. All it required was for him to order that the Pandavas be given back their lands. Then war would be averted.

"However, O king," Krishna continued, "if you do not pursue this line, then disaster is certain. All the kings present here, as well as those in Virata, will slay one another mercilessly. Your sons or those of Pandu will also die. Consider how you will feel, O king, when news of either of their deaths reaches you."

When Krishna stopped speaking, several of the rishis stood up, one after another, and gave their opinions. All of them warned Dhritarashtra that entering into war against the Pandavas would be calamitous.

Duryodhana looked defiantly around the hall. Caring nothing for either Krishna's or the *rishi*'s advice, he loudly exclaimed, "I am whatever God has made me! How can I change my nature? Whatever is destined to happen, will happen. That also lies in God's hands."

Duryodhana looked at the rishis and smiled. They were always saying how God controlled everything. The Kaurava prince had no argument with that.

Hearing his son's outburst, Dhritarashtra appeared uncomfortable. He called for water, and after sipping a little, he said, "O Krishna, O rishis, greatly wise men all of you, I also desire peace. However, my hands are tied. My son will not obey me nor any of his elders. Try to change his mind, for that is the Kurus' only hope."

Krishna looked toward Duryodhana, who sat nonchalantly rubbing the mosaic floor with his foot. He looked back at Krishna with a half smile. In a gentle voice, Krishna said, "O Duryodhana, best of the Bharatas, I wish only for your good. Your obstinacy is vicious, frightful, and destructive to all. It will not lead to your happiness. Make peace with your cousins. This is desired by your father, by your elders, by the rishis, by myself, and by the Pandavas as well. Such a peace will lead to your lasting fame, and all your desires will be fulfilled. However, if you choose to follow the advice of inferior and foolish men—men such as Karna, Shakuni, and Dushasana—then how can you expect any good fortune?"

Karna frowned. He respected Krishna, and his berating words toward him were painful. It was hard to understand why Krishna was pleading on behalf of the Pandavas. Duryodhana was the son of the ruling Kuru king. Why, then, should he not have first claim to the whole kingdom? The Pandavas should themselves come humbly to him and ask for some lands to rule. The magnanimous Duryodhana would surely accord them some territories if they dealt with him nicely. But why should he accede to their demands made through messengers, accompanied by threats of force?

Seeing Duryodhana's indifference, Krishna's tone became sterner. "How can anyone face the enraged Bhima and live? Could anyone return home after coming out to fight with Arjuna? He has already vanquished the gods, Gandharvas, Daityas, and Danavas. Do not seek war with him and his brothers unless you desire your dynasty's obliteration, as well as your own."

Duryodhana said nothing. Finding Krishna's advice intensely annoying, the prince glared around the hall. He resembled a heap of burning coals.

One by one, Bhishma, Drona, and Vidura stood up and concurred with Krishna. Then Dhritarashtra himself spoke again, telling his son to make peace. "Go with Krishna and bring back the Pandavas. Be blessed by the ever-virtuous Yudhishthira and embrace Bhima to your bosom. Offer your blessings to Arjuna and the twins, and live happily as cousin brothers. Do not disobey me, dear son. The time has come to cease all hostilities."

The thought of embracing Bhima, his mortal enemy, made Duryodhana grimace. He had heard enough. Jumping to his feet, he exclaimed, "Everyone criticizes me and praises the Pandavas. What is my fault? I have done nothing wrong at all. Yudhishthira lost at dice, fair and square. In any event, he should never have been given half of this kingdom. That mistake was made when I was younger and had little influence. It has now been rectified. The kingdom belongs to my father, Dhritarashtra—and I, his humble servant, aim to keep it that way. I will not be moved by any threats or attempts at coercion. If the Pandavas want any part of the kingdom, they will have to fight for it. As a kshatriya, fighting is my duty, and I will not abandon that duty out of fear or anything else."

Duryodhana looked around the hall and spoke in measured tones as he concluded his speech. "O Krishna, know that as long as I rule the kingdom on my father's behalf, I will not give the Pandavas even as much land as can be pierced by the point of a needle."

Krishna rebuked Duryodhana, reminding him of his many acts of antagonism against the Pandavas and, especially, Draupadi. "O Kurus, I am thinking now of my debt to Draupadi. That chaste lady purchased me for all time when she cried out to me in this assembly. Her honor will surely be avenged."

Duryodhana pulled a face and snorted. He jumped up and stormed out of the hall, followed by his ministers and brothers. Krishna then said, "O Kurus, your only hope is to bind and imprison Duryodhana. Otherwise, destruction faces you."

All eyes turned toward Dhritarashtra, but the blind king remained silent. He could only remonstrate with his son; he could not follow it up with any action. Unless he gave the order to implement Krishna's suggestion, there would be war.

Outside the hall, Duryodhana began to confer with his close associates. Between them, they had made a plan to capture Krishna. Duryodhana felt that now was the moment. If left much longer, Krishna may convince his father to do something foolish. He gave the order for his men to enter the hall and surround Krishna. As the soldiers began entering through all of the hall's broad doorways, he went back in himself.

Seeing what was about to happen, Krishna called out to Duryodhana, "O Kaurava, out of folly you think me alone and vulnerable. See now the truth."

Krishna laughed and, as he did, his body flashed like lightning and grew to a huge size, seeming to fill the hall. Many gods began to emanate from him. Brahma came from his head, Shiva from his chest, and Agni from his mouth. Indra and many other celestials also appeared. All five Pandavas were also visible, standing by Krishna's side. Sparks flew and brilliant light, along with clouds of smoke, issued from his terrific form.

The warriors closing on Krishna with drawn swords fell back in astonishment, shielding their eyes. Almost everyone in the assembly looked away, for only the rishis, along with Bhishma, Drona, Vidura, Sanjaya, and Satyaki, were able to look upon Krishna as he displayed his universal form. He also gave Dhritarashtra the vision to see him, and the old king was able to witness numerous celestial rishis and brilliantly shining gods standing before Krishna and offering prayers.

Outside the hall, a fierce wind suddenly blew up and the sky became overshadowed. Thunderclaps reverberated and the earth shook. With the hall in a tumult, Krishna withdrew his mystical form and signaled for Satyaki to join him. Taking Satyaki's hand, he then walked out of the hall and mounted his chariot, and as he did so, the various disturbances ceased. The sky cleared and the wind died down to a gentle breeze. All the leading Kurus followed Krishna outside, folding their palms in respect. Vidura led the king out of the hall, where he stood before Krishna's chariot and said, "O Janardana, you have seen the influence I wield over my sons. I have tried my best. Do not blame me if war should ensue. I desire only peace."

Seated on the back of his great chariot, which was covered with white tiger skins and decorated with hundreds of golden moons, Krishna smiled down on Dhritarashtra. Looking around at the other Kurus, he said, "O descendants of Bharata, you have witnessed everything; how the uncultured Duryodhana walked out, and how the great lord of the earth has declared his powerlessness in the matter. Now, with your permission, I must return to Yudhishthira."

The chariot moved off, picking up speed as it went down the broad highway. Sending up a cloud of dust and with a great rumbling sound, it went out through the city's southern gate and in a short time was out of sight. Slowly, the Kurus went back into their palace.

Krishna's peace mission had failed. War was certain.

Twenty-three

ETERNAL WISDOM
ON THE BATTLEFIELD

AFTER KRISHNA HAD left Hastinapura, Kunti began thinking about Karna. It seemed that either he or Arjuna would soon die. Or perhaps one of her other sons would perish at Karna's hands. The mighty son of Surya had no idea that the Pandavas were his brothers. He would show them no quarter in the upcoming war. Most probably, though, he would die himself. By opposing Krishna, he had little chance of survival.

Feeling affection for her first-born child, Kunti felt it was time he learned the truth. She had never felt it possible to tell anyone before now. Nor had it been necessary. From the day she first saw Karna at the martial arts display it was clear to her that he was doing well. Duryodhana had given him a great kingdom, and he had been accepted as one of the Kauravas. But now it looked like his allegiance to Duryodhana would soon prove his undoing. Kunti therefore went early one morning to the Ganges, where Karna was performing his devotions to the sun god. As he came out of the river, he was surprised to see the Kuru queen waiting for him. He greeted her with folded palms. "O noble lady, to what do I owe this honor? How can I serve you today?"

Kunti looked at her son, who stood with the sacred river water running from his powerful body. She recalled again how she had placed him in that same river many years ago. Tears came to her eyes as she spoke. "O my child, there is something you must know. I am your mother. You were conceived in me by Surya, your worshipable deity."

Kunti's voice trembled as she described how, as a maiden, she had feared she would tarnish her family's reputation if she kept her child. "I thus cast you away into this river. O dearest child, my heart was breaking. I prayed to the Lord that you would be safe. By his grace, you were found and adopted by Adhiratha and his good wife."

Karna gazed in shock at Kunti. He could say nothing. There was no possibility that Kunti was lying, for her adherence to virtue and truth was famed throughout the world. Karna dropped to his knees and held his head. He already knew that Adhiratha had found him one day on the bank of the Ganges. Seeing Karna's natural bodily armor, the charioteer thought that he must have been abandoned by the gods themselves. Karna had often wondered about his natural parents but had never thought, for a moment, that Kunti might be his mother. He looked up at her, shaking his head in amazement.

"It is true, child. You are the Pandavas' brother— indeed, the eldest of them. You should go and join them. Do not follow avaricious and deceitful men. You will be ruined. Follow instead the path of virtue and unite with your brothers."

Karna was still unable to reply. He felt confused. It seemed that Kunti was genuinely distressed out of affection for him and fear for his welfare. But why had she not said something sooner? It was too late now. How could he abandon Duryodhana after all the Kaurava had done for him? Whether or not the Pandavas were his brothers, he now had no choice but to fight them.

Struggling with his raging thoughts and pushing aside the natural affection that was rising in his heart for his mother, Karna composed himself and said, "I believe your words, good lady, but I cannot take your advice. It is hard for me to accept that you are my well-wisher. By abandoning me at birth, you have done me a great harm. I have been denied the rites of a kshatriya and labeled a suta. Now, when danger threatens your other sons, you finally come to me."

Karna got to his feet and glanced up at the sun. No wonder he had always felt such a strong attraction for the worship of that deity. He looked back at Kunti, who stood with tears streaming down her face. Taking a deep breath, he said, "I will not leave Duryodhana. He is the lord of my life. Still, your visit to me will not prove fruitless. In the upcoming war, I will not kill any of your sons other than Arjuna, even if I overpower them. But if I can, I will certainly slay Arjuna, and thereby win lasting fame. Or, dying at his hand, I will attain the celestial regions. There can be no other way."

Shaking with emotion, Kunti reached out to Karna. He stepped forward uneasily and she embraced him, saying, "The Kurus will soon be destroyed in a fierce fight. Remember then your promise to me, dear son. Be blessed. I shall go now."

As Karna bowed to her, the sorrowful Kunti walked quickly back toward the city. It was plain that at least one of her sons would soon be dead.

*   *   *

The Pandavas were hardly surprised when Krishna returned unsuc-
cessful from Hastinapura. It had never seemed likely that Duryodhana
would have a sudden change of heart. Urged on by Krishna, Yudhishthira
began at once to arrange for war. After some consultation with his brothers
and Krishna, he selected Dhrishtadyumna to become the overall commander of his forces. As the huge army mobilized itself, the city of Virata was
filled with a great clamor. The cheers and shouts of men, the blasts of
conchshells, the cries of elephants, and the beating of drums were tumultuous. Along with his fighting forces, Yudhishthira arranged for another virtual army of cooks, doctors, engineers, and all kinds of other skilled work-
ers to support his troops. The whole assembly marched out of Virata in a
line extending for many miles and resembling a sea moving across the face
of the earth. At its head were Bhima and the twins, with Dhrishtadyumna
right behind. Yudhishthira rode in their midst on a splendid war chariot, and
Arjuna rode next to him, with Krishna driving his chariot.

Many brahmins accompanied the procession, continually reciting
Vedic hymns extolling the virtues of righteous battle. The warriors were joyful, seeing that either a glorious victory or death and ascent to the higher
planets now awaited them.

The army gradually made its way to the Kurukshetra plain where the
battle would take place. They arrived there after six days and set up camp
around Lake Hiranvati. Soon, a city of tents had been erected, and the
Pandavas waited for the Kuru leaders to come and discuss with them the
rules of engagement. Thereafter, the war would commence.

In Hastinapura, Duryodhana's forces were also on the move. Personally
marshaled by him, they loaded up their weapons onto thousands of chariots.
Bows, arrows, axes, lances, spears, spiked clubs, maces, and heavy darts were
loaded, as well as bombs, bullets, and many other types of explosive missiles,
along with the machines for launching them. There were large baskets full
of poisonous snakes and vats filled with molasses and sand that would be
heated and hurled at the enemy.

Moving up and down his almost unending line of chariots, horsemen,
infantry, and elephants, Duryodhana was elated. How could the Pandavas
even look at such an army? It resembled the surging ocean during a full
moon. With its countless heroes all clad in brilliant armor and bearing their
gleaming weapons, it shone brightly. The Kaurava leader sat aboard his
immaculate war-chariot, emblazoned with golden images of suns and many
kinds of fierce beasts and equipped with every conceivable weapon.

When all the arrangements were underway, Duryodhana went to Bhishma and said, "O Grandfather, none can equal you in either virtue or prowess. You are always the Kurus' best protector. Therefore, please become our leader in this war. March at our head, like Kartikkeya leading the celestials."

Bhishma looked across at Duryodhana, who stood before him with folded palms. The day he had feared had finally arrived—war among the Kurus. From the moment Draupadi had been insulted, Bhishma had foreseen it. He had also known that he would have to oppose the Pandavas. Aside from his vow to protect Hastinapura's throne, after years of living under Dhritarashtra's keep, he felt obliged to fight for him, even though it meant fighting alongside Duryodhana. Raising his gloved hand, he said, "I shall command your army, O ruler of men, but you should know one thing. The Pandavas are as dear to me as the Kauravas. I will not slay any of them."

Duryodhana had expected that from Bhishma. It did not matter. As long as the Kuru grandfather wrought havoc among the Pandavas' troops, as he undoubtedly would, other warriors could deal with the Pandavas directly. Karna would settle his score with Arjuna. And as for Bhima. . . . Duryodhana fingered the golden mace by his side. His time would soon come.

"There is another thing you should know," Bhishma continued. "There is no warrior, not even myself, who can match Arjuna's power. With Krishna by his side, he cannot be conquered by the combined armies of the gods and the demons."

"We shall see," Duryodhana replied with a smile. He had not been impressed by Krishna's display of mystic power. Any magician or yogi could have done the same thing. So far, Krishna had not done much to save the Pandavas from losing their kingdom. And without fighting, there would little he could do in the war.

"To Kurukshetra, then! Victory will be ours!" Duryodhana's shout filled his troops with joy. They roared and clashed their weapons, and the immense army began to move off, slowly heading out of Hastinapura, with the prince at their head. The earth trembled as they marched out, eager for the fight to commence.

Arriving after some days at Kurukshetra, they set up camp a few miles away from the Pandavas. Duryodhana immediately called for a war council, and the leading members of his army assembled in his great tent. He then said to Bhishma, "O great hero, with yourself and Drona as our leaders, I do not fear even the gods. It is time to plan our strategy. Tell me, then, of the strengths and weaknesses of both ourselves and the enemy."

Bhishma rested a hand on his ivory-handled sword. "Listen as I describe to you the power of all the warriors assembled here for battle. There are rathas, who are capable of contending with a thousand other fighters; *maharathas*, who can contend with ten thousand; and then there are *atirathas*, who can fight with sixty thousand or even an unlimited number at once."

Bhishma named many of the fighters on both sides, grading them in terms of their power. On Duryodhana's side, he named Drona, Kripa, Kritavarma, Ashvatthama, and the prince himself as *atirathas*. He also described the Pandavas as invincible fighters, stressing again Arjuna's power. "With his Gandiva bow, knowledge of mystical weapons, celestial chariot, impenetrable armor, and inexhaustible quivers, and especially with Krishna by his side, he is unapproachable in battle by anyone other than Drona or myself. Also, he is young, while we are old and worn out. He will range through your army, causing tremendous devastation."

The kings in Duryodhana's tent, who heard Bhishma describing Arjuna, felt their arms shorn of power and hanging down uselessly by their sides. Bhishma then went on to speak about Shikhandhi. "This one is actually the reincarnation of a princess who was formerly kidnapped by me for the sake of my brother Vichitravirya. Filled with an intense hatred for me, she died thinking only of my death and has taken birth as Drupada's son."

Bhishma told the whole story. Many years ago, he had kidnapped the three daughters of King Kashi, intending to bring them to Hastinapura as wives for his brother. One of them, however, named Amba, had already given her heart to another king. Bhishma had therefore sent her to him, but that king had then rejected her, saying, "You have been sullied by another man's touch."

The distraught Amba had gone into the forest and practiced severe austerity to gain Shiva's favor. The god had finally appeared and blessed her that in her next life she would become a man who could kill Bhishma. The Kuru grandfather explained that he had heard the story from Vyasadeva. "It seems that Amba was first born as Drupada's daughter, and only in her youth, by Shiva's grace, did she become a man. For this reason, I will not face him in battle, even if he comes before me desiring my death. This is my vow. I will not attack women, those with women's names, or even those who appear to be women. Shikhandhi is actually a woman, but she has somehow taken a man's form."

The kings looked with respect at the noble Bhishma. He would certainly not break his vow. They would need to work hard to ensure that Shikhandhi did not get any opportunity to face him alone. As night gradually fell, they sat discussing their strategy. Battle would commence the next morning.

*   *   *

Early in the morning, the commanders of the two armies met to agree on the rules of engagement. Warriors should only fight with equals and with equal weapons. No blow should be struck without any warning, and one fleeing from the fight should not be assailed. The many servants and physicians on the battlefield should not be harmed. The generals spoke for some time and then stood up to leave for their positions at the head of their armies. Doubting that the deceitful Kauravas would follow the rules they had made, Dhrishtadyumna said, "O Kurus, we will not be the first to break these codes. However, if we see that you do not observe them, then we, too, shall disregard them."

Shining like fire in his golden armor, Dhrishtadyumna then mounted his chariot and headed out onto the field. He began to arrange his forces into a needle formation, with himself, Bhima, and the twins at its point. Yudhishthira was positioned in its center, surrounded by many powerful chariot fighters. Near him was Arjuna, with Shikhandhi by his side. The Pandavas knew that their success depended upon overpowering Bhishma as soon as possible. As Arjuna advanced, Hanuman let out tremendous shouts from his banner, causing the horses and elephants to pass urine and dung in fear.

Seeing the Pandavas' formation, the Kauravas arranged themselves in a counter-array. Bhishma was at their head. Seated on a huge chariot, with white headdress, white banner, and a white umbrella over his head, he looked like a white mountain. Behind him came Duryodhana, riding on the back of a great elephant the color of a blue lotus. Bards and singers surrounded him, chanting eulogies, and he was protected by thousands of highly trained fighters.

Looking across at the Kuru forces, which resembled the ocean rolling toward him with the banners of countless heroes for its sharks, Yudhishthira's heart sank. He turned to Arjuna and said, "O mighty-armed one, how shall we ever overcome this army? The grandfather cannot be slain by anyone at any time, and numerous other fiercely powerful fighters support him. This battle seems hopeless."

Arjuna encouraged his brother. "Battles are not won by prowess alone, O sinless one. Virtue also plays a part. Wherever there is righteousness and truth, and wherever Krishna is found, there will be victory."

Yudhishthira was not entirely sure if his cause was so righteous. Had it not been his own foolishness that had ignited the conflict? Was it not his desire for kingdom and wealth that impelled him now to fight? But Krishna's presence was certainly reassuring. The fact that he was behind the war was the conclusive argument in Yudhishthira's mind. He nodded in agreement with Arjuna, who then moved off toward the front of the army.

Dhrishtadyumna, at the head of the Pandava forces, gave the order for the conchshells to be blown to signify the start of battle. Arjuna and Krishna blew long and mighty blasts on their celestial conches. Bhima and the twins also blew to their full power, and the combined sound of all those conches carried over to the Kauravas, making their hearts tremble. They responded with blasts of their own. Drums were beaten and trumpets blown, creating a tumultuous sound across the battlefield.

Arjuna then said to Krishna, "My Lord, infallible one, please drive my chariot closer to the Kauravas. Let me see the enemy positions and who has come out today, wishing to please the evil-minded Duryodhana."

Krishna urged the horses on, and the fine chariot rumbled out into the middle of the field. Krishna raised his hand toward the Kauravas and said, "Just behold all the Kurus assembled here, O Partha."

Arjuna gazed across the field. The whole Kuru army was indeed present. But he, too, was a Kuru. How could he bear arms in a life or death conflict with his own kinsmen? Suddenly the grim finality of the situation struck him. He began to feel overwhelmed with apprehension. Here were Bhishma, Drona, Kripa, and so many others whom he had loved since childhood and who had loved him in return. In order for Yudhishthira to be victorious, all of them would have to be killed. The thought was too much for Arjuna. He felt as if his limbs were dissolving. His mouth was dry, and he said to Krishna in a wavering voice, "O Keshava, I do not think I can fight. What good can come from killing one's own relatives? It seems that only sin and misfortune will result from this war."

Arjuna's bow slipped from his hand, and he sat down in his chariot. He had no heart for the fight. Virata had been different. He had had no intention of killing his kinsmen there, nor had the Kuru elders fought to their full power, anyway. But now there would be no mercy. Only one side would be returning from this war.

Tears streamed from Arjuna's eyes as he spoke. "O Keshava, I cannot fight for a kingdom bereft of all those I love! What happiness will it bring?"

Arjuna was overcome with compassion. Bhishma was exactly like his father, and Drona was equally dear. So many other kind and gentle elders were also present. Even Duryodhana and his brothers were pitiable because they were so foolish. Sweat broke out on Arjuna's brow as he implored Krishna, "If we kill learned elders, men who are our gurus, will not sin overcome us? The whole of society will go to hell, as it depends upon the elders for the perpetuation of religious practices."

Arjuna spoke passionately, his various arguments based on his understanding of morality. Finally, he slumped in his chariot and said, "I do not care if the Kauravas slay me unarmed and unresisting. I cannot fight."

Krishna smiled as he looked down at the weeping Arjuna. This was certainly an uncharacteristic display from the fierce warrior. Still holding the chariot reins, he said, "How have you given way to such weakness, Arjuna? It does not befit one who understands life's true values. O great hero, rise up. Do not yield to this impotence. It leads only to degradation."

Arjuna was bewildered by Krishna's unequivocal dismissal of all his arguments. He voiced his doubts. "My dear Krishna, I can understand the necessity of killing sinful enemies, but some of these men are highly respectable. They are superiors and should not even be offered a verbal fight, never mind slain."

Arjuna gazed into Krishna's implacable face. Clearly, he was not impressed with Arjuna's arguments. Arjuna knew that ultimately he would have to follow Krishna's direction. Deciding to his open his heart to his dear friend, he said, "O Krishna, it is plain that I cannot determine right from wrong. I am completely confused. You are my only hope. Please instruct me; tell me why I must fight. I surrender to you as a disciple."

Krishna smiled broadly, pleased that Arjuna was ready to accept him as a teacher. As the two armies stood off, waiting to see what Arjuna was going to do, Krishna began to instruct him. He began by explaining that Arjuna's arguments were based on a misconception. The Pandava warrior was not recognizing that the body is only a temporary covering for the soul. Ultimately, the soul's welfare is more important than the material body's. Arjuna needed to understand how to act for the benefit of the soul, and that would be in everyone's best interests.

"The eternal soul is a part of the Supreme Spirit. He belongs in the eternal spiritual world, a place of unlimited happiness—not here in this temporary and miserable material world." Krishna had put down the reins and was standing before Arjuna with his hand raised as he spoke. "You must therefore act in ways that take you and, indeed, everyone else, toward that spiritual world."

Krishna explained that everyone's ultimate welfare lay in pleasing the Supreme Lord. "And, my dearest friend, I am that Lord. Everything, both material and spiritual, emanates from me. All things rest on me, like pearls on a thread. I am the beginning, middle, and end of everything. All beings owe their existence to me and depend upon me for their lives. Therefore, try to act only for my pleasure."

Arjuna listened attentively as Krishna described how he is everyone's greatest well-wisher. He alone knows how the souls came into the material world and how they can get out again. Through Krishna's grace, the veil of ignorance covering the living beings can be gradually removed, and they can realize their true nature as his eternal loving servants.

"In illusion, or maya, people think their happiness will come from serving their own senses, from pursuing their mental fantasies," Krishna told Arjuna, "but this always leads to suffering. Permanent happiness will only be found when one gives up this illusion and turns to me."

Krishna instructed Arjuna for almost an hour. Arjuna posed many questions, which Krishna answered with profound and timeless wisdom. For Arjuna's benefit, Krishna again displayed his majestic universal form, giving the Pandava the ability to see it in all its splendor. Arjuna felt his doubts being dispelled. There could be no doubting Krishna's supremacy. Understanding that if Krishna wanted him to fight, it must be the best thing, not only for him, but even for those who might die at his hands, Arjuna felt reassured. Krishna would not misdirect him, he felt certain. Although not easy, it was still his duty to fight.

Looking across at Bhishma's chariot, Arjuna said, "Dear Krishna, my illusion is gone. I shall do exactly as you have instructed." He picked up his bow and asked Krishna to take the chariot back to the front of the army. The war was about to begin.

Twenty-four

THE SLAUGHTER BEGINS

As THE ARMIES were on their way to Kurukshetra, Dhritarashtra sat anxiously in his palace, cursing his blindness. In reality, he should be leading the Kurus into battle. After all, he had brought about the war. Perhaps, if he had gone out and seen the Pandavas arrayed for battle against his sons, he might have stopped the hostilities and peacefully handed them their kingdom. But he could only sit and wait. The king called for Sanjaya and asked him what was happening. "Have the armies reached Kurukshetra? O Sanjaya, destiny is all-powerful. Although I could see Duryodhana's folly, I could not bring myself to restrain him. Surely this war has been divinely ordained. Can it, therefore, be so terrible? After all, what greater honor is there for a warrior than to die in battle?"

Sanjaya sighed. He loved Dhritarashtra but found his tendency to avoid responsibility frustrating. They had been through it so many times. Maybe now, however, as he faced imminent ruin, he might realize the truth. "It is said that man proposes and God disposes, O king," Sanjaya said. "The Lord gives us the results of our own acts, good or bad. But he also has his own desires. It is only when we understand and surrender to those desires that we can be truly happy. Otherwise, we act sinfully and end up suffering."

As Sanjaya spoke, the sage Vyasadeva entered the chamber. He came before Dhritarashtra and said, "O great king, your sons and most of the other warriors are at the end of their lives. All this has been arranged by time. It is inevitable."

Vyasadeva then told the king that he could bestow upon him divine vision that would enable him to see the battle, but Dhritarashtra replied, "I have no wish to see my sons die, O great sage. Let me just hear of the battle."

"So be it. I shall give the vision to Sanjaya. He will see every part of the war. O king, know one thing: victory follows righteousness. In Hastinapura, the omens are bad."

Vyasadeva described the portents he had seen, and Dhritarashtra became alarmed. He pleaded with the sage not to blame him for what had happened. "I tried my best to bring my sons to the path of virtue."

Becoming angry, Vyasadeva chastised the king. "The great slaughter of men that is about to occur has its root in you. You could still prevent it. Give the order now for the Pandavas' kingdom to be returned, and the war will end before it begins."

Dhritarashtra hung his head. He could make no reply. In his heart, he still hoped beyond hope that his sons might somehow be victorious. Knowing this, Vyasadeva said, "Do not think that a superior-sized army will necessarily win a battle. Even fifty well-trained men, who do not retreat and who work well as a team, can defeat an entire army. Victory in any battle is uncertain. Ultimately, as you have heard so many times, virtue is the decisive factor."

Leaving the king silent, the sage walked out of the chamber, his wooden sandals clacking on the marble floor. Sanjaya closed his eyes and began to see within himself the scene unfolding on the battlefield. He described it to the king, relating to him the conversation that took place between Krishna and Arjuna. Hearing Krishna describe himself as the supreme power, and hearing also how he again manifested his universal form, Dhritarashtra felt his hopes for victory fading. Even with the assistance of the great Kuru fighters, what chance did they stand of overcoming such a power?

"What did my sons and the Pandavas do after Krishna spoke?" Dhritarashtra asked. Fearing the worst but still hanging on to a slender hope of success, the king sat rapt in attention as Sanjaya began to describe in full detail all the events as they occurred on the battlefield.

*   *   *

As Arjuna's chariot made its way back to his army, the men sent up a great cheer. They had watched with apprehension as he remained stationary between the two armies, obviously overcome by some kind of uncertainty. Now it seemed he had regained his resolve. His bow was raised and he was moving into position. Horns, bugles, drums, and conchshells were sounded in a continuous uproar.

Just as the battle was about to begin, Yudhishthira removed his armor and climbed down from his chariot. As his brothers and the other warriors looked on in amazement, he walked across the field toward the Kauravas. Unarmed and unprotected, he made his way straight to Bhishma's chariot.

The Kauravas started laughing. "It seems this wretch has been overcome with terror. He has come to beg Bhishma for mercy."

Paying no heed to those jeers, Yudhishthira approached Bhishma with folded palms. The old Kuru chief got down to greet him, and Yudhishthira immediately clasped his feet, saying, "O invincible hero, kindly grant us permission to fight with you. Please bless us."

Bhishma smiled. Yudhishthira was properly observing the ancient code, which required that before fighting with an elder, one should offer respects and seek his permission. "O son of Kunti, fight and obtain victory," he replied. "Alas, O child, although I know your cause is just, I must oppose you. Surely, men are slaves to wealth. Thus do I stand here helplessly. Still, I wish to do you good. Ask anything from me, and it will be granted."

Tears came to Yudhishthira's eyes. In a choked voice, he said, "O Grandfather, tell us how you may be slain."

Standing before Yudhishthira in his polished silver and gold armor, Bhishma was a formidable figure. Although he was over a hundred years old, he had lost none of his power. His gilded bow stood by his side, almost as tall as he was. Placing a hand on Yudhishthira's shoulder, he said, "There is no man present here who can slay me, even if aided by the king of the gods. The time for my death has not yet come. Approach me again later and I will answer your question."

Yudhishthira bowed again and then walked toward Drona, who got down from his chariot to greet him. Offering respects to his martial teacher in the same way, he asked his permission to fight. Like Bhishma, Drona blessed Yudhishthira. "O king, how can you be opposed?" he said. "With Krishna as your guide, your victory is assured. Alas, I am a slave to Kuru wealth and cannot fight for you, but ask from me some boon."

Moved by affection, Yudhishthira falteringly replied, "O preceptor, please tell me how you may be defeated."

"As long as I stand with upraised weapons, you will never obtain victory," Drona answered. "Neither man nor celestial can stand before me as I scatter arrows in all directions. Only when my weapons are lowered can I be overcome. O king, I will lay down my arms when I hear terrible news from a credible source."

Drona held up a hand in blessing and then remounted his chariot. Thinking about his words, Yudhishthira went over to Kripa to seek his permission and blessings. As he came near Kripa's chariot, a surge of grief overwhelmed him. Clasping his hands, he stood before his old teacher with head bowed, tears streaming down his face. First Bhishma, then Drona, and now Kripa—three men who were like fathers to him, and who all had to be killed. Yudhishthira could not recall a single harsh word or deed from any of them.

Seeing Yudhishthira's plight, Kripa gently said to him, "O great king, go forth and obtain victory. Waste no time trying to kill me, for I am unslayable. My father, Gautama Rishi, has blessed me so. But every day I will rise from sleep and pray for your victory."

Yudhishthira went finally to Shalya, who was Madri's brother. Duryodhana had reached him first with his plea for assistance, and the noble-minded Shalya had felt unable to refuse. After giving his permission for the fight, he looked sadly down at his nephew and said, "I have become obliged to the Kauravas. O child, may you win everlasting fame and glory. I wish only for your success."

Yudhishthira walked slowly away and returned to his own forces. After again donning his armor and mounting his chariot, he called across to the Kauravas. "If any of you wish to join us now, before the battle begins, you are welcome. Step forward."

In addition to his hundred sons from Gandhari, Dhritarashtra had one other son who had been born from a maidservant. This prince, Yuyutsu, had never shared Duryodhana's evil mentality. When he heard Yudhishthira's offer, he called back, "I will join with you. O sinless one, will you accept me?"

"Come, come," Yudhishthira replied. "Fight against your foolish brothers. It seems their line will soon rest on you."

Duryodhana glared in silent fury at his half-brother as he made his way across to the Pandavas. Drums were beaten and trumpets blown. The moment for the battle to start had arrived. All the warriors sent up a great cheer. Now it was either victory or a glorious death. There was no third possibility. The two armies closed on each other like two great oceans coming together. Bhima raced ahead of the Pandava forces, sending up tremendous cries that struck terror into the Kauravas' hearts. Whirling his mace above his head, he resembled a furious tornado as he tore into his horrified foes. At last, the time to vent his long-pent-up wrath had arrived.

Taking heart, the Kauravas responded with their own battle cries and rushed toward Bhima with their weapons raised. Other Pandava warriors came up alongside him and a fierce general conflict was soon raging. Neither side flinched nor turned back. The twang of bowstrings and the slap of the strings against leather arm-protectors sounded everywhere, like continuous gun shots. The air was full of long-shafted arrows that glanced off the warriors' case armor. Spears, darts, clubs, and iron balls rained down on both armies. The fighters roared and blew their conches, weapons clashed, animals screamed, infantry thudded across the field with heavy steps, chariot wheels clattered, and drums were beaten to create a deafening cacophony of sound. With total disregard for their lives, the warriors rushed at each other in a frenzy.

Many omens were seen as the battle commenced. Thunderclaps sounded and the sky flashed red and blue. A shower of putrid matter dropped from the heavens and a terrible wind blew. Bolts of lightning struck the earth. Undeterred, the warriors fought on with full force. Powerful chariot fighters met together, discharging volleys of deadly arrows. Infantry fought infantry, smashing and hacking at one another with their maces and swords. Elephant riders came against other elephants, their great beasts trumpeting in fury, while horsemen charged each other with their long spears extended.

The great heroes on both sides engaged with their chosen foes. Bhima singled out Duryodhana; Dhrishtadyumna assailed Drona; Sahadeva attacked Shakuni; Arjuna engaged with Bhishma. Many other mighty heroes clashed as the first exchanges of the war took place. Men fell in thousands, their heads and limbs severed. The ground quickly became muddy with blood. The warriors' jewels and gold ornaments sparkled from the mire, like stars shining in the firmament.

Divisions of Rakshasas marched out on both sides. Ghatotkacha led a huge force for the Pandavas, while a mighty Rakshasa named Alambusha led them for the Kauravas. These awful beings tore their human opponents to pieces creating a terrible carnage. The battlefield assumed the appearance of Yamaloka, Death's grim abode. Men screamed in pain, like souls condemned to the tortures of hell. They fought as if possessed by demons. No quarter was shown. In that confused melee, soldiers slew even their own kinsmen as their shouts of identification were lost in the general din.

Bhishma broke free from Arjuna's attack and plowed into the Pandava army. His chariot, marked with an ensign bearing a palm tree, carved through the enemy troops, leaving a trail of slaughter in its wake. His arrows sped in all directions. Anyone who came before him was immediately slain. The old Kuru warrior seemed to be possessed of a new life. He appeared to be dancing in his chariot as he fought. His arrows were fired with such power that they sent even great elephants tumbling to the earth.

After the first day's fighting, tens of thousands of men lay dead. Due mainly to Bhishma's exertions, the battle went the Kauravas' way. Hearing of it from Sanjaya, Dhritarashtra felt cheered. But then he felt guilt. Surely, it was sinful to revel in the death of so many men. And how could he relish the hope that his own nephews may be crushed? He felt trapped. Either way, victory or defeat, he would suffer. Sitting with head bowed, he lamented, "What good will come of this, Sanjaya? Alas, Vidura was right. The noble Bhishma and Drona spoke well. I should have heeded Krishna's words."

The second day of the battle began like the first, with Bhishma wreaking havoc. Seeing the powerful Kuru hero carving through the Pandava forces, Arjuna became infuriated. How could he be so committed to Duryodhana's evil cause? Arjuna said to Krishna, "O Janardana, go quickly to where Bhishma stands. It seems he is bent on massacring our entire army. I shall kill him without delay."

"Be on your guard," cautioned Krishna. "I shall now take you to him."

Arjuna began to fight his way past the contingent of chariot fighters assigned to protect Bhishma. The Pandava fired his arrows in an endless line. The twang of his bow, the slap of the string on his leather fences, and the whistling of arrows leaving his bow made one continuous sound. He whirled about in his chariot, striking down the warriors who assailed him from all sides.

Bhishma saw Arjuna's standard coming toward him. Hanuman's frightful cries were distinctly audible, even from a great distance. Soon Arjuna's chariot, with its four cream-colored steeds, broke through the troops surrounding Bhishma. Arjuna blew his conch in a challenge to the Kuru warrior. Bhishma looked across at Arjuna. He felt a surge of affection and love. In his mind, he offered respects to Krishna, marveling at how he had become a chariot-driver for his friend. Awed, Bhishma was almost overpowered with his feelings for Krishna. But, focusing on his duty, he became resolved in battle and continued to fire off his deadly arrows at the Pandava forces.

Drona, Kripa, and Duryodhana were fighting alongside Bhishma, and they attacked Arjuna. Many other powerful warriors, supporting Bhishma, also trained their weapons on the Pandava. "Stay, stay! Fight with me! Be on your guard!" came the shouts from all quarters.

Unperturbed by that multiple attack, Arjuna smiled. Within seconds, he sent arrows at each and every one of his assailants. They reeled about in their chariots as the shafts loosed from the Gandiva thudded into them. Rallying themselves, they fought back with fury. Arrows flew everywhere as the one Pandava contended with dozens of other warriors. Seeing this fight, other Pandava heroes came to Arjuna's aid and engaged the great Kuru fighters. At the same time, hundreds and thousands of Kaurava warriors advanced toward Arjuna. Encountering Arjuna's furious assault, they resembled the ocean lashed by a storm. Their armors were torn off and their bows shattered. Standards were sent crashing to the ground, and chariots were smashed to pieces. Bodies pierced with dozens of arrows lay every-where. Viewing Arjuna as Death incarnate, many warriors jumped from their chariots and ran desperately away from him.

Duryodhana went up to Bhishma and called out, "O sire, do something quickly. Arjuna is slaying our men like a farmer reaping wheat. For your sake, Karna has laid down his arms; otherwise, he would surely check the enraged Pandava."

Bhishma was reluctant to engage in direct battle with Arjuna. Aside from his deep affection for Pandu's son, he also knew that with Krishna on his side, Arjuna could not be overcome. But seeing Duryodhana's pleading expression, Bhishma felt impelled, bound by painful duty. Ordering his char-ioteer to face Arjuna, Bhishma cursed, "Fie on a warrior's duty!"

Seeing Bhishma turn toward him, Arjuna focused his attention on the old Kuru chief. Still enraged, he shot ten, then a hundred, and then a thou-sand arrows at him. Bhishma countered all those arrows with his own. Arjuna then fired so many shafts at him that Bhishma appeared covered by a network of arrows. Bhishma expertly dispelled those arrows and quickly counterattacked Arjuna. The two heroes cheered one another as they fought. Neither could gain any advantage over the other.

Struck on the breast by a number of arrows, Krishna bled and appeared like a red-blossoming kinsuka tree as he dexterously drove Arjuna's chariot, confounding Bhishma's aim by describing various circular motions. Bhishma also wheeled rapidly about the field, and the two fighters resembled a pair of angry lions circling one another. The ground trembled beneath the char-iot wheels and seemed about to split open. Many other warriors stood by, watching in amazement. They could not detect the slightest flaw in the techniques of either combatant. Much of the time, both of them were invis-ible beneath clouds of arrows. In the sky, the celestials looked on and said, "These two cannot be defeated by any earthly or heavenly foe. This fight will surely never end."

As Bhishma and Arjuna fought, many other fierce encounters took place elsewhere on the battlefield. Drona and Dhrishtadyumna contended in a fight that was no less spectacular. Each pierced the other with steel-tipped shafts and roared in fury. Conscious of his destiny to kill Drona, Dhrishtadyumna constantly sought an opening, but the preceptor repeated-ly thwarted his attacks.

Bhima had entered deep within the Kalinga army. Laughing all the while, he unleashed thousands of arrows that cut down his foes on all sides. Those shafts released from Bhima's huge bow passed clean through the bod-ies of men and horses. The Kalingas fought him fearlessly but were slaughtered like so many deer encountering a lion. In a terrible battle, Bhima met the Kalinga king, who was mounted on a heavily armored elephant. The beast screamed and tried to gore Bhima with its sharpened tusks. Finally, Bhima leaped from his chariot with his blue-bladed sword held high. He brought it down on the king's head with all his power. The king was clean-ly sliced into two pieces, which fell on either side of his mount. Bhima then severed the elephant's trunk, and the blood-soaked beast toppled over and died.

Jumping clear of the falling elephant, Bhima rushed at the remaining Kalingas. He moved with the speed of a hawk, his gleaming sword flashing. Severed heads and limbs flew everywhere. The Kaurava troops were terri-fied. Bhima jumped forward and backward, spinning and somersaulting through the air. Exhibiting every kind of move with his sword, he resembled a frenzied dancer and left a trail of carnage in his wake. His enemies shook with fear. Before long, thousands of Kaurava warriors lay slain, hacked to pieces by Bhima. Amid the blood and gore were pieces of armor and shat-tered chariots, as well as golden housings and shining bells from the backs of elephants.

The Kaurava forces fled in panic from Bhima. Seeing this, Bhima roared triumphantly and blew repeated blasts on his conch. That sound reverberated around the field, causing the hair on the Kauravas' bodies to stand erect. As they dashed away in all directions, twilight fell and the battle ended for the day. The two armies disengaged and withdrew from the field. Jackals and vultures, crying in glee, began to gather around the slain and mutilated warriors. Fatigued from the fight, the soldiers wearily made their way back to their camps.

Twenty-five

THE OLD WARRIOR

THE BATTLE RAGED on for over a week, with a great slaughter of men on both sides. Goaded on by Duryodhana, Bhishma created mayhem among the Pandavas' forces. So, too, did Drona and the other principal Kuru warriors. On the opposite side, the Pandava heroes, headed by Bhima and Arjuna, cut down the Kauravas in the tens of thousands. Remembering his vow to slay all of Dhritarashtra's sons, Bhima targeted them at every opportunity. Duryodhana wept tears of frustration and anger as he saw his brothers hacked down by the remorseless Bhima. The Kaurava prince longed to check him but found himself hardly able to approach the raging Pandava warrior. Even when backed up by a number of other mighty Kuru fighters, Duryodhana was still repulsed by Bhima whenever they met.

Hearing of his sons' deaths from Sanjaya, Dhritarashtra lamented pitiably. He tossed about on his throne and let out great sobs. "Destiny is chastising me. Surely, Bhima will slay every one of my sons. Alas, I am sinking into an ocean of distress."

After eight days of fighting, Duryodhana was feeling disheartened. He had hoped that by now his army would be quite on top, but things were not going well. Perhaps the Danavas were assisting him; it was hard to say. Certainly, a great number of the Pandava forces had been slain, but the Kauravas had also sustained huge losses, even more than their foes. His eleven great divisions were now no more than six. The Pandavas had to be stopped or Duryodhana's whole army would soon be decimated. Bhishma and Drona were his best hopes, but they were too soft on Pandu's sons.

Thinking in this way, Duryodhana went to Bhishma on the evening of the eighth day and said, "O grandsire, it seems we can do nothing to prevent the Pandavas from annihilating us. They continuously smash apart our formations and grind down our forces. I think the gods are favoring them."

Bhishma sighed. It was bad enough that he was forced to fight the Pandavas, but to also have to constantly face Duryodhana's accusatory remarks made it much worse. The old fighter raised up his two powerful arms, which were covered with lacerations and scars. "See here the evidence of my endeavor, O king. I have exerted myself to the best of my ability and the limit of my strength. Tens of thousands of warriors lie slain by me. However, neither I nor any other man can kill the Pandavas. They are protected by virtue and by the very Lord of virtue himself. What can exertion achieve?"

Bhishma felt compassion for Duryodhana. His foolishness was certainly pitiable, and now he was perhaps starting to become a little humble. At the very least, he was being humbled by the Pandavas' might in battle. Maybe he would see sense and make peace with his cousins before everything was lost. That, though, seemed unlikely. More probably, he would fight to the very last man—and still not surrender anything.

Duryodhana could guess Bhishma's thoughts. "I do not believe the Pandavas are invincible. However, I know that you certainly are. You cannot be killed until you desire death yourself. With your assistance, we could vanquish the gods and demons combined. How, then, can five mortal men survive against you?"

With folded palms, Duryodhana beseeched Bhishma. Tears flowed from his eyes. Dropping down and holding Bhishma's feet, he said, "O lord, please be merciful to me. Slay the Pandavas, even as Indra slays the demons. Make good your promise to always protect the Kurus."

Bhishma looked away from the prince. Protect the Kurus? Duryodhana seemed prone to forget that the Pandavas were also Kurus. Indeed, they might soon be the only surviving Kurus.

Duryodhana's imploring voice went on, "O son of Ganga, if, out of hatred for me or love for the Pandavas, you feel unable to slay them, then please stand down from this fight. Let Karna come out. He has vowed to kill at least Arjuna."

Bhishma was stung by Duryodhana's words. What did the prince think Karna could achieve that he could not? Had Duryodhana already forgotten Karna's previous encounters with Arjuna? What would it take to convince him that his hopes were futile? Perhaps, if he saw for certain that even the so-called invincible Bhishma could not kill the Pandavas, then he might relent.

Bhishma reached down for his beautiful gem-encrusted quiver. It was filled with long golden shafts fletched with buzzard feathers. Bhishma took out five arrows fitted with crescent heads. Spreading out a cloth on the ground, he carefully placed the arrows on it. The old Kuru leader then closed his eyes and began uttering Vedic mantras. After a few minutes, he opened his eyes and looked at Duryodhana. "O king, I have imbued these five arrows with all my ascetic power. Tomorrow, I shall fight a battle such as has never been witnessed before. I will attack the Pandavas and seek to kill them all, each with one of these shafts. Only Krishna can save them, but he has vowed not to fight. Let us see what happens now."

Bhishma felt certain that Krishna would find some way of saving the Pandavas. He would need to. The Kuru chief would give it his all. Surely then, when he failed, Duryodhana would realize the futility of his cause.

Duryodhana jumped to his feet, beaming. This was what he wanted to hear. He clapped his hands and repeatedly praised Bhishma. Then, thinking of Krishna, he became pensive. The Yadu prince was tricky. Looking down at the five arrows, Duryodhana said, "Let me keep these arrows tonight. I will guard them carefully and give them to you tomorrow at the beginning of the battle."

Feeling joyful, Duryodhana took the arrows and retired to his own quarters for the night. Surely now the Pandavas were doomed. Bhishma was famed for keeping his word. He would certainly try his best to kill all five brothers with his infallible arrows. And Krishna was only protecting Arjuna. Even if he broke his word and started to fight, how would he save the others? Smiling to himself, Duryodhana lay down to rest.

*   *   *

Yudhishthira sat in his tent, surrounded by his brothers. After eight days of fighting, the battle seemed to be going his way. The Kauravas had sustained huge losses and were down to half their original number. His own losses had not been so great, and now the two sides were almost equal. But the Pandava king felt little joy. So many men were dying so that he might regain his kingdom. Soon the world would be full of widows and orphans. It was a terrible tragedy. Yet what choice was there? He had tried everything to bring about peace. Now he was only doing his duty by fighting—a duty endorsed by Krishna. Doubtlessly, some divine plan was being enacted. Yudhishthira often needed to remind himself of that. He looked over to Krishna, who sat amidst the Pandava brothers like the full moon surrounded by glowing planets.

Appearing thoughtful, Krishna began to address Yudhishthira. "O great hero, you are becoming successful in this fight. Your army is crushing the

Kauravas. We can expect them to resort to every desperate means to reverse the situation. Even now, I sense that they are devising some deadly scheme."

Krishna looked over at Arjuna. That day's battle had seen the death of Iravan, Arjuna's son by a Naga princess whom he had married during his yearlong pilgrimage. Iravan had brought a division of powerful Naga warriors to the fight, but he had been killed after a terrific contest with Alambusha. The only consolation had been that Ghatotkacha had then killed Alambusha, throwing his severed head onto Duryodhana's chariot. But Arjuna was seized with grief for his slain son. Krishna comforted him. "Shake off this sorrow, O hero. Your son has ascended to regions of unending bliss. What greater end is there for heroes than to die in battle?"

Tears fell from Arjuna's eyes. The Pandava felt pained that he had been unable to help his son. He had been far away from Iravan when he'd been killed. Duryodhana's tactic each day had been to detail a vast division of warriors—the fierce Samshaptakas and Narayanas—to engage with Arjuna and keep him away from the principal Kuru fighters. It was only when he returned from the battle that he heard the awful news. But Krishna was right. No one should lament the death of a hero in battle. It was an end that all kshatriyas longed to achieve.

"Take heart, Arjuna, for there is something you must now do," Krishna continued. "You must go to Duryodhana and call in the favor he owes you."

Arjuna widened his eyes in surprise. Go to Duryodhana? He remembered well enough the time when the Kaurava had promised him a boon. It had been when Arjuna had rescued him from the Gandharvas. Disheveled and humiliated, Duryodhana had tried to salvage his pride by saying he would later return the favor, when Arjuna was himself in need. Krishna must have decided the time had come. Arjuna was curious. "I will do whatever you say, O Krishna. Tell me what I should ask from him."

Krishna told Arjuna about the five arrows. "Go at once and ask Duryodhana to give them to you."

Arjuna stood up and left immediately. Alone and unarmed, without any fear that he would be assailed, Arjuna entered the Kaurava camp. By night, the warriors would often come together as friends, and the guards greeted Arjuna respectfully, taking him through the rows of torchlit tents, straight to Duryodhana's quarters in their midst.

The Kaurava prince sat up in surprise as Arjuna entered. "Welcome, O hero. What brings you here at such a late hour?"

Arjuna reminded him about the favor he was owed. "I have come for that now, O king. Please give to me the five arrows you took from Bhishma today."

Shocked, but bound by his word and thus unable to refuse, Duryodhana reached down and lifted the arrows. Placing them across his outstretched palms, he offered them to Arjuna. "How did you know?" he asked.

"The all-knowing Krishna informed me," Arjuna replied, taking the arrows. He then took his leave from the bemused Duryodhana and made his way back to his own camp. The Kaurava was left sitting on his bed, shaking his head. Krishna was a cunning opponent. Was he really the Supreme? How else could he have known about the arrows? But still, he seemed so human. If he was God, he could surely end the war in a moment, having the earth open up and swallow all the Kauravas. It did not make any sense. Duryodhana lay down again and stared at the now empty cloth where the arrows had lain. How would Bhishma keep his promise now?

*   *   *

The next morning, when Bhishma heard how Arjuna had taken the arrows after being sent by Krishna, he smiled wryly. It was not a surprise. Krishna would always find some way to save his followers. Gazing across at the Pandavas' array, Bhishma pulled on his leather finger protectors. "Krishna has made my promise false, for I cannot imbue another five arrows with the same power. However, I will still fight to my utter limit. I will target Arjuna alone. If Krishna does not give up his own promise not to fight, he will see his beloved friend slain today."

Seeing Bhishma's grim determination as he rode out for battle, Duryodhana's hopes rose. Even if Arjuna alone was killed, the Pandavas would be finished. But Bhishma would need to overcome his affection for Arjuna. Duryodhana thought again of the Danavas. Let them possess Bhishma now. Let them charge him with all their demonic fury. Shouting out his battle cry, Duryodhana began ordering the leading Kuru warriors into positions where they could guard Bhishma as he fought.

The two armies closed again for the ninth day of battle. Shrieking birds of prey flew above the armies as they charged. The sky seemed ablaze, a strong wind blew, and a shower of stones rained down. The horses and other animals shed tears and stumbled as they ran. Everything portended a terrible massacre, but the warriors rushed, unflinching, into the fight. They fell upon one another with shouts and roars, thrusting and hacking remorselessly with their long swords and daggers. The sky was filled with wave after wave of arrows. Countless spears sped through the air like silver- and gold-winged serpents.

True to his word, Bhishma began a great slaughter of men. He resembled personified Death bent upon destroying all beings. Arrows flew from his bow in unending lines. Bearing down upon Arjuna, he swept aside the warriors in his path. Before the sun had reached the meridian, he had slain ten thousand chariot fighters. They lay about the field with their armors, standards, and chariots lying around them, shattered.

Seeing the carnage caused by Bhishma, Krishna said to Arjuna, "O Partha, the time has come to face Bhishma. Remembering your duties, do not hesitate. Slay him now, before he destroys your army."

Arjuna, who himself had been smashing apart the Kaurava forces, felt heavy with sorrow. He looked across at Bhishma. "A warrior's duty is a burden indeed, O Krishna. Killing even those who should never be killed, he relentlessly seeks wealth and honor. Still, my highest duty is to please you, O Lord. Take me, then, to the grandfather. I will slay him."

Krishna urged on Arjuna's celestial steeds, and the chariot wheeled around to face Bhishma. Seeing him heading for an encounter with the Kuru commander, the afflicted Pandava troops sent up a cheer. Bhishma yelled out his battle cry and immediately shot a hundred shafts at Arjuna. But Krishna dexterously maneuvered the chariot away from the arrows. Arjuna shot a crescent-headed shaft that cut Bhishma's bow in two. He immediately strung another, but in an instant, Arjuna had sundered that one also. Bhishma called out to him in admiration, "Excellent! Well done!"

Bhishma's charioteer swung his chariot around, and the Kuru hero strung a third bow and began to assail Arjuna with countless shafts. Covered with a blanket of arrows, Arjuna was struck all over, and he reeled under the force of Bhishma's attack. Many arrows also pierced Krishna, and he bled from his wounds, like a dark mountain giving forth a stream of red oxides.

Simultaneously as he attacked Arjuna, Bhishma maintained a steady assault on the Pandava army. His long steel shafts sped in all directions. They passed clean through the bodies of warriors, horses, and elephants. Laughing loudly, Bhishma spun around in his chariot, his bow constantly bent into a circle. He resembled the Destroyer himself. Wailing soldiers fled in all directions, terrified for their lives.

Arjuna found himself unable to exert himself to his full power. He countered Bhishma's attack only half-heartedly. Seeing this, Krishna felt anxious. If Bhishma were not checked, he would slaughter everyone on the field. He was seized by a demonic rage. By employing celestial weapons, he released a countless number of death-dealing shafts. They flew indiscriminately across the field, mowing down everyone in their path. A constant stream of them shot toward Arjuna. Krishna became thoughtful. It was obvious that Arjuna was unable to overcome his affection and respect for Bhishma. The Kuru warrior was sorely afflicting him. Arjuna lamely resisted and was therefore threatened with imminent death. Krishna decided he had to act himself to stop Bhishma.

Krishna threw down the reins of Arjuna's chariot and leapt down. He took up a nearby chariot wheel and raised it above his head, as if it were his favorite weapon, the Sudarshan chakra. He began to run toward Bhishma as a lion might run at an elephant. His yellow silk garment fluttered in the dusty air like lightning dancing in a thundercloud. Krishna's bodily effulgence lent luster to the wheel, and it glowed like the primeval lotus that gave birth to Brahma. His dark arm was like the lotus stalk, and his beautiful face, shining with beads of perspiration, was like its filament covered with dew.

Struck with transcendent emotion on seeing this wondrous sight, Bhishma lowered his weapons. His limbs trembled and tears flowed from his eyes. The Lord of all the worlds was breaking his promise to protect his beloved friend. Bhishma called out to him, "O Supreme One, I bow to you. Strike me down at once. Killed by you, I will obtain the greatest good fortune. My fame will be celebrated forever."

Arjuna was aghast. It was his fault that Krishna was apparently forsaking his vow. The Lord had not taken up any weapon, but he had nevertheless entered the fray. Foolish men would no doubt condemn him for his seeming falsity. Arjuna could not have that on his conscience. He had to rectify his omission in not giving his all to the fight with Bhishma. Jumping from his chariot, he ran after Krishna.

Coming close to Bhishma, Krishna furiously shouted out, "You are the root of this great slaughter of men. A wise minister should check a wicked king by any means. If words fail, then force should be used."

As Krishna addressed Bhishma, Arjuna caught up to him. He hurled himself forward and caught hold of Krishna's legs. Krishna continued running, with Arjuna clinging onto him.

Still seized with wonder and love for Krishna, Bhishma answered, "You always speak the truth, O Lord. What can I say? Surely destiny is all-powerful."

Dragged by Krishna, Arjuna dug his feet into the earth. Krishna gradually slowed and finally came to a stop after taking ten steps with Arjuna. The Pandava implored him. "O Lord, stop! Do not break your promise. I swear by my sons and brothers that I shall fight to my full strength. You will see me do battle as never before."

Krishna lowered the chariot wheel, still glaring angrily at Bhishma. Throwing the wheel aside, he then turned and walked back to his chariot with Arjuna. At that moment, the sun reached the western horizon and hostilities were ended for the day. The warriors on both sides withdrew, marveling at the wonderful incident between Krishna and Bhishma. The Kuru warrior himself thought only of Krishna. The image of him running in anger with the upheld wheel was forever imprinted upon Bhishma's heart.

*   *   *

As the Pandavas returned to their camp, Yudhishthira felt intense anxiety. Bhishma was obliterating his forces. He would have slain even Arjuna if Krishna had not intervened. The terrible Kuru fighter had clearly left behind all his affectionate feelings for the Pandavas. If he was not soon checked, their defeat seemed certain.

After the five brothers and their allies had taken their seats in Yudhishthira's tent, he consulted with Krishna. "O Keshava, what can we do about Bhishma? We can hardly even look at him as he stands with upraised weapons. Not even the most powerful gods could face him. In confronting him, we are like insects rushing into a blazing fire."

Yudhishthira hung down his head. He had no heart to carry on with the war. But Krishna encouraged him. "Throw off this grief, O king. You have warriors even greater than the gods on your side. If Bhishma worries you, then fear not; I shall personally kill him. Riding out on a single chariot, I will end his life myself."

Krishna declared his love for Yudhishthira and his brothers. Gazing at them with affection, he said, "Whoever is inimical to you may consider me an enemy. Arjuna is my friend, relative, and disciple. For his sake, I would cut off and give away my own flesh. He, too, would give up his life for my sake."

Yudhishthira was moved by Krishna's words, but he argued, "It cannot be you who slays him, Lord. Your promise should not be falsified, as it almost was today."

Yudhishthira recalled Bhishma's words to him at the start of the battle. "I think Bhishma himself will tell us how he can be defeated. Let us go to him and ask."

As he contemplated Bhishma's death, Yudhishthira felt a wave of grief. He let out a sob. "Alas, how vile is a warrior's duty! We must now seek to slay he who became our father when we were fatherless children. He who has always sought our good—even he must be killed by us now."

Krishna gently consoled the distraught Yudhishthira. Becoming more firm, he said, "Take heart, O king. Bhishma has chosen to follow Duryodhana, thereby ensuring his death in this war. You are right. We must go to him and ask him how he can be killed. That noble hero will certainly tell us."

Krishna suggested that all five brothers go, along with himself. They all took off their armor and went at once to the Kauravas' camp. Bhishma's face lit up with joy as they entered his tent. He waved toward the ornate seats arranged around him on fine silk rugs. "Welcome, all of you. Please be seated. What do wish from me? Consider it done, even if it is extremely hard to accomplish.

Yudhishthira stood before him with folded palms. Gazing at Bhishma's old face, which smiled back at him with obvious affection, the Pandava felt his throat choke up. He was unable to speak for some moments. Krishna placed a hand on his shoulder to encourage him. Taking a deep breath, Yudhishthira knelt before Bhishma and inquired, "O mighty hero, how can we vanquish you? I asked you this before, and you told me to come again. Please tell me then, O greatly wise man, the means to defeat you in battle. It seems to us that you are utterly invincible."

Bhishma nodded slowly. As he looked down at Yudhishthira, he felt his heart move. Pandu's virtuous sons were surely undeserving of any suffering. It could only be by some supreme arrangement of the Lord that they were being subjected to so much misery. The old Kuru felt it to be a cruel twist of fate that he had to be an instrument of that suffering. Glancing across at Krishna, who had seated himself nearby, he replied to Yudhishthira, "You are correct, O king. As long as I stand with weapons raised, you will never achieve victory. Only when I lower my weapons am I approachable. Listen, then, to my vow. I will never raise my weapons against the weaponless, the helpless, the frightened, the surrendered, or a female."

Bhishma then specifically referred to Shikandhi, saying that he would cause his downfall. "This one was formerly a woman and bears undying hatred for me. I will not strike him, even if he attacks me. Therefore, place him in the forefront of the battle, assisted by Arjuna, and assail me with all your power. This is your only chance."

Yudhishthira thanked Bhishma and got to his feet. The others also rose, and Bhishma rose with them. Bidding each other fond farewells, they parted company, and the Pandavas headed back to their camp. They rode silently through the darkness, dreading in their hearts the arrival of the following day, when Bhishma would be slain.

Twenty-six

Two Generals Fall

A S THE SUN rose on the tenth day of battle, the clamor of countless conchshells, drums, and trumpets again filled the air. The two armies arrayed themselves for battle and then rushed at each other with loud shouts. Duryodhana, aware that the Pandavas would target Bhishma, had ordered many of the foremost Kauravas to protect him. Bhishma realized that this might be his final day in battle, and he began to exert himself for one last, supreme effort. Once more, he began a vast slaughter, his arrows flying out in great showers. Defying his advanced age, he fought as if he were a youth. He wheeled about on the terrace of his chariot with his bow constantly twanging. The beleaguered Pandava forces felt there were dozens of Bhishmas fighting them, and they scattered in fear.

Seeing the destruction of his forces, Dhrishtadyumna detailed a number of Pandava heroes to engage with Bhishma's escort. Arjuna then began to advance toward Bhishma, accompanied by Shikhandhi. As they came within range of the Kuru grandfather, the powerful Shikhandhi, remembering his former life and enmity with Bhishma, roared out an angry challenge and fired a dozen fierce shafts at him. They struck Bhishma on his arms and chest, piercing through his armor. Bhishma, although angered, only smiled and called out, "O Shikhandhi, I will not fight you. The great creator made you a woman, and even now, I accept you as such."

Shikhandhi was infuriated. Determined to make Bhishma retaliate, he released another volley of arrows and called back, "I care not for your words—they simply hide your cowardice! Stay and fight with me now. You will not escape with your life."

But Bhishma turned away from him and attacked the warriors surrounding him. Invoking celestial missiles, he massacred them by the thousands. Numerous Kauravas came forward to protect him from attack. Arjuna met them and began cutting them down with arrows shot from the Gandiva. Many of the principal warriors from both sides entered the fray.

Ferocious duels took place on different parts of the field. At the same time, Bhishma and Arjuna maintained a huge slaughter of troops. Keeping Shikhandhi close by, Arjuna relentlessly bore down on Bhishma. Great Kaurava heroes came before him, one after another, but Arjuna beat them back.

A vast horde of barbarian fighters, clad in animal skins and clutching bludgeons and spears, then rushed at Arjuna. Mounted on wild horses, they came at him from all sides. Their spears and spiked arrows rained down in thousands. Krishna wheeled the chariot around and pulled it clear of the attack. Arjuna then invoked a mystical weapon that sent sheets of razor-headed shafts at his assailants. Cut to pieces, they dropped down with terrible cries, covering the field with their bloodied corpses.

Arjuna rode around his slain foes and kept driving toward Bhishma. The Kuru grandfather was protected by Duryodhana, Kripa, Shalya, and a number of Dhritarashtra's other sons. Arjuna's four brothers came up to engage them, leaving the way clear for Arjuna to attack Bhishma. The two great heroes then met like a pair of enraged lions. They covered each other with clouds of arrows. Each invoked celestial weapons, which the other neutralized with his own. Both warriors put aside all feelings of affection and fought to their full power. They praised each other's prowess as they contended remorselessly, looking for even the slightest weakness in the other. But neither could find any gaps in his opponent's defenses.

Thousands of warriors closed on Shikhandhi, trying to keep him away from Bhishma. Drupada's valiant son pressed on without the least fear. He carved a path through the Kauravas, his gaze fixed on Bhishma.

Bhishma seemed to be sporting as he battled Arjuna. At the same time, he trained his arrows on the surrounding Pandava forces. They fell in hundreds and thousands as the Kuru warrior released his unstoppable shafts. But thousands more warriors kept coming at him. Like clouds covering the sun, they surrounded his chariot. They rained down arrows, spears, battle-axes, spiked maces, darts, bludgeons, and steel javelins.

Hard-pressed under the assault, Bhishma smiled. He wished only for a hero's end. His armor was shattered, and blood flowed from his numerous wounds. Oblivious to the pain, he fought on, slaying hundreds of his attackers. Arjuna marveled how, even under such a fierce attack, the Kuru chief was a formidable foe. He continuously spun around in his chariot, covering himself from every side. Arjuna fired numberless shafts, but Bhishma cut them down again and again.

As Shikhandhi came up to his side, Arjuna sensed that Bhishma's end was near. Placing Shikhandhi in front of him, he closed on Bhishma. With a perfectly aimed arrow, he cut Bhishma's bow in two. Both Arjuna and Shikhandhi released keen-pointed shafts that deeply pierced the Kuru hero. They killed his charioteer and horses, bringing him to a halt on the battlefield. With a crescent-headed arrow, Arjuna cut down his tall standard.

Bhishma immediately took up another bow, worked with gold, but Arjuna shattered it as well. Bhishma hurled a great lance at Arjuna, but the Pandava cut it to pieces with five swift arrows. Seeing Arjuna thwarting all his weapons, Bhishma became resigned to his fate. It was the end. He looked with love at Krishna, who was dexterously guiding Arjuna's horses. What use was there in trying to overcome such a power? That was something Duryodhana should have realized a long time ago.

Resolving to go down fighting, Bhishma launched himself into one last effort. He spun around in his chariot, lifting and stringing another bow in a matter of seconds. He shot a volley of arrows at both Arjuna and Shikhandhi. They replied with dozens of short-range shafts that pierced Bhishma's powerful frame, like snakes entering their holes in a mountain. Bhishma was stunned, and he reeled back on the terrace of his chariot. Although struck by the arrows of both his assailants, he considered that only Arjuna's shafts were capable of bringing him down. He rallied himself and stood to face the attack with his bow drawn to a full circle. But when he saw that Shikhandhi had come directly in front of him, he lowered his bow.

Arjuna immediately took his opportunity. He fired razor-sharp arrows that left the Gandiva in a continuous line. Bhishma was pierced in every part of his body. Finally, overcome by Arjuna's unrelenting assault, he toppled from his chariot. Before the Kauravas' shocked eyes, he dropped to the earth, like a mountain cleft by a thunderbolt. He lay on the ground, fully supported by the arrows protruding from his body. Staying alive by his own will, he determined to wait till the sun reached its auspicious northern course before leaving his body.

The Kauravas were utterly confounded. They dropped their weapons and ran about in confusion. As the sun set, they fell to the ground and wailed. Some of them swooned, and others stood as if frozen to the spot. Hearing the terrible news from Duryodhana, Drona dropped from his chariot in a faint. When he came around, he ordered the Kauravas to withdraw, and they made their sorrowful way back to their camp.

The Pandava forces blew conches and danced on the battlefield in delight. At last, their scourge had been brought down. But Arjuna was deeply saddened. Along with his brothers, he approached Bhishma and asked if there was anything the old Kuru desired. Bhishma told them not to grieve for him. He had achieved an end desired by all heroic warriors. By his father's boon, he was able to remain alive. When the sun moved to the north, he would quit his body and attain the higher planets.

Praising him, the Pandavas walked around the fallen hero in respect and then, as Bhishma entered a state of yogic meditation, they headed back to their camp. They felt their victory could not now be far away.

*   *   *

Hearing of Bhishma's fall, Dhritarashtra was inconsolable. For a long time he wept. Consumed by remorse, he fell from his throne and tossed about on the marble floor of his chamber. "Is my heart made of stone that it does not shatter upon hearing this news?" The king's loud lamentations echoed throughout the palace.

In the Kaurava camp, there was total despair. Even Karna cried out loud when he heard of Bhishma's fall. Despite his frequent strong words toward him, Karna could not deny Bhishma's nobility and power. He knew also that the Kuru grandfather had spoken only with his best interests in mind. But now he had fallen. Karna looked toward his weapons. His time had come.

As the sun rose on the eleventh day of battle, the Kauravas installed Drona as their new commander. Seeing the martial preceptor leading out his forces, Duryodhana felt renewed hope. The battle raged on again with full force. The great heroes on both sides continued to create carnage among the armies. Countless men were sent to Death's abode. Many lay on the field, laughing as their lifeblood ebbed away and they approached the heavens. Drona, Karna, Kripa, and Ashvatthama headed the Kauravas' attack, and they tore into the Pandava divisions, while Bhima, Arjuna, and other mighty warriors among the Pandavas smashed through the Kaurava ranks.

With the loss of Bhishma, the Kuru forces were dispirited and they began to succumb to their mighty foes. Duryodhana became increasingly frantic. He begged Drona to find some means to overcome the Pandavas. "Even if all the brothers cannot be slain—and I have come to accept this— then, at least, try to capture Yudhishthira. Or slay some other great hero among his forces."

Drona then spread the Kauravas out in a great, impenetrable array, hoping to surround and capture Yudhishthira. But his plan was thwarted when Arjuna's son Abhimanyu broke through the formation, leaving a trail of destruction right through the heart of the Kuru army. The sixteen-year-old warrior was as powerful as his father, and the Kauravas had no answer to his attack. At last, in sheer desperation, they broke the rules of battle. Six of the Kauravas' mightiest fighters closed in on Abhimanyu. Simultaneously attacking him from all sides, even when he was without his chariot and weapons, they eventually managed to bring him down. Finally, Dushasana's son slew him with a great blow from his mace.

At that time, Arjuna had again been strategically removed from the main battle by Drona's arrangement. The other four Pandavas had been held back by Jayadratha, who was strengthened by virtue of the boon he had acquired from Shiva. Arjuna was devastated when he discovered that his son had been so mercilessly and unfairly killed. Wild with fury, he made a terrible vow to kill Jayadratha. "It is his fault that my son now lies dead. Had my brothers reached the boy, he would surely have been saved. For this mean and despicable act, the Sindhu ruler will pay with his life. Whoever tries to stop me will proceed with Jayadratha to Death's kingdom. If I do not kill him before sunset tomorrow, I will enter fire and give up my own life."

Hearing of Arjuna's vow, Duryodhana arranged for Jayadratha to be protected by his whole army. There followed an astonishing fight, during which Arjuna single-handedly wiped out a quarter of the remaining Kauravas. With Krishna's divine assistance, he broke through their army and reached Jayadratha. When, at last, Arjuna approached the Sindhu monarch, Krishna created an illusion of sunset just before the sun had actually reached the horizon. The mighty Kuru warriors surrounding Jayadratha thus lowered their weapons with great cheers, believing that Arjuna had failed. Krishna then withdrew his illusion. In the ensuing confusion, Arjuna slew the Sindhu monarch, even as Duryodhana and his best fighters looked on.

At the end of the day, a greatly relieved Yudhishthira embraced Krishna, tears flowing from his eyes. "O Govinda, all things are possible for those whom you favor. Our enemies are drowned in a sea of grief, and we are delivered from a fearful danger."

Among the Kauravas, there was only increasing despair. After thirteen days of fighting, their army had been reduced from eleven great divisions to three. Millions of men had been killed. Still, Duryodhana would not relent. He blamed Drona for Arjuna's success in killing Jayadratha. "Surely you are being soft on our enemies. It is my fault. I should have known better. Blinded by my greed for wealth, I trusted you, even though I knew of your love for the Pandavas."

Drona had heard such reproaches repeatedly from the desperate Kaurava prince. He sighed wearily. Pulling off his long gloves, he bared his sinewy arms, which were covered with wounds. As the physicians began

tending them, he said, "What point is there in piercing me with barbed and
sarcastic words, O king? I have told you again and again that no one can kill
Arjuna. After seeing even Bhishma brought down, I am convinced that we
are doomed. The dice that Shakuni threw against the Pandavas are returning now as blazing arrows. You were warned so many times. How did you
expect your heinous sin in insulting Draupadi to go unpunished?"

Drona looked with pity at the miserable Duryodhana. Half of his brothers had been slain by Bhima. Why was he so obstinate? The old martial
teacher knew that the fight would only end with Duryodhana's death, even
if he were the last man standing. Drona stood up to leave for his quarters.
In his burnished gold armor, he shone like the sun. Encouraging the gloomy
Duryodhana, he said, "I cannot abandon my duty, loathsome though it may
be. Tomorrow you will see me give everything to the fight. With weapons
ablaze, I shall stand at the head of your army one more time. Hear my vow:
Until the remaining Pandava forces are slain, I shall not remove my armor."

Duryodhana felt cheered. There was still hope. The Pandavas' divisions had also been decimated. The two armies were still roughly equal. If
Drona was determined, victory could surely be achieved, especially if Karna
fulfilled his vow to kill Arjuna. Duryodhana looked over at his friend. "O
great hero, I think it is time for you also to display your full prowess. You still
have Indra's infallible weapon. Use it to bring down Arjuna, and victory will
be ours."

Karna was circumspect. Having seen the incredible way that Arjuna
had fought past the whole Kaurava army, he wondered if Drona's assessment
of the Pandava might be right. Perhaps it really was impossible to slay
Arjuna. . Certainly, with Krishna by his side, he was a highly formidable
opponent. So far, Krishna had managed to keep him clear of Karna and his
deadly Shakti weapon. But sooner or later they would meet. What would
Krishna do then? Indra had said that the Shakti would not fail, and the
gods' words were always truth. Indeed, if Krishna really was the Supreme
God, then it was he who made good the gods' oaths.

"I will do all that a friend can do," Karna said, looking across at Indra's
glowing weapon, which he had respectfully worshipped each day since
receiving it from the deity. "I shall spare no effort. In my view, though, destiny is supreme. Despite our vast army, filled with invincible warriors, we
have not yet been successful. We have tried everything against the
Pandavas. Still, those steadfast heroes stand against us, full of vigor and
power. This is all due to our adverse destiny. Let us see, then, what fate
decrees for us tomorrow. I shall train the Shakti on Arjuna as soon as
possible."

But throughout the fourteenth day of battle, Karna again found no opportunity to approach his mortal enemy. Many other Pandava warriors kept him engaged. Terrific duels took place between the heroes on both sides. Bhima bore down on Dhritarashtra's remaining sons like Yamaraja himself. Before Duryodhana's horrified eyes, he picked them off, one by one. He ranged among the Kauravas like a furious tempest. His mace could hardly be seen as it whirled around him. Men, horses, and chariots flew through the air. Terrified, the Kaurava soldiers ran screaming from the field. No two men were seen running together as they fled from the frenzied Bhima. "This one is not human!" they cried, as Bhima laughed almost insanely.

Elsewhere, a frightening battle took place between Ghatotkacha and Ashvatthama. Both were past masters in the use of mystical weapons. Bhima's son conjured innumerable illusions on the battlefield, making hordes of terrible-looking Rakshasas appear. He fought from the sky and assumed many different forms. At one point, he appeared like a towering mountain, with a fountain at its summit that incessantly showered spears, darts, swords, and blazing arrows. The Kauravas were hacked to pieces. They cried out to Drona's son for protection. Ashvatthama fearlessly countered Ghatotkacha's attack. Invoking celestial weapons, he managed to beat back the huge Rakshasa and destroy much of his force.

Karna constantly sought an opportunity to encounter Arjuna, simultaneously wreaking havoc among the Pandava army. With both conventional and celestial weapons, he slew thousands of men. Becoming totally enraged, Bhima finally put him to flight after a mighty battle. But Karna regrouped and came again to the fray. Encountering Bhima once more, he engaged in another great fight. Honoring Arjuna's vow, Bhima did not wish to kill him, and he eventually decided to leave the fight. Karna pursued him, but he, too, remembered his promise to Kunti and thus made no attempt to kill Bhima. From his chariot, he derided the Pandava, who was on foot, and hit him with the end of his bow. "Why do you flee, O weak and impotent fool? Your prowess lies only in eating. The battlefield is no place for a boy like you. Run quickly to Arjuna and Krishna. Seek their protection."

Bhima seethed but held himself back. Karna would soon meet his destined end. The Pandava wrung his hands together in fury. He watched silently as Karna moved off into the thick of the battle. Arjuna was not far away; it would not be long now. Turning back to the fight, Bhima set his mind on destroying Dhritarashtra's remaining sons.

In separate encounters with the twins, Karna again managed to somehow gain the upper hand, but on both occasions he honored his promise to Kunti. He even managed to overpower Yudhishthira after meeting him in fierce single combat, but still did not press home his advantage. There was only one Pandava he wanted to slay. He glanced again and again at the Shakti missile.

The sun set, but the battle raged on. Three-quarters of the warriors on both sides had been slain. It was obvious that the war would soon be over. Darkness fell with both sides frantically seeking victory by the light of thousands of torches. Waves of flaming arrows lit up the sky, revealing ghastly scenes below. Wrecked chariots were ablaze everywhere, and they silhouetted the dark forms of countless warriors locked in deadly combat. The stench of blood filled the air, along with the battle cries and screams of the warriors and the clash of weapons.

Seeing Karna plowing through the Pandava forces, Krishna said to Arjuna, "It seems that Karna is intent upon destroying our whole army. Someone has to stop him. But I feel you should wait. He still has the Shakti weapon. Lo, there in the distance is Ghatotkacha. Order him to face Karna. It is night now, and the Rakshasa's power will be doubled. Other than you, he may be the only one who can check Karna."

Arjuna looked toward Ghatotkacha's immense chariot, drawn by a hundred demonic beasts. Having recovered from his defeat at Ashvatthama's hands, Bhima's son was returning to the battle. He was accompanied by ten thousand huge-bodied Rakshasas, whom he had summoned from the nether regions. When he heard Arjuna's request, he smiled and turned toward Karna. Roaring out his awful war cry, he shot a hundred steel-pointed shafts at him, and a fearful battle ensued between the two great warriors.

The fight raged on for a long time. Despite employing all his skills and power, Karna could not gain the upper hand. Ghatotkacha fought with unrestrained fury. Remembering Karna's viciousness toward his father and uncles, the Rakshasa fixed his mind on killing him. Karna was forced back. His horses and charioteer were slain, and he stood in his immobile chariot, trying to fend off the Rakshasa's relentless assault. Observing the battle, Duryodhana began fearing for Karna's life. Ghatotkacha was impervious to all of Karna's weapons, even his most powerful celestial missiles.

When the Rakshasa at last leapt from his chariot and rushed at Karna with his scimitar raised high, the horrified Duryodhana called out, "Use the Shakti, Karna! It is your only chance."

Karna knew his friend was right. The demon would almost certainly slay him if he did not stop him. What use would the Shakti be against Arjuna then? Karna snatched the weapon from its golden case. Uttering the mantras, he placed it on his bow and immediately fired it at the onrushing

Rakshasa. The weapon flew like a fireball at Ghatotkacha. He saw it coming and quickly expanded himself to a vast size. The missile struck him on the chest and passed through his body. With a shout that reverberated around the entire battlefield, Ghatotkacha died. His massive body dropped to the ground, killing thousands of Kauravas.

The Pandavas cried out in dismay. But Krishna began to laugh and clap his hands. Arjuna looked at him in surprise. "Why this display of levity at such a terrible moment, O Keshava?"

Krishna replied, "Now that Karna has discharged the Shakti, you may consider him slain and the Kauravas defeated. Ever since I heard he had received that weapon from Indra, I felt anxious, because your life was in dire danger. Now my fear has gone. Karna has lost both his natural armor and his deadliest weapon. The weapon has returned to Indra and cannot be used again. Now he is like an infuriated serpent, filled with venom but stupefied by incantations." Arjuna remembered that it had been Krishna who had suggested that Ghatotkacha confront Karna. The Pandava realized that, yet again, he was alive only due to Krishna's protection. There was no doubt that, without Krishna's assistance, the war would have ended by now—but not with a Pandava victory.

Having fought well into the night, the warriors on both sides were grateful when Arjuna suggested they rest until sunrise the next day. The lay down on the battlefield wherever they had been fighting. A bright moon rose in the clear sky, illuminating scenes of destruction everywhere. With all the surviving men and animals sunk in sleep, it appeared as if both armies had been utterly destroyed. But as the sun rose on the fifteenth day, they gradually stirred and took up their positions to continue the battle.

True to his word, Drona ranged about the field causing complete chaos among the Pandava army. In great battles, he slew both Virata and Drupada. When he saw his father killed, Dhrishtadyumna was consumed by grief and anger. The Panchala prince thought only of his destiny to be Drona's slayer. He went after the Kuru preceptor, determined to take his life. But Drona resisted all of his attacks. He held off even Arjuna, as the Pandava released upon him every celestial weapon in his arsenal. At the same time, he carried on slaughtering the Pandava forces in the tens of thousands.

Witnessing Drona's power, Yudhishthira began to despair. He consulted with Bhima and Arjuna. "Drona will finish our whole army. How can he be checked?"

Krishna looked grave. He replied to Yudhishthira, "This is the truth, O king. Drona can scorch us by his mere glance. But he has already given us the clue how he may be stopped. He must lower his weapons, and this he will do after hearing some highly disagreeable news. I think if he hears that his son, Ashvatthama, is killed, he will desist from the fight."

Arjuna's turned sharply toward Krishna. "I cannot accept this, O Keshava. How can we deceive the noble preceptor in such a way?"

Bhima, however, liked the idea. He ran at once into an elephant division and slew a beast that he knew shared the same name as Drona's son. The Pandava then raced over to Drona and repeatedly called out, "Ashvatthama is slain!"

Drona lowered his bow. He stared at Bhima. Could his words be true? The preceptor found them hard to accept. Ashvatthama, with his brahminical power and vast martial knowledge, was virtually invincible. Bhima was known to be capricious. He could easily speak a falsehood in anger or jest. Drona did not want to believe him. He lifted his bow again and continued to fight.

Seeing this, Krishna exhorted Yudhishthira to go to Drona and confirm Bhima's report. "Save us from Drona, O king. In this case, untruth is certainly better than truth. Speaking falsehood in order to preserve life is not sinful."

Yudhishthira was hesitant. In his entire life, he had never uttered even an ambiguity. Yet, here was Krishna telling him to speak a direct lie. Krishna's direction had to be followed. It was the only way to prevent Drona from destroying the entire Pandava force. Reluctantly, Yudhishthira went over to Drona and called out, "Ashvatthama is dead!" adding inaudibly, "the elephant."

Hearing those words from Yudhishthira, Drona felt as if his heart had dissolved. It had to be true. Yudhishthira could never tell a lie. Drona's arms fell limply to his sides. He called out to Duryodhana, "O king, I am laying down my weapons. This world and all its wealth no longer hold any attraction for me. Fight with all your power, for I shall now depart."

Distracted by grief, Drona sat down in his chariot and wept. He closed his eyes and gradually calmed himself. Entering into a mystical trance, he left his body through yogic power and ascended to the higher worlds.

Dhrishtadyumna had been contending with Drona. When he saw him seated in meditation, Drupada's son leapt down from his chariot, clasping a long sword. He rushed over to Drona's chariot and lopped off his head with a sweeping blow. Roaring in joy, he picked up the head and threw it toward the Kauravas.

Duryodhana was mortified. Along with all his generals and men, he fled from the cheering Pandavas. Yudhishthira looked with mixed feelings at the body of his old teacher. With him slain, the Kauravas must surely give up all hope. But it had taken deceit to finally bring him down. That thought hurt Yudhishthira—especially that it had been he who had told the lie. Nevertheless, the Kauravas had been the first ones to use unfair means when they slew Abhimanyu. They should expect no less in return, as had been agreed at the outset. And following Krishna's direction could never be sinful.

Seeing that the sun had set, Yudhishthira ordered his troops to withdraw, and the two armies again retired for the night.

Twenty-seven

A FITTING END

URYODHANA SLEPT ONLY fitfully on the fifteenth night. He tossed and turned, his mind wracked with anxiety. What was happening? First Bhishma and now Drona—two warriors whom even the celestials could not have brought down. Even though they fought with all their power—and perhaps also were inspired by the Danavas—still the Pandavas had overcome them. What force did those five brothers have on their side? How would they ever be defeated? Surely, it had been a mistake to antagonize them, but at this point, there was no turning back. When so many great heroes had been slain for his sake, he could hardly abandon the fight now. Death or victory were the only choices. And all was not yet lost. There was still Karna. In the morning, he could take command of the remaining Kauravas. Perhaps, with a last great effort, he would kill Arjuna.

As the sun rose on the sixteenth day, the two armies once again arrayed themselves for battle. Having installed Karna as their leader, the Kauravas roared out their battle cries and charged at the Pandavas. They were met by their unflinching foes, and a savage battle was soon underway again.

Fired by his position as commander, Karna fought as never before. He careered into the Pandava army, sending blazing arrows in all directions. Soldiers, horsemen, charioteers, and elephant fighters were ruthlessly cut to ribbons. Ashvatthama, who burned with a desire to avenge his father's cruel death, supported him.

Arjuna engaged with the last of the Samshaptaka and Narayana armies, with whom he had been contending throughout the war. Still observing the rules of fair combat, he did not employ the terrible weapons of the gods. However, this was his only restraint. The Pandava fought without mercy. Seeking to end the war, he slaughtered his foes with waves of searing shafts fired from the Gandiva.

Bhima continued to slay Dhritarashtra's sons, one after another. Relentlessly, the two armies ground each other down. By noon on the seventeenth day, less than half a million men were left from the original six million.

When Arjuna had at last overcome the immense armies that the Kauravas had deployed against him, Krishna urged him to confront Karna. "Strike down this wicked-minded fool. Frustrate Duryodhana's hopes and end the war. How can Karna live after meeting you with the Gandiva in hand?"

Krishna's words stirred Arjuna. He was ready for the fight. Just ahead of him, he could see Karna's tall standard cutting through the Pandava army. Arjuna scowled and took a firm grasp on his bow. As Krishna urged on his steeds, he began mowing down all the troops that were in his way.

Seeing Arjuna advancing toward their general, a number of Kaurava heroes rushed against him. Kripa, Kritavarman, and half a dozen of Duryodhana's brothers all attacked him at once. But Arjuna was in no mood to be checked. He furiously beat back his assailants. Rows of chariot fighters charged him and were struck down by volleys of straight-flying shafts. Huge elephants rocked toward him, and they, too, were butchered by Arjuna's deadly arrows.

Karna saw his adversary from a distance. He knew the time for their final confrontation had arrived. One of them would not return from this fight. Karna gazed respectfully at his indomitable enemy. Driving Arjuna's chariot through the ranks of bejeweled warriors, Krishna resembled a dark cloud in the star-studded firmament. Behind him, Arjuna looked like second cloud, sending forth streaks of lightning as he fired his arrows. Karna spoke to his charioteer, "Take me toward Partha. His time has come, as well as that of Krishna. I will soon slay those two warriors-and then the entire Pandava force."

Duryodhana saw his friend advancing toward Arjuna. He quickly detailed all the most powerful Kauravas to support Karna. They rushed in a body at Arjuna and were met with swift arrows that struck them on every part of their bodies. Bhima came up to join his brother and was assailed by Duryodhana's twenty remaining brothers. At their head was Dushasana. Seeing that evil-minded prince, Bhima licked his lips and smiled. Dushasana roared in anger and shot at Bhima a brilliant arrow worked with gems and gold. It hit the Pandava full on the chest, with a sound like thunder. Bhima was stunned, and he dropped to his knees in his chariot, clinging on to his standard pole for support.

The Kauravas rained down arrows and other weapons on the stricken Bhima. Thinking their mortal foe to be slain, they cheered. But Bhima soon regained his senses and stood again for battle. He glared at Dushasana and shouted, "Strike me while you still can, O wretch! Soon you will lay down your life. I long to drink your blood. Feel now the force of my mace!"

Bhima's chariot swung toward the prince, who frantically discharged numerous arrows at him. Bhima beat down all the arrows with his whirling mace. Leaping from his chariot, he charged at Dushasana. The prince hurled a blazing dart at him with all his strength, but Bhima smashed it to pieces. In moments, he was upon his enemy. He struck a terrific blow to his forehead, which threw him out of his chariot to a distance of twenty paces.

As Dushasana struggled to his feet, Bhima unsheathed his sword, running over to him. He kicked him in the face and sent him crashing back to the ground. Taking hold of his arm, he wrenched it upward and, with a sweep of his sword, severed it and raised it high into the air.

"Here is the arm that seized Draupadi's sanctified hair," he yelled. The Kauravas watched in horror as Bhima then tore open Dushasana's chest and, with cupped hands, drew his blood to his mouth. As he stood up with blood running down his face, they ran pell-mell away from him, crying out in terror, "Save us from Bhima! Surely he is a bloodthirsty Rakshasa!"

Bhima turned toward Arjuna and Krishna and called out, "I have redeemed my pledge and avenged Draupadi. Soon I will fulfill my other vow, when I crush Duryodhana. Only then will peace be mine."

Ten of Dushasana's brothers rallied themselves and rushed at Bhima. The Pandava quickly remounted his chariot. Firing off razor-headed shafts decked with gold wings, he slew all of his assailants. Among them was Vikarna. Remembering how that prince had spoken out during the gambling match, Bhima lamented greatly at having to slay him. He jumped from his chariot and, folding his palms, he circumambulated the fallen Kaurava. "O hero, I have fulfilled my vow and my duty as a kshatriya by slaying you. May you attain the regions of the righteous."

Karna had been shocked to witness Dushasana's killing, but he controlled himself and prepared to fight with Arjuna, who still bore down on him. As the two great warriors came face to face, the gods assembled in the sky to watch. Celestial horns were sounded, and flowers fell on both combatants.

The two heroes began a fierce exchange of arrows. Bent upon each other's death, they stood like two suns risen for the destruction of all the worlds. Their bows, drawn constantly to a circle, resembled the sun's corona, and their arrows blazed from their bows like sunbeams.

The battle raged for a long time with neither warrior gaining an edge. They each invoked celestial weapons, which the other countered. While fighting together, each maintained a ferocious assault on the other's supporting troops, killing thousands. Karna gave his utmost to the fight. Charged with the power of his illustrious heavenly father and inspired with a burning desire to defeat his lifelong foe, he fought as never before. But just as it seemed that he might be overpowering Arjuna, the curses that had been leveled at him took effect.

Seeing his opportunity when Arjuna was reeling from a sustained attack, Karna tried to invoke the powerful Brahmastra weapon. But he could not remember the incantations. His guru's words came back to him: "When you are in dire need of your most powerful weapon, you will be unable to summon it."

Crying hot tears of frustration, Karna fought on with a blazing fury. He then saw that, true to the brahmin's imprecation uttered long ago, his chariot wheel was sinking into the earth. The chariot came to a halt and could not be moved. Confounded by this crippling disability, he leapt down and heaved desperately at the wheel. Unable to budge it even slightly, he called out to Arjuna, who was closing on him, "O hero, do not kill me like a coward. Remember virtue. No noble fighter slays a disadvantaged enemy."

Krishna smiled. He called back to the stricken Karna, "It is good that at last you think of virtue, O Karna. It is a shame, though, that you could not remember it on those occasions when you cheated and abused the Pandavas—especially when their chaste wife was so grievously insulted. Where, too, was this virtue when you and the other Kuru heroes ruthlessly killed the boy Abhimanyu? If all that is your idea of virtue, then do not waste your time invoking it now."

Karna hung down his head. He tried again and again to free the wheel, but it was hopeless. Krishna urged Arjuna not to hesitate. "Strike down this wicked man at once. He deserves no mercy."

Perspiration flowed freely from Karna's forehead as he grappled with his wheel. Realizing that he could not free it, he spun round and took up his bow. He took up a long steel arrow and discharged it with all his power, uttering mantras all the while. It flew at Arjuna like a thunderbolt and struck him full on the chest. Arjuna reeled. Krishna again urged him to waste no time in killing his enemy. "This one should not be spared. Cut off his head before he remounts his chariot."

Arjuna then took out an arrow fitted with an anjalika head, shaped like folded palms. Placing that golden-shafted arrow on his bow, he invested it with the power of Indra's Vajra weapon. As he drew it back to his ear and took careful aim, an eerie silence enveloped the battlefield. All the warriors froze. The sky seemed to shake, and the rishis watching from the heavens cried out, "All peace! All peace!"

Arjuna held the arrow for a moment and muttered, "If I have ever practiced penance and respected my elders, then let this arrow slay Karna." He then let it go, and it streaked toward Karna, shining like the sun. It caught him on his broad and powerful neck. His head was instantly severed and thrown to the earth, where it lay with its gold earrings gleaming. His trunk collapsed to the ground, gushing blood. To everyone's amazement, a brilliant light left his body and rose up to merge with the sun.

The Pandavas were overwhelmed with joy. Dancing on the battlefield, they blew their conches and gazed in wonder at the fallen Karna, who resembled a mountain struck down by a bolt from heaven. Krishna praised Arjuna, and Yudhishthira came to his side, warmly congratulating him over and over. Yudhishthira wept tears of happiness and relief. His greatest fear was gone. The war was now all but over. Surely, the Kauravas' end was very near.

Duryodhana fell from his chariot. He beat his chest and rolled about in grief, tears flowing down his face. The other Kauravas surrounded Karna and cried out in sorrow. They walked around his body in respect and were joined by the Pandavas. As the day ended, the sun god went in grief to the western hills, shedding his last rays on his fallen son's body.

*   *   *

As the eighteenth day dawned, the Kauravas were almost totally in despair. Duryodhana had been up most of the night, inconsolable. He sat alone in his tent, gazing at Karna's empty seat. When the sun rose, he wearily dragged himself up to perform his morning ablutions. Distracted with grief, he made his way out of his tent to consult with his remaining ministers. As he thought about the way that Karna had been slain, his grief gave way to anger. His friend had been ruthlessly murdered as he stood deprived of his chariot. It had to be avenged. He strode toward his chariot, tightly grasping the long sword by his side.

Kripa tried advising Duryodhana that it was time to make peace with the Pandavas and accede to their demands. They now possessed a superior force, and before long the Kaurava army would be rooted out. But Duryodhana was resolute. "Everything is now on fire. I have created an enmity with the Pandavas that will be ended only with either their death or mine."

Installing Shalya as his commander, Duryodhana gave the order to march out once more. The remnants of his army cheered and headed out to fight, a glorious death now staring them in the face. Swarming out over the field, the two armies collided with roars and the clash of weapons.

On Krishna's advice, Yudhishthira headed straight for Shalya, intent on sending him to the higher regions. Sahadeva, remembering his vow at the dice game, sought out Shakuni. Arjuna engaged with Ashvatthama and Kripa. And with frightful shouts, Bhima rushed at the last of Dhritarashtra's sons. At the same time, both armies continued to grind each other down. Once again, the battlefield became a quagmire, thick with blood and entrails.

The fight between Yudhishthira and Shalya resembled that between two tigers fighting in the forest over a carcass. They circled and feinted with speed and grace. Each wounded the other with swift arrows. For a long time, Shalya displayed remarkable prowess. He withstood Yudhishthira's attack, and simultaneously slew thousands of Pandava troops. Gradually, though, Yudhishthira began to overpower him. He shattered Shalya's armor and broke down his standard. Killing his charioteer and horses, he stopped him in his tracks.

Shalya took up a polished steel sword and rushed at Yudhishthira. Seeing his foe charging at him with ferocious yells, Yudhishthira raised a glowing golden dart. Shouting, "You are killed!" he hurled it with all his power. The dart flew at Shalya like a meteor dropping from the sky. It struck him on the chest and passed clean through his body. Blood shot from Shalya's mouth, nose, and ears as he dropped to the earth. Like a dear wife rising to embrace her beloved spouse, the earth seemed to rise up to meet Shalya. Having enjoyed her for so long, the Madras monarch finally fell into her embrace and died.

Duryodhana knew the war was over. Bhima had slaughtered all of his brothers. After a fierce fight, Sahadeva had killed Shakuni and all his Gandhara warriors, and Arjuna was wiping out the last of the Kaurava forces. Gripped by utter despair, the Kaurava prince turned and fled from the battlefield. His mind was a maelstrom of mixed feelings. Genuine regret for having neglected the advice of his elders fought with boiling anger against the Pandavas. It had been a miscalculation to confront them in the first place—some kind of inconceivable cosmic power was obviously aiding them—but now they had slaughtered everyone he had held dear. Karna's death particularly rankled. His killing had been highly unrighteous. So, too, had Drona's. But it was too late to do anything now. Everything was lost.

Racing away from the field, Duryodhana came across a great lake. He dived in and swam to the bottom. By yogic power, he solidified the water and remained underneath. He needed time to rest and recover. After that, he could decide what action to take.

Unknown to Duryodhana, there were still three Kaurava warriors surviving—Kripa, Ashvatthama, and Kritavarman—but when they saw that Duryodhana had fled, they also ran from the battlefield. On their way they encountered Vyasadeva, and the *rishi* told them where to find Duryodhana. They went to the lake and called out to their leader. Ashvatthama exhorted him to come back to the fight. "We are still ready to confront your enemies, O king. Rise up! We shall certainly slay them today. Indeed, I will not remove my armor till I see the Pandavas and all their troops killed. My father's death will be avenged."

Duryodhana had lost all heart for the battle. He shouted back, "O mighty-armed ones, it is fortunate that you still live. I, too, am fortunate to have such devoted followers. When morning comes, I will join you. Let me rest for now."

Some hunters were in the forest nearby. When they heard the discussion between Duryodhana and Ashvatthama, they realized that the prince was hiding in the lake. Knowing that Yudhishthira would likely reward them for that information, they went quickly to tell him.

The Pandavas had returned to their camp, after unsuccessfully searching for Duryodhana. Learning from the hunters where he had gone, they set off at once to find him. The war would not be over till he had either surrendered or been slain.

As the Pandavas approached Duryodhana's hiding place, accompanied by their remaining forces, the other three Kauravas heard them from a distance, and they ran into hiding. Reaching the lake, Yudhishthira looked with wonder at the solidified water and said to Krishna, "Just see how the deceitful Duryodhana hides in fear. However, he will not escape me now."

Yudhishthira shouted out to Duryodhana to come out and fight. "Why are you trying to save yourself after millions have died for you? Coward! Face the consequences of your acts. Death is better than such dishonor. Fight with us. Either govern the world, having won victory, or, slain by us, embrace the cold earth."

The Pandavas surveyed the scene. Waterfowl walked across the solid surface of the lake, mystified by its sudden change. A breeze rustled through the surrounding trees, which were covered with bright blossoms. After the heat and dust of the battlefield, the brothers felt soothed simply by seeing that picturesque region.

After some moments, Duryodhana shouted back from the lake bottom. He asked Yudhishthira to wait some time while he rested. But Yudhishthira was insistent. "You shall not be spared today. Rise out of this lake or we shall drag you out. Finish what you have started. Killed by us, you will ascend to the heavens."

Angered, and with his pride wounded, Duryodhana decided to fight. The lake water swirled and bubbled, and the prince suddenly emerged. With his great mace on his shoulder, he looked like a mountain rising from the ocean. He looked around at the Pandavas and their forces, and laughed. "Here I am, ready to send you all to Death's abode. But how can I, one man, fight so many at once?"

Bhima grasped hold of his own mace and started forward. He was ready to smash Duryodhana's head at once, but Yudhishthira raised a hand to check him.

Yudhishthira smiled. "The time has come for you to pay for your crimes, wretched-minded one. We should kill you now as you killed Abhimanyu, but I will give you a chance. Select any one of us and fight with the weapon of your choice. If you win, you may keep the kingdom. Otherwise, proceed to heaven."

Yudhishthira was convinced that Krishna would protect him and his brothers. But Krishna glanced at him in surprise. It was a rash offer. Duryodhana was matchless with his mace. Even Bhima would be hard pressed to beat him.

Duryodhana laughed again. "I care not which of you fights with me. Take up a mace, any one of you. I will kill you at once and then all of your brothers, one by one."

Bhima looked achingly at Yudhishthira. "Permit me to slay this wretch, O lord," he begged. "I shall end this war. Your victory is assured."

Yudhishthira placed a hand on Bhima's massive shoulder. "Be it so. Go forward and deal him the punishment he so richly deserves. Fulfill your vow. But be careful. He is no mean opponent."

Bhima and Duryodhana glared at one another. Both had always known it would come to this. Anticipating this day, Duryodhana had spent many hours in Hastinapura practicing with his mace on an iron image of Bhima. The two men whirled their maces above their heads and marched back toward the battlefield. Like a lion and an elephant meeting in the forest, they stood to face each other. "Recall now all your depraved and sinful acts, O worst of men," Bhima spat out to his sneering enemy. "The final reckoning has come. All your brothers are dead, and now you, too, will follow the path taken by them. Your pride and your hope for the kingdom will today be crushed by me."

Duryodhana raised his mace and smiled. "What use are these words? How can you defeat me? See here my mace, like the summit of Himavat. Having already obliged you to become a cook in Virata and Arjuna to become a eunuch, I shall today pound you both to death."

The two enraged fighters slowly circled one another. Every muscle in their bodies was tensed. Their eyes resembled glowing embers. Clenching and unclenching their hands around their maces, they watched for an opportunity to strike. Suddenly, they both leapt forward. Their maces collided with a deafening crash. Showers of sparks flew upward. Like two furious bulls, they roared and grappled together. Both exhibited graceful moves, spinning, feinting, and leaping high. As the celestials looked on, the two mighty fighters contended to the limits of their power.

For some time, neither could land a blow on the other, but gradually they began to penetrate each other's defenses. Blows landed with loud thuds. Both men were sent reeling, but they quickly recovered and resumed their positions. They knew every move and displayed the full range of their skills. The onlookers gasped and cheered.

Bhima's mace resembled Yamaraja's death-dealing staff. It sounded like the rushing wind as it fell upon Duryodhana. The Kaurava moved with blinding speed and dexterity. His own mace swung with such speed that it sent forth tongues of fire.

Unknown to Bhima, Duryodhana had been blessed with a special strength by his mother. Gandhari had known that her son would eventually meet Bhima in a mace fight. She had thus summoned him to come naked before her. The Kuru queen knew that by her glance, imbued with all her ascetic power, she could render Duryodhana's body invincible. But the prince had been unable to appear naked before his mother. He had worn a loincloth, and thus, his upper thighs had not been strengthened. The rest of his body, however, was impervious to Bhima's strikes. The Pandava stared in amazement as Duryodhana remained standing, even after receiving his most powerful blows.

Gradually Duryodhana gained the upper hand. He repeatedly smashed Bhima, laughing all the while. Bhima grew wild with anger. Rocked by Duryodhana's powerful blows, he perspired and breathed like a snake.

Krishna could see that Bhima was avoiding striking his foe below the belt. Although he had made a vow to break his thighs, it appeared that Bhima first wanted to defeat Duryodhana in a fair fight. But Krishna knew about Gandhari's blessing. Knowing that Bhima's only chance was to smash

Duryodhana's thighs, he caught the Pandava's eye and then slapped his own thigh.

Bhima understood Krishna's sign. It was clear that Duryodhana would not be defeated in any other way. The Kaurava was taking his best shots and coming back for more. Remembering his vow, Bhima circled his foe. After another furious exchange of blows, Bhima suddenly stepped back and swung his mace round by its long sling. As he expected, Duryodhana leapt up to avoid the blow. Bhima quickly pulled back his mace, as the prince somersaulted in the air. The Pandava then stepped forward and again swung his mace in a great arc, his huge biceps glistening with sweat as they were fully exerted. As Duryodhana dropped back to the ground, he was caught across the thighs by Bhima's onrushing mace. The iron mace, which could only be lifted by three strong men, smashed Duryodhana's thighs like a thunderbolt smashing a pair of trees. The Kaurava fell flat on the earth, screaming in pain.

The fight was over. Duryodhana was mortally wounded by Bhima's tremendous blow. He could hardly move. The Pandavas sent up a great cheer. Krishna clapped his hands and applauded Bhima. Still seething, Bhima looked down at his fallen enemy and lifted a foot to place it on his head. Yudhishthira called out, "No, Bhima! Desist. Do not insult our cousin in this way." He knelt by Duryodhana's side. "O child, the hostilities are over. Due to your pride, avarice, and folly you have suffered this calamity. Millions of heroes lie dead for your sake. Now you shall follow them. It is we who should be pitied, not you. Surely, you will reach the heavens, while we shall have to remain here in this world of suffering, surrounded by grieving widows."

Tears flowed from Yudhishthira's eyes as he thought of the war's terrible toll. He stood up and was comforted by Krishna. Duryodhana said nothing. He writhed in pain, both from his wounds and from the thought of how he had been defeated. Yudhishthira's gently spoken words did not make him feel any better. He looked over at Krishna and angrily cried, "I saw your sign to Bhima. You are deceitful and sinful! It is only thanks to your cunning that the Pandavas have won this war."

Grimacing in pain, the Kaurava fell back, his face covered in perspiration. Krishna retorted, "O fool, have you forgotten that it was I who came to Hastinapura, trying to save you from the war in the first place? Do not rail uselessly. You are receiving the consequences of your own deeds and nothing else. Your wicked acts against the Pandavas, against their wife, and against Abhimanyu, have come back to you today."

Duryodhana was unable to make any reply. He lay gasping, his mace by his side. As the sun set, Krishna suggested to the Pandavas that they return to their camp. Bidding farewell to Duryodhana, they departed, leaving the Kaurava prince to await his death.

Twenty-eight

POWERFUL EMOTIONS

OF THE TWO great armies, all that remained were less than a thousand Pandava troops. Filled with joy at having finally attained victory against the mighty Kurus, they wearily returned to camp. As the eighteenth night fell, they lay down their weapons and rested. Krishna had suggested to Yudhishthira and his brothers that they spend the night in the Kauravas' camp, in accordance with tradition. As the victors, it was now their prerogative to take possession of all the Kauravas' property. They also needed to provide leadership and protection to the Kauravas' many servants and women who were at the camp. Accompanied by Krishna, the five brothers entered Duryodhana's great tent and rested there for the night.

Out in the forest, Kripa, Ashvatthama, and Kritavarman were resting beneath a large banyan tree. Having found the fallen Duryodhana, they had been infuriated when he told them how he had been defeated. The prince encouraged them to continue the fight the next day. Completely fatigued, they had then collapsed beneath the tree. But Ashvatthama could not sleep. He still burned with a desire for vengeance. As he gazed up at the tree branches, he saw a great owl suddenly swoop down from the sky. There were many crows asleep in the branches, and the owl began killing them as they slept. Watching those slain birds dropping from the tree, Ashvatthama began to reflect. Perhaps this was a sign from destiny. There was little chance that he and his two companions could defeat the Pandavas. But now they would be buried in slumber. Of course, killing sleeping men was generally forbidden, but these were sinful enemies. They had to be punished by any means possible.

Drona's son sat up, and woke the other two men. When they heard his plan, they sat in silence, too shamed to reply. After some moments, Kripa said, "O hero, we have tried our best to defeat the Pandavas, but destiny decreed that it be otherwise. Duryodhana has met with calamity due to his own foolishness. As his followers, we, too, have been sunk in sorrow. I cannot see the point in any further fighting, especially by such a sinful means. Let us now return to Hastinapura."

But Ashvatthama was resolute. His mind was set upon slaying his enemies, and he was not interested in any arguments. He made that clear to Kripa. Again, the old Kuru tried to dissuade him. "If you must fight, do so in fair combat. Wait till the morning. We will then join with you."

Ashvatthama stood up and reached for his weapons, his silver armor glinting in the moonlight. "No. We cannot possibly win in an open encounter. I am going now to their camp. Catching them unawares, I will slay them like animals. That is all they deserve.

Kripa and Kritavarman watched in dismay as Drona's son mounted his chariot. Kripa tried hard to dissuade him from his dark plan, but Ashvatthama was unmoved. He headed off into the night. But when he reached the Pandavas' camp, he encountered a strange-looking being at the gates. Tall and frightful, he was draped with a blood-soaked tiger skin and had a black snake around his neck. In his awful face there were a hundred eyes, and his huge mouth seemed to be ablaze.

Fearful for his life, Ashvatthama immediately attacked him. He launched all his most powerful weapons at the terrible-looking creature, but they had no effect. Drona's son saw that his arrows were all consumed, while the being stood unmoved.

Realizing that this was almost surely the great god Shiva, whom he had long worshipped, Ashvatthama got down from his chariot and prostrated himself on the ground. The being then spoke in a thunderous voice. "O child, I am Shiva. I have protected Pandu's sons throughout this war. Out of love for Krishna, I am always inclined to his worshippers. But now the Pandava warriors are being assailed by time. They have carried out the plan of Providence, relieving the earth's burden, and now their own destined end has arrived."

Shiva held up a huge sword. "O son of Drona, take this weapon. It is ordained that you shall be the instrument of their destruction. Empowered by me, you will kill them all."

Ashvatthama stood up and took the brilliant sword, which had a handle set with gems. Shiva then vanished from the spot. Feeling himself infused with enormous strength, Ashvatthama smiled and raised the sword. He silently entered the Pandavas' camp and at once began to slay the sleeping warriors. Taken by surprise, they jumped from their beds and fumbled for their weapons. Ashvatthama slew them without mercy. In one tent, he found five warriors sleeping together. Believing them to be the Pandavas, he joyfully crept up to their beds. With great blows from his sword, he killed them, one by one. He then ran on, laughing hideously and swinging his bloodied sword. In less than an hour, he had killed everyone in the camp. He then severed the heads from the five men he believed were the Pandavas. They would make excellent trophies to show to Duryodhana. The Kaurava would at least die knowing that his enemies were also slain.

After placing the heads in his chariot, Ashvatthama rode quickly to where Duryodhana lay. The sun was rising, and he saw the prince looking pale, obviously close to death. Carnivorous beasts were circling him, and Ashvatthama scared them away. He placed the heads near the prince and said, "My lord, your enemies are killed. Here are their heads."

Duryodhana lifted his head slightly and smiled. He replied with difficulty. "Well done, O son of Drona. You have accomplished what even Bhishma, Karna, and your own father could not. Well done."

Duryodhana reached out and took hold of one of the grim-looking heads, its face a mask of shock. The prince found it hard to believe that the Pandavas were dead. It was difficult to tell their identities from the appearance of the heads, but there was one way he could know. Exerting the last of his strength, Duryodhana squeezed the head, and it immediately collapsed. He did the same with the other four. In disappointment he said, "These are not the heads of the Pandavas. Those brothers have heads like iron. Even my hardest mace blow could not smash Bhima's skull. It seems you have killed their five teenage sons. Alas, this was a heinous act. Who will now continue the Kuru line?"

Repeatedly gasping, "Alas, alas," Duryodhana slumped back. His head fell to the side and he gave up his life. Ashvatthama was filled with dismay and sorrow. With the sunrise, he had felt Shiva's power leave him. There was no question of confronting the Pandavas now. They would soon be looking for him. He remounted his chariot and headed into the forest, unsure which way to run.

* * *

Soon after sunrise the Pandavas saw Dhrishtadyumna's charioteer run panic-stricken into the Kuru camp. Somehow he had escaped the massacre. The brothers listened in horror as he told them what had happened during the night. They cried out in grief. Yudhishthira was particularly afflicted. The soft-hearted Pandava felt personally responsible for the killing. He was the cause of the whole war, for it had taken place just so that he could become king. Well, now he was king—but what a poisoned chalice. All his beloved elders, friends, cousins, and now even his sons were dead. He dropped to his knees and spoke in an agonized voice. "An already bitter victory has become even more bitter. What happiness will we enjoy with all our friends and kinsmen dead? What will become of Draupadi? How will she live when she hears that her five sons are slain?"

Taking their distraught wife, the five brothers went quickly to their camp. They were met by gruesome scenes. Mutilated bodies were strewn everywhere. When Draupadi saw her beheaded sons, she fell senseless to the ground. Coming round again, she wept uncontrollably. Her body shook violently. Looking toward Arjuna and Bhima, who had Krishna by their side, she declared, "I will not move from this spot until Ashvatthama is punished. Slay him like a beast! If he does not pay for this crime, I will give up my own life."

Krishna agreed. "Ashvatthama must certainly be caught. He is wrathful, wicked, and cruel. Let us leave at once."

Krishna and Arjuna set off from the camp in Krishna's personal chariot. They sped off into the forest, looking for signs left by Ashvatthama. Finding his trail, they gave chase and soon caught up to him. When Ashvatthama saw them approaching, he was terrified. He immediately invoked the Brahmastra and released it with all his power. A circle of brilliant white light began to emanate from his chariot. Seeing this, Krishna spoke urgently to Arjuna. "O hero, in his blind panic, the wretched fool has indiscriminately fired the Brahmastra. This missile can destroy the whole world. Counter it with your own weapon, and then withdraw both of them."

Arjuna quickly followed Krishna's instruction. He released another Brahmastra, and it joined with Ashvatthama's missile. The weapons came together like two suns in the heavens, and a dazzling light filled the sky.

Seeing his weapon confounded, Ashvatthama realized his end was near. He thought of wreaking one last violent act against the Pandavas. Knowing that Abhimanyu's wife, Uttara, was pregnant, Ashvatthama decided he would try to slay her unborn child. With mantras, he could redirect the Brahma missile toward her womb. Her child was the Pandavas' hope for the future. It would break their hearts if he were killed. Concentrating his mind, Drona's son directed his missile toward Uttara.

Not realizing what Ashvatthama had done, Arjuna recited the mantras to withdraw his own weapon, and the brilliant light subsided. In the Pandavas' camp, Uttara suddenly felt herself in great danger. Her limbs trembled and she fell to the ground. She immediately began praying to Krishna. "O all-powerful Lord of the universe, please protect me. In this fearful world of death, you are the only shelter."

Hearing her prayer even as he stood on Arjuna's chariot, Krishna, who had understood Ashvatthama's intentions, at once expanded himself by his supreme power. In a mystical form, he entered Uttara's womb. As the Brahmastra approached, he deflected it and neutralized its power. Uttara saw a glowing light approach her and then shoot harmlessly up into the sky.

After he had withdrawn the Brahmastra, Arjuna fired another weapon that bound Ashvatthama with strong cords. He then jumped down and dragged him by his hair onto Krishna's chariot. Although longing to kill him, Arjuna was reluctant to slay his teacher's son. Drona's death had already given Arjuna great pain, and killing his only son was difficult. He turned to Krishna, who was urging him to kill Ashvatthama at once. "I feel unable to slay this wretch, O Krishna. Let me take him before Yudhishthira, and he can decide what to do."

Krishna agreed, and Arjuna dragged the bound Ashvatthama onto his chariot. Arriving back at the camp, he threw him at Yudhishthira's feet. "Here is the killer of our sons. What should be done with him?"

When Draupadi saw the miserable-looking Ashvatthama, she felt compassion. Her desire for vengeance dissipated, and she said, "O Arjuna, release him. He is a brahmin and your guru's son. Do not make Drona's wife weep like I am weeping. Show him mercy."

Yudhishthira applauded his wife's words, but Bhima argued that Ashvatthama should be killed at once. "He has mercilessly slain sleeping boys! What kind of brahmin is that? Why should he spared?"

Krishna looked at Arjuna, who was standing over Ashvatthama. "O Partha, you must find some way to satisfy both your wife and your brother."

Arjuna drew his sword and raised it, taking hold of Ashvatthama's hair with his other hand. Draupadi gasped as he brought the razor-edged sword down in a sweeping arc, but Arjuna severed only Ashvatthama's topknot, with its shining, jewel-encrusted clasp. Presenting the jewel to Draupadi, he said, "O beautiful lady, this fellow is now as good as dead. Cutting off a warrior's hair is equal to killing him, and this jewel was the repository of all Ashvatthama's power."

Ashvatthama seemed to shrivel as his hair was cut. He collapsed to the ground, and Krishna said to him, "Cruel son of Drona, you shall be known as a coward and a wretch. For three thousand years you will wander this earth, afflicted with disease and reviled by men everywhere. Having thus received the consequences of your acts, you will finally rise to the higher regions. Now go."

Ashvatthama got up and slunk away, his head hanging down. Krishna then consoled the Pandavas and Draupadi, instructing them with eternal spiritual truths. After this, Yudhishthira arranged for the funerals of all the slain warriors, and he and his brothers went to the Ganges to make offerings for the departed souls.

*   *   *

Having heard of the war's conclusion and Duryodhana's destruction, Dhritarashtra and Gandhari sat mutely in their palace, seized with unbearable grief. Every one of their sons was dead. The Kuru house was destroyed. Bhishma, their greatest well-wisher and esteemed elder, lay dying out on the battlefield.

Sanjaya tried to console the grieving king and queen. He repeated the words of Vyasadeva—that everything had been ordained by the gods. "Duryodhana was an incarnated expansion of Kali, the evil spirit of the dark age. By divine arrangement, he marshaled the demonic elements who were burdening the earth and then led them to destruction."

Gandhari's breast heaved as she loudly sobbed. The Kuru queen accepted Sanjaya's words. She had always known that her son was evil-minded. He should have been abandoned at birth. But somehow the gods had a different plan. Now it was complete. More than six million warriors were dead, among them hundreds of kings.

Along with all Hastinapura's citizens, Dhritarashtra and his wife made their sorrowful way to the Ganges to offer oblations for the dead. When they arrived at the river, they saw the Pandavas nearby. Seeing their elderly uncle and aunt, the five brothers went before them and bowed down to the ground. Dhritarashtra wept as he heard them announce their names. He embraced each of them with difficulty. When he heard Bhima's name, he was overcome with anger. Krishna saw this, and he pushed Bhima aside as the blind king was about to embrace him. With his mystic power, Krishna at once brought the iron statue of Bhima from Duryodhana's palace. He had it appear in front of Dhritarashtra, and the king seized it in a furious embrace. Before everyone's astonished eyes, he crushed the metal image into tiny fragments. Choking and vomiting blood, he slumped to the ground.

Sanjaya knelt by the king's side and gently raised him. "Do not act in this way," he chided.

Having vented his wrath and feeling sure he had killed Bhima, Dhritarashtra cried out, "Alas! What have I done?"

Krishna told him not to grieve. "You have only smashed Bhima's image, O king. Give up your spite and be peaceful. How will killing Bhima bring back your sons?"

Dhritarashtra hung his head in shame. Helped by his servants, he walked down to the river and silently took bath. There was nothing he could say. He had been advised by everyone to reject Duryodhana and his foolish schemes. Now he was reaping the sure result of that omission.

Gandhari was also struggling with her anger. When the Pandavas came to offer her their respects, she said to Bhima, "Could you not have spared even one of my sons? How will I and my blind husband survive in this world without any support?"

The Kuru queen then thought of Krishna. She felt her anger rise even more. So many times she had heard the rishis describe how he was the all-powerful supreme person, who was kindly disposed to all living beings. Why, then, had he allowed so many men to be slaughtered? When Krishna greeted her, she said to him, "The Kuru dynasty has been rooted out, O Keshava, even before your eyes. Why did you permit it? For this neglect, I curse you that your own dynasty will die in the same way, slain in a fratricidal war."

The Pandavas were shocked. What was Gandhari thinking? How could anyone curse Krishna? But Krishna smilingly said, "O chaste lady, your words will not prove false. No one can kill the Yadus. Therefore, when the time comes for their departure, they will kill each other. I thank you for this curse."

The Pandavas were deeply saddened. The thought of Krishna's departure was unbearable. And another fratricidal war? It was too much to contemplate. But the Lord must have some plan. Thinking about Krishna's words, the brothers then left Gandhari and met with their mother. Kunti was trembling with emotion as she embraced her sons. She praised Krishna again and again for saving them. As the brothers made their way to the river to offer oblations, she walked behind. Thinking of Karna, she wept silently. Looking up at her other sons, she decided t was time to tell them the truth. Taking a deep breath, Kunti said, "O heroes, please offer an oblation for Karna. That great hero was Surya's son, born of myself. He was your eldest brother."

The five brothers stopped in their tracks. They turned and looked at their mother, their mouths falling open. Yudhishthira shook his head in amazement. He recalled how, on several occasions, he had noticed a marked similarity between Karna's feet and those of Kunti. He had wondered about that, but never dared think that Karna might be his brother! But now it was confirmed beyond doubt. He threw up his arms and cried out, "O Mother, how were we never told? How did he become your son? O noble lady, tell us everything. Hearing this news, my grief rises like the ocean at the full moon."

Kunti told her astonished sons the whole story. When she had finished, she fell sobbing to the ground. Yudhishthira gently raised his mother and stroked her forehead. "Dear Mother, you must have suffered so much."

The brothers then entered the Ganges to make their offerings. Krishna came to the grief-stricken Yudhishthira and told him, "Karna knew his true identity. I tried once to convince him to take your side, but he would not be moved. Even his father, Surya, tried, and so did your mother. But Karna was unshakable in his determination to support Duryodhana."

Yudhishthira still felt that he should have been informed. His mother should have trusted him. So much bloodshed might have been avoided. As he came out of the river, Yudhishthira said, "O Mother, I do not blame you for your silence. Surely, you were moved by supreme destiny. But I feel you should have confided in me. I therefore say that from this day on, no woman will be able to keep a secret."

When all the rituals had been completed, Yudhishthira sat with his brothers and Krishna. It was time for him to again assume rulership of the earth. But he felt unable. The enormity of the war burned into his heart. There were now millions of bereaved women and children. Yudhishthira felt directly to blame. He sat staring vacantly at the earth. Was his sovereignty really so necessary? For all his faults, Duryodhana had been an efficient enough administrator, even maintaining the brahmins with abundant wealth. Now he, his brothers, the Kuru elders, and countless other kings were dead. Yudhishthira wept. Perhaps it would have been better to have stayed in the forest.

Heaving a deep sigh, Yudhishthira voiced his feelings. "Like dogs fighting over a piece of meat, we have waged war for the kingdom. Now, we no longer desire that meat. I will throw it aside. The whole endeavor was useless. I do not want to take the burnt remnants of the war, won at the cost of so many lives. Let me retire to the forest. Let Bhima or Arjuna become king."

Yudhishthira's brothers regarded him with dismay. They had fought hard to win back his kingdom. What comparison was there between him and Duryodhana? Under Yudhishthira's rule, the people would not only be materially well situated but, much more importantly, they would be properly led toward ultimate salvation. The faithless Duryodhana could never have directed them in such a way.

One after another, Yudhishthira's brothers argued that he should not hesitate to become king, but he remained unmoved. During the discussions, many rishis came to join them. Finally Vyasadeva spoke, and he also argued at length that it was Yudhishthira's duty to become king. Hearing the immortal sage speak, Yudhishthira at last began to accept that he should ascend the throne, especially as the sage again made it clear that the war had been directly arranged by the Lord. Yudhishthira understood that no sin had accrued to him as a result of the war, but he still had doubts about kingly duties themselves—were such duties not fraught with sin? Being a king entailed possessing and enjoying wealth, attacking and subduing other kings, as well as various other seemingly violent and selfish acts. He looked toward Vyasadeva. "O great sage, it is said that a king is even culpable for the sins committed by men in his kingdom. What should I do? I have no wish to be covered by sin, thus incurring the Lord's displeasure."

Yudhishthira glanced over at Krishna, who had sat silently listening to the discussion. Vyasadeva also turned toward Krishna, inviting him to speak, but Krishna only smiled and raised a hand for the sage to continue. Vyasadeva then said, "O king, if you wish to hear of morality and the duties of kings, you should approach Bhishma. He is still living, and there are none in this world who understand morality better than he does. He will clear all your doubts."

Hearing Bhishma's name made Yudhishthira feel even more aggrieved. Tears again sprang to his eyes. "How can I go before my grandfather now? He was deceitfully slain by me."

Krishna placed a hand on Yudhishthira's shoulder to reassure him. "You should do as the sage has suggested. Bhishma will surely be pleased to see you, and he will certainly clear your doubts."

Krishna's words finally convinced Yudhishthira. He replied, "So be it. I shall get myself duly consecrated by the brahmins and then go to the Kuru grandfather."

For the good of the world, the Pandava then stood up and prepared to go to Hastinapura. His brothers cheered, and together they set off for the city.

Twenty-nine

DELIVERANCE

AFTER THE INSTALLATION ceremony was completed, Yudhishthira left to see Bhishma. He went out of Hastinapura accompanied by his brothers, Krishna, Dhritarashtra, Gandhari, and thousands of other citizens. All of them longed to see the old Kuru hero one last time. Reaching Kurukshetra, they were met by dire scenes of destruction. The field was littered with wreckage. Skulls lay everywhere, like brilliant white conches. There were countless skeletons, picked clean by the buzzards and jackals. But as the party approached Bhishma, they saw that the whole area where he lay was aglow with effulgence. He was surrounded by rishis, and his body shone like the setting sun.

The Pandavas and Krishna dismounted from their chariots and went on foot to see the fallen Kuru. They offered him prostrate obeisances and then sat around him. Krishna, with tears running down his face, said, "O hero, I trust that your mind and understanding are as clear as ever. It is indeed wonderful that you are able to remain alive in this condition. Who else in all the worlds could do this? Your devotion to truth, penance, charity, and virtue is without equal."

Krishna then told the Pandavas that Bhishma was in fact an incarnation of Dyau, the leader of the highly powerful celestials known as the Vasus. He explained how it came to pass that Dyau had taken a human birth, and when he had finished, he turned again to Bhishma and said, "O great one, kindly destroy Yudhishthira's grief and doubts. He is overcome with anguish due to the death of his kinsmen and elders. The gentle king is reluctant to take his rightful position as the world's ruler. Reassure him, O Bhishma. Explain to him everything about duty and morality, for you are the best of all speakers."

Bhishma, who still lay on the bed of arrows protruding from his body, raised his head slightly and looked into Krishna's face. "Obeisances to you, O divine Krishna. You are the supreme cause of everything. I am now aware of your all-pervasive universal form. O Lord, be merciful to me. Pray tell me what is best for me now. I only desire to reach your eternal abode."

Krishna reassured Bhishma that he would surely rise to the highest regions of spiritual bliss. He asked him again to speak to Yudhishthira. "Tell him all you know. When you leave this world, your great knowledge will leave with you."

Bhishma was doubtful. "How can anyone speak on religion in your presence, O Lord? What is more, I am in too much pain. My mind is clouded, and I can hardly discern anything. I think you should speak."

Bhishma was shaded from the hot sun by a large umbrella. The brahmins surrounding him softly chanted Vedic mantras, and a servant stood by his head, fanning him with a whisk. Although feeling great discomfort, Bhishma wept tears of joy as he gazed at Krishna. He felt unlimitedly fortunate. The Supreme Lord had personally come to see him as he lay dying.

Krishna again reassured Bhishma. "By my grace, you will feel no more pain. Your memory and intelligence will be perfect. All your knowledge will appear before you like fish seen in a crystal clear pond."

As Krishna spoke, a shower of flowers fell from the sky. Celestial instruments were heard, and a cool, fragrant breeze began to blow. Everything became peaceful. Even the animals and birds were silent.

Bhishma then began to speak. He began by explaining that Yudhishthira and his brothers, being faithful and devoted souls, were always protected by God. Thus, they emerged successful from all kinds of tribulation. The Kuru grandfather assured Yudhishthira that everything was happening according to the Lord's inscrutable will. No one should lament for such inevitabilities. He looked up at Krishna. "Vasudeva's son, Krishna, is the supreme controller. He is all-knowing but unknowable. Accepting everything as his inconceivable plan, you should do your duty, firmly adhering to virtue."

Bhishma spent some time speaking about Krishna. He described how Krishna acted only for the good of all beings. The Lord made no discrimination in terms of bodily designation. He had no material purpose to fulfill. All of his acts were transcendental. As he spoke, Bhishma was absorbed in ecstatic feelings of love, and tears flowed from his eyes. "Krishna is equally disposed to all, and yet he has come before me now because I am his unflinching servitor."

When the sun set, everyone went to their encampment. They lived there for more than fifty days as Bhishma delivered his instructions to Yudhishthira. He answered all of the Pandava's questions to his full satisfaction. Yudhishthira felt his doubts and fears being removed. Gradually, the

sun moved toward its northern declination. When at last it reached the
northern hemisphere, Bhishma had finished. He then thought of departing.
Gazing lovingly at Krishna, who stood before him manifesting a four-armed
form and dressed in glittering yellow garments, he prayed, "Let me now
invest my full consciousness in you, O Lord. May my mind remain fixed on
the memory of you running toward me with chariot wheel held high, your
face smoldering with anger and your silk garments flowing in the wind."

Bhishma went on praying to Krishna as the sun reached the meridian.
He then said his final farewells to the Pandavas and closed his eyes. His
breathing stopped, and he entered a trance. Suddenly, his life air shot out
from the crown of his head and went into the sky like a blazing comet. The
rishis saw him leave his body in a shining spiritual form and enter Krishna's
eternal abode. Yudhishthira and his brothers sat in silent respect, shedding
tears. After some minutes, conchshells were blown and drums beaten.
Demonstrations of honor and respect were made by all present, and the
gods showered flowers from the sky.

With great sadness, the Pandavas performed the last rites for their
grandfather. After wrapping his body in silken cloth and smearing it with
scents and sandalwood pulp, they placed it on the funeral pyre. Everyone
cried out as the body burned. Finally, his ashes were consigned to the
Ganges, from whence he had first taken birth. The river goddess rose up
from her waters to receive her son's remains. Yudhishthira and his brothers
then returned to Hastinapura to begin the task of ruling over the kingdom.

*   *   *

Krishna stayed with the Pandavas for some time, continuing to reassure and console the still-grieving Yudhishthira. Finally, he took
Yudhishthira's permission and returned to Dwaraka. The Pandava king was
deeply saddened at Krishna's departure, but, encouraged by Krishna's
words, he applied himself to his duty with full determination. Yudhishthira
was the embodiment of justice and virtue. Due to his piety and expert leadership, his people wanted for nothing. The gods co-operated with him, and
thus, there were not even any natural calamities. Rain fell in season and
crops grew abundantly. The people were not afflicted by disease, anxiety, or
even excessive heat and cold. They enjoyed long lives and, following their
king's example, practiced virtue. At the end of their lives, they went straight
to higher regions.

In time, Uttara gave birth to a son, who was named Pariksit. As
Dhaumya performed the name-giving ceremony, he said, "This child was

saved by Krishna while still in the womb. He will therefore be known as Vishnurata, 'one who is always protected by the Lord.' Growing to be an irresistible hero, he will rule the people exactly like Rama in ancient times. He will expand the fame of your family like Bharata himself."

Filled with joy to hear these and other such descriptions, the Pandavas felt assured that a worthy heir to the throne had been born, and their grief at losing their own sons was assuaged. Yudhishthira then thought of consolidating his position as emperor. There would be some kings—relatives of those who had sided with Duryodhana—who would be inimical. Yudhishthira did not want anyone to cause another catastrophic war. He decided to perform a sacrifice similar to the Rajasuya, which would re-establish him as the world's ruler. A challenge horse was sent out to roam the earth, and Arjuna followed it with a large force of men. Anyone who would not accept Yudhishthira's position was soon subjugated by Arjuna. Within a few years, the entire earth was again under the Pandavas' sway.

Many years passed without incident. Feeling compassion for Dhritarashtra and still respecting him as his elder, Yudhishthira treated him as a superior. His opinion was sought on all matters of state. He and his wife were honored by everyone in the royal household—except Bhima. Unable to forget the many ills that the Kauravas had done to him and his brothers, Bhima only reluctantly offered Dhritarashtra respect. Inwardly, he resented the royal treatment that Yudhishthira accorded him. Bhima would look for opportunities to give pain to the old Kuru leader. Sometimes, he would stand within earshot of Dhritarashtra and, slapping his arms, would loudly say, "With these two mace-like arms I have crushed all of the blind king's sons."

Dhritarashtra silently tolerated these utterances, not wanting to disturb Yudhishthira. His wife also said nothing. She accepted Bhima's painful words and behavior as the inevitable reaction to her and her husband's past acts.

More than thirty years elapsed after the war. Vidura, who had gone on an extended pilgrimage when the war had started, came back to Hastinapura and was received with great affection by the Pandavas. Vidura told them about his travels and the many spiritual instructions he had heard from the rishis at the holy places. He stayed in the palace for some time. Seeing the condition of his blind brother, he felt pity for him. He could see that Bhima was often giving him pain and also that Dhritarashtra still felt remorse for having failed to check his foolish sons.

Finding an opportunity to speak alone with his brother, Vidura said, "O king, it is well past time that you retired. You are living now on the charity of your former enemies. All your family members are dead, and death is fast approaching you. You should leave at once. Come with me to the forest and spend your final days in penance and meditation."

With strong words, Vidura exhorted the blind king to give up his material attachments. Dhritarashtra was convinced by his arguments. On the next full moon night, he and Gandhari left with Vidura and went to the forest. Kunti also went with them. For many years she had been spending her days in prayer, fasting often and living very simply. The party left secretly, telling no one. It was always the accepted custom to retire to the forest without announcement at the end of life, for death itself never made announcements when it arrived.

When the palace residents saw that their elders had left, they cried out in sorrow. Yudhishthira felt especially saddened. "Alas, where is our beloved mother? And where, too, is my esteemed uncle? Surely, the old king has gone away in grief. Although he accepted us when we were fatherless children, I repaid him by killing all his sons."

At that time, Narada came to the palace. He told the Pandavas that Dhritarashtra and the two ladies had gone with Vidura. They would soon leave their bodies and ascend to higher regions. "O king, do not lament for anyone, for everyone is under the Lord's control. Ultimately, it is he who brings men together and disperses them. We are all helplessly moved by God's infallible laws. His will is supreme; therefore, all men should simply worship him and take his shelter. This is always their best interest."

Narada went on instructing the Pandavas. He explained that affection for other living beings based upon their bodies was illusory. "No one is anyone's father, son, uncle, or anything else. We are all eternal parts of the Lord, living only temporarily in different bodies."

When Narada had finished instructing the brothers, he took their leave and then rose into the sky and vanished. They felt consoled but realized that their own retirement was also drawing close. As predicted by Dhaumya, Pariksit had grown into a powerful and competent prince. Yudhishthira installed him as the heir apparent and, some time after Dhritarashtra's departure, he began thinking of leaving for the forest himself. But before he left, he wanted to hear news of Krishna's plans. He knew that Gandhari's curse, accepted by Krishna, would have to take effect. Soon the Yadu dynasty would be gone, along with Krishna. Yudhishthira therefore sent Arjuna to Dwaraka to see Krishna one last time. Perhaps Krishna might even be persuaded by his dear friend to make a final visit to Hastinapura.

But as the months passed after Arjuna's departure, Yudhishthira grew increasingly anxious. He began noticing many inauspicious omens. The seasons appeared out of order, and men were abandoning their duties. Constant disputes arose between the citizens. They seemed to be overcome with pride, anger, and greed.

Yudhishthira spoke with Bhima. He could understand the omens. "O man with a tiger's strength, I fear that Krishna's departure is near. Just see how the jackals howl at the rising sun. The air is filled with the shrieks of owls and crows. In the temples, the deities seem to perspire and tremble. It looks as if they are about to leave at any moment. O hero, the earth was fortunate to be marked with the Lord's footprints. All these signs indicate that this will no longer be."

Not long after Yudhishthira's discussion with Bhima, Arjuna returned. He appeared dejected, and tears flowed from his eyes. His face was pale, and he could hardly look at anyone. Yudhishthira felt almost afraid to ask him what he had discovered in Dwaraka. He placed an arm around Arjuna's shoulder to comfort him. "Dear brother, how are our friends and relatives in Dwaraka? Are they well?"

Yudhishthira asked after many members of the Yadu family and then about the welfare of Arjuna himself. He was hoping that somehow his worst fear would not be confirmed. When he finished speaking, Arjuna made no reply. His limbs trembled, and he buried his face in his hands and wept. Managing at last to compose himself, he said, "O king, I have just lost him whose separation for even a moment would render all the universes void and lifeless. The Supreme Personality of Godhead, Lord Krishna, has left this world."

Absorbed in thoughts of his friend, Arjuna recounted at length the many incidents when Krishna had protected him and his brothers. He recalled the intimate moments that he had spent with Krishna. "We would eat, sleep, and loiter together. Joking and sporting, I would sometimes laughingly reproach him when he spoke of his prowess. He would never take offense, even though the greatest of the gods cannot approach the smallest fraction of his power."

Arjuna broke off, unable to continue. He covered his face again. His brothers sat stupefied with grief. There was complete silence, broken only by Arjuna's stifled sobs. After some time, Yudhishthira asked him to relate how Krishna had left. Arjuna again composed himself and described what had happened. He narrated how all the Yadus had gone for a pilgrimage to Prabhasa, a holy place on the coast. After performing sacrifice and worshipping the gods, they had partaken of the wine that had been offered in sacrifice. Influenced by destiny, they became intoxicated and began brawling among themselves. The fight became heated, and they lost all compunction and restraint. Father slew son, and brother, his brother. By Krishna's will, and in accord with Gandhari's curse, all of them were soon killed. "Only Krishna and Balarama survived that terrible fight. Then they, too, by their own mystical powers, left this world. Thus, I am utterly undone. Distracted with grief, I somehow made my way back here, a wanderer with a vacant heart."

The brothers sat looking downward. All they could think of was Krishna. They felt that without him their lives were meaningless. Yudhishthira eventually said, "We should now retire. In the morning I will formally hand over the kingdom to Pariksit. Then we shall leave for the Himalayas."

When Draupadi heard the news about Krishna, she, too, was overcome with grief. She made up her mind to follow her husbands. As they walked out of the city, clad in ascetic garb and surrounded by sorrowing citizens, she went behind them. They walked northward, traveling for many days. Finally, reaching the great Himavat Mountain, they began to ascend its steep paths. As they climbed upward, their bodies became emaciated with fasting and worn out from their journey, but none of them stopped or looked back. They began to fall, one by one, and give up their lives, their minds fixed on attaining ultimate liberation. Knowing that the self was different from the perishable body, they cast off all material attachment and lamentation.

At last, only Yudhishthira survived. As he climbed higher up the mountain, he saw that a dog had begun to follow him. It stayed at his heels for some time as he continued to climb. Suddenly, he saw Indra's blazing chariot ahead of him. With a great sound, it descended to the mountain. Indra approached Yudhishthira and said, "Climb aboard, O Bharata hero. I will take you to heaven."

Dazzled by the god's brilliance, Yudhishthira folded his palms and replied, "I have no desire for heaven, O lord. Nor can I leave my brothers and chaste wife, who have fallen on this mountain."

"You will soon see them all in their self-same bodies. Come with me."

Yudhishthira pointed to the dog that had sat down by his side. "This creature has taken shelter of me. How can I abandon it now?"

Indra laughed. "There is no place in heaven for dogs. Leave it here and we shall go."

"No, I cannot. I have vowed never to abandon one who seeks my shelter."

Despite Indra's entreaties, Yudhishthira made it clear that he would sooner forsake heaven than leave the dog. Then, before Yudhishthira's eyes, the dog transformed into Dharma. Seeing his father standing before him, Yudhishthira fell to the ground in obeisance. Dharma raised him up and said, "Your virtue is without compare. I examined you at Dwaitavana and you answered every one of my questions. Today you have shown the perfect example of morality. O king, go with Indra. Regions of bliss await you."

Yudhishthira mounted the chariot, which then rose into the sky. He saw many celestial beings surrounding him, praising both him and Indra. The chariot entered Amaravati, Indra's heavenly abode, and descended into a shining mansion. Hosts of mind-stealing Apsaras danced to the exquisite music of the Gandharvas. All sorts of celestial food and drink lay on many gold tables. Pious souls, with glowing bodies of great beauty, enjoyed themselves everywhere.

Yudhishthira was not attracted to any of the sights or sounds. Even on earth, he had always controlled his senses, seeking instead the transcendental happiness of spiritual realization. The Pandava knew that sensual pleasure, even in heaven, was temporary and followed inevitably by suffering. Not seeing his brothers anywhere, he asked Indra where they had gone. The god then commanded some of his servants to take Yudhishthira to them. The servants led him onto a path that led away from heaven. As they walked, Yudhishthira found himself enveloped in darkness. A fetid smell wafted on the air, and swarms of wasps, gnats, and mosquitoes flew about. Through the gloom, Yudhishthira saw a wasteland covered with rotting corpses. Crows and vultures with iron beaks picked at those bodies, while many kinds of evil spirits with grotesque forms moved around, wailing hideously.

Yudhishthira was astonished. He turned to his guides. "Where are we? Why have you brought me here?"

Indra's servants replied that they were taking him to his brothers. He then heard voices around him. "O king, we are pleased to see you. Simply by your presence, we feel uplifted and our suffering is dispelled."

"Who are you?" Yudhishthira called out.

From all sides the voices called back, "I am Bhima. I am Arjuna. I am Nakula. I am Sahadeva."

Yudhishthira was shocked. How had this happened? What had his brothers ever done to deserve such a hell? Wondering if he was dreaming or had perhaps become insane, Yudhishthira told his guides to leave him. "If my brothers are here, then I shall not leave them."

The celestials went away, and Yudhishthira stood alone, thinking of Krishna. Was this some other part of the Lord's plan? As the Pandava stood in thought, the whole region suddenly grew bright. He again saw Indra coming toward him, accompanied by the other principal gods. The terrible visions of hell vanished and were replaced with heavenly landscapes. To his amazement, Yudhishthira saw that he was now in a beautiful garden of celestial flowers and blossoming trees.

Indra smiled. "O best of men, be peaceful. Neither you nor your brothers are in hell. It was your one act of deception that made you see that dark region. No man can ever perform good deeds alone. Those whose piety is great will first receive the fruit of their sins, and then they will enjoy very great happiness."

Indra explained that the sin of lying to Drona had obliged Yudhishthira and his brothers to see hell. Now that they were freed of that slight stain, they could remain in heaven for vast amounts of time. Yudhishthira's performance of the Rajasuya entitled him to enjoy Indra's celestial opulences for as long as Indra himself.

"Bathe here in the Mandakini, and you will attain a celestial form, O king." Indra pointed to the clear waters of the nearby river. Yudhishthira entered the water, and when he emerged, he felt all his grief and anxiety gone. In a resplendent form, he followed Indra into his palace. To his great joy, he saw Krishna seated on a fine golden throne, manifesting a beautiful four-armed form. Arjuna was worshipping him, and his other brothers were surrounding him. Close to Indra sat Pandu in a dazzling splendor. Draupadi was also present, in a brilliant form resembling the Goddess of Fortune. Numerous Siddhas, Charanas, and other perfected celestial beings were praising the Lord, along with thousands of rishis. Yudhishthira saw Narada among them, and he asked the sage, "How long will I and my brothers remain here?"

Narada replied that by their practice of virtue, they had earned an almost endless stay in heaven. "However, O king, you and your brothers are eternal associates of Krishna. You will go with him wherever he goes."

Explaining that the Lord is forever appearing in one material world after another, Narada said, "The Lord manifests his activities with pure souls like you, thus attracting all men back to him. No one can fully understand his pastimes. Although seeming to become involved in human affairs, he is always aloof, acting only to save all souls from their suffering. In illusion, men do not recognize him, being too attached to material enjoyment."

Yudhishthira felt an overwhelming joy. He was certainly not attached to material things. All he wanted to do was be with Krishna. Nothing else seemed to matter. Heaven and its pleasures were nothing by comparison—indeed, it would be hell without Krishna. Yudhishthira knew that his brothers and Draupadi felt the same. Gazing lovingly at Krishna's face, he wondered where they would go next.

GLOSSARY

Acharya: Teacher.

Anjalika: An arrow with a head shaped like folded palms.

Apsara: Heavenly nymph of great beauty.

Arghya: A drink offering made to respectable persons consisting of honey, milk, and ghee.

Ashram: Dwelling where one practices spiritual life and asceticism.

Astra: Celestial weapon.

Asura: Celestial demon.

Atiratha: A warrior able to fight with sixty thousand warriors simultaneously.

Avatara: An incarnation of God who descends to the material world.

Balarama: Krishna's elder brother, accepted by the Vedas as a manifestation of God.

Bharata: A powerful king after whom the earth was named. Later kings in his line, the "Bharata dynasty," are sometimes referred to by the same name. (It is also a name often used, even currently, to refer to the Indian subcontinent)

Brahma: The creator of the universe (in the Bhagavat Purana it is described that he was born from a cosmic lotus flower). The term "brahma" is also used to refer to spirit.

Brahman: The supreme spiritual energy.

Chakra: Circular weapon with razor-sharp edge.

Champaka: Tree bearing a beautiful yellow blossom.

Charana: A class of celestial noted for their singing ability.

Dakshina: The charity given to a priest at the end of a sacrifice or to a guru in appreciation for lessons learned.

Daityas: Celestial demons, enemies of the gods.

Danava: A class of powerful celestial demon.

Datura: Poisonous plant.

Destroyer: Time personified is also known as the Destroyer.

Dharma: Religious duty. Also, the name of the god of religion.

Gandharva: A class of celestial.

Kali: The last of the four Vedic ages, an age of hypocrisy and quarrel. Also, one of the four dice throws in the Vedic game (the other three being Krita, Treta, and Dwapara—the names of the other three ages).

Karma: Work performed with a selfish desire for the result; also the actual results of work.

Kaurava: Descendent of Kuru—but a name particularly applied to Dhritarashtra's sons and their followers.

Kshatriya: The warrior and ruling class.

Kumbhaka: Yogic technique for stopping breathing.

Kuru: A powerful king of ancient times who founded the Kuru dynasty.

Maharatha: A warrior capable of contending with ten thousand other warriors.

Maya: The illusory potency of God, personified as a female deity, who is also known variously as Durga, Bhadrakali, etc. Also, the name of the architect among the Asuras.

Mridanga: A two-headed drum.

Pandava: Son of Pandu.

Prapti: A mystic power that allows one to fetch objects from distant places.

Pratikamin: Chief servant.

Pratismriti: A mystical power enabling one to perform supernatural deeds.

Rakshasa: Powerful man-eating demon.

Rajasuya: The greatest of all sacrifices, which establishes its performer as emperor.

Rasa: A celestial drink.

Ratha: Chariot fighter who can contend with a hundred others.

Rishi: A powerful ascetic.

Sabha: An assembly hall.

Siddha: A class of celestial; literally, "perfected being."

Soma: A plant juice considered to be a drink of immortality, used in Vedic rituals.

Suta: A class of men generally employed as charioteers.

Swayamvara: A ceremony in which a woman selects her own husband from a number of suitors.

Tirtha: Place of pilgrimage.

Vasu: A class of celestial

Yadu or Yadava: A member of the Yadu dynasty founded by the king of the same name.

AUTHOR'S NOTE

FROM SPEAKING WITH various reviewers and other readers of my books, I have understood that for many people *Mahabharata* is mythology. Even where the validity of its ethical and spiritual instructions is accepted, quite often the story itself is still regarded as little more than a fictional vehicle for presenting those instructions.

Yet for millions of others, *Mahabharata* is much more than mere fiction. Followers of the Vedic scriptures regard *Mahabharata* as historical fact and, indeed, a part of the Vedas. It includes the *Bhagavad-gita*, a highly regarded spiritual treatise that sets out the essential Vedic theology. *Mahabharata* basically narrates the details of events that surrounded the narration of *Bhagavad-gita* and is therefore an important text in the Vedic canon. However, if we cannot accept the *Mahabharata* story as factual, then its spiritual credibility may well be undermined. I feel this is a shame since, for me, the beauty and value of *Mahabharata* lies mainly in its spirituality.

I do recognize the problems. There are many details in *Mahabharata* that a modern reader will find hard to accept: gods, demons, mystic powers, warriors with superhuman abilities, and so on. Without doubt, there is much that is beyond the experience of most, if not all, of us. How, then, can it be believed and accepted by any reasonable person? In answer to this, I would like to offer some considerations from the viewpoint of a follower of the Vedic tradition.

Before doing so, however, I will admit that, after thousands of years, it is probable that some of the *Mahabharata's* details are not entirely accurate. There are now numerous versions, and many of these have been principally preserved through oral traditions, so variance in detail is hardly surprising. Perhaps here and there creative poets have embellished the text, and perhaps the odd verse of the original has become lost. But, by and large, the main narrative and many of the finer details remain and are common to most versions. So-called critical editions of the text have been produced, which include only the verses occurring in all versions, yet even these tell the same basic story that I have written here.

So how can we accept the veracity of this story? Let us first consider the question of epistemology, i.e., how do we know anything? When our reasoning is stretched beyond its limits we can react in one of two ways: Either we can reject the new information that challenges our present assumptions, or we can take another look at those assumptions. "What do I believe and why do I believe it? Are the things I accept as true actually factual? How have I acquired my knowledge?" These days great importance is given to the empirical method; 'seeing is believing.' For the most part, science today works in this way—via the inductive process of understanding, which depends upon observed phenomena. But this is not the most reliable method. Our senses, upon which we depend for our observations, can easily be fooled. We see the sun in the sky as a small disc, but in truth it is a planet far larger than the earth. Clearly, our senses do not necessarily perceive the truth.

In addition to the problem of faulty senses, which make our information about the universe questionable in the first place, we are also struggling to translate that information into a clear picture of reality. Scientists are forever grasping for the truth, for a deeper and fuller understanding of what they see. New theories are always being found and old ones challenged. Much of what was believed a few hundred years ago is now rejected. Perhaps even what we learned at school as children has now been superseded by a better understanding.

Yet, throughout all our quests for knowledge there remains one process that never fails: hearing from an authority who already knows the truth. In fact, this is how most of us learn anything at all. We hear from our parents, teachers, books, radio, TV, newspapers, and so on. We may have more or less faith in any of these sources, but ultimately, hearing from them shapes our belief systems and understanding. Most of what we know or think we know has been gleaned from one authority or another. We know that the sun is a huge planet millions of miles away, because we have faith in the scientists who told us, not because we have been to the sun and seen it for ourselves.

Of course, we will more readily accept something as truth when it is confirmed by our direct experience. This principle applies even in the case of things that we may not fully understand. Let me explain by giving an example: I am a regular user of e-mail and the Internet. However, its technology is far beyond my comprehension. I have neither the time nor inclination, nor probably even the ability, to learn computer science. Nevertheless, I have been told that an e-mail message, when it is sent, is broken into small pieces of information that are then transmitted to their destination by various electronic grids. Jumbled and dispersed throughout the vast information superhighway, as it is now called, these bits of information finally somehow reassemble themselves into the original message. I have no idea how this happens; it seems almost miraculous to me, but I do see that letters sent by me are received intact at the other end—and vice versa. Seers of computer truths have explained the technology and, because I see that it works, I accept this, even though it leaves me bewildered.

In the same way, then, the Vedas are dealing with another kind of technology. Basically, it can be described as the science of mantras. By chanting various Sanskrit mantras one is able to invoke higher powers. The sound vibrations of the mantras, when properly chanted by a qualified person, have an intrinsic potency that can summon ethereal beings such as gods, Gandharvas, and other celestials. These supernatural beings can then, at our behest, empower us to perform extraordinary feats, such as those described in *Mahabharata*.

Now I have to be honest and admit that I have no personal experience of the above. I have not seen any gods, nor any celestial weapons being released, and I have no mystic powers. However, I do have personal experience of one part of the *Mahabharata*—the *Bhagavad-gita*. This also describes a science, in fact the spiritual science of self and God- realization. By following the scientific directions of the *Bhagavad-gita*, which, by the way, also includes the chanting of mantras, I have been able to experience the practical results. I see that my mind has become peaceful, my material desires have diminished, and my realization of the spiritual knowledge presented in the *Bhagavad-gita* is gradually developing. I can see for myself the truths contained in that text.

As with my computer example, though, I may not fully understand how or why this is happening. But seers of spiritual truths have explained it to me, and on the strength of my personal experience, I accept what they say. And because I see that the most important part of the *Mahabharata* is verifiable by direct perception, I have no reason to doubt the other parts that as yet are not verified by my experience.

It is a question of judging a thing by its results. By accepting *Bhagavad-gita* and *Mahabharata* as truth and trying to follow their directions, we will achieve one result, as I have already mentioned. On the other hand, by following other authorities who may decry the Vedas—newspapers, TV, atheistic scientists, etc.—we will get quite a different result. Our desires for material pleasure increase without limit and can never be satiated. We become increasingly disturbed, frustrated, and ultimately depressed and defeated in our lives.

This, then, is *Mahabharata's* message. If the *Bhagavad-gita* is the practical instruction manual, then the *Mahabharata* itself is the illustrated how-to-do, and indeed, how not-to-do. We see the example of the Pandavas, who endeavor to follow Krishna's instructions as given in the Bhagavad-gita. Although undergoing difficulties, they remain faithful to those instructions and in the end they emerge victorious and blessed with all good fortune. On the other hand, Duryodhana and his brothers care nothing for Krishna's instructions and choose instead to pursue their own whims and desires. Thus, they meet with ruin.

Accepted from the viewpoint of faith, Mahabharata becomes a profoundly illuminating work, which can be read repeatedly. Within its pages one can discover deeper and deeper layers of meaning. Of course, this is a much-shortened version, but I hope that from reading it you are inspired to delve into the longer book that I have written, and also the full text of the Bhagavad-gita, which I was not able to include. I recommend Bhagavad-gita As It Is, by A.C. Bhaktivedanta Swami. It is this text that I have referenced for its spiritual instructions, and I offer my respectful obeisances to its esteemed author.

I would also like to offer my respectful thanks to Kishari Ganguli and Manmatha Datta, two fine scholars whose Mahabharata translations provided my main source material for this book.

As always, I am open to feedback from my readers, which can be sent via the publisher. I admit that there may well be faults in my writing, and I beg your tolerance. Let me know if you have seen any mistakes and I will correct them in future editions.

Krishna Dharma

ILLUSTRATED STORIES AND RELIEF SCULPTURE DEPICTING INDIA'S GREATEST SPIRITUAL EPIC

Dive into the magnificent treasury of India's glorious past! Exquisitely crafted high-relief sculpture brings to life the essential beauty, splendor, and nobility of the *Mahabharata*, India's greatest spiritual epic. A feast for the eyes, *Art Treasures of the Mahabharata* is a collection of captivating photographs of the monumental work of sculpture that forms the Mahabharata Experience—part of the Glory of India project, now on view in New Delhi. Based on the trials and tribulations of the noble and virtuous Pandavas as well as their heroism and prowess, each intricately sculpted panel is accompanied by the dramatic story it depicts and the original line drawing upon which it was based, including scenes of high adventure, intrigue, and romance. Enjoy this stimulating pictorial journey into India's distinguished past and the magnitude of its timeless epic, the *Mahabharata*.

$24.95 ♦ £17.99 ♦ ISBN 1-887089-21-7 ♦ 8.5" x 11"
♦ Hardbound ♦ 80 pgs. ♦ 24 b&w illustrations ♦ 45 color photos

Mystical Stories
From the Mahabharata

Twenty Timeless Lessons in Wisdom and Virtue
By Amal Bhakta

Immortality... Invincibility...
Curses... and counter-curses...
Old age transformed into youth...
In *Mystical Stories from the Mahabharata*, Amal Bhakta has distilled from India's greatest spiritual epic a collection of gripping stories filled with adventure, romance, intrigue, and timeless wisdom. In his vivid storytelling style, Amal Bhakta brings to life some of the *Mahabharata's* most fascinating and exhilarating adventures. These extraordinary tales of heroes and heroines, devils and demons, will inspire, challenge, and motivate us to live up to the highest ideals and values.

"[He] has retouched the stories very little... leaving [them] to work their own magic. The *Mahabharata* is a treasury too little known to the West, and these selections can only help to bring it to a wider audience. Highly recommended."
—*Library Journal*

"Jewel-like stories of heroes and heroines that sparkle not only with adventure and romance but with deep spiritual meaning. *Mystical Stories from the Mahabharata* offers a new moral compass that enables us to chart a better course for ourselves, individually and collectively."
—Michael A. Cremo, Co-author of *Forbidden Archeology*

$17.95 ♦ £12.99

ISBN 1-887089-19-5 ♦ 6 x 9 ♦ Hardbound ♦ 264 pgs. ♦ 26 b&w illustrations

By
His Divine Grace
A.C. Bhaktivedanta
Swami Prabhupada

The *Bhagavad-gita* is the concise summary of India's spiritual teachings. Remarkably, the setting for this classic is a battlefield. Just before the battle, the great warrior Arjuna begins to inquire from Lord Krishna about the meaning of life. The *Gita* systematically guides one along the path of self-realization. It is the main sourcebook for information on karma, reincarnation, yoga, devotion, the soul, Lord Krishna, and spiritual enlightenment.

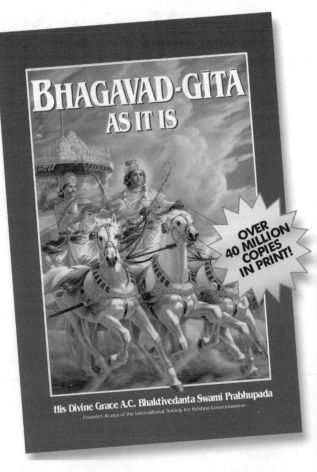

Bhagavad-gita As It Is **is the best-selling edition in the world!**

"*Bhagavad-gita As It Is* is a deeply felt, powerfully conceived, and beautifully explained work. I have never seen any other work on the *Gita* with such an important voice and style. It is a work of undoubted integrity. It will occupy a significant place in the intellectual and ethical life of modern man for a long time to come." —Dr. Shaligram Shukla, assistant Professor of Linguistics, Georgetown University

"When doubts haunt me, when disappointments stare me in the face, and I see not one ray of hope on the horizon, I turn to *Bhagavad-gita* and find a verse to comfort me; and I immediately begin to smile in the midst of overwhelming sorrow. Those who meditate on the Gita will derive fresh joy and new meanings from it every day." —Mohandas K. Gandhi

Deluxe edition with translations and elaborate purports:

$24.95 ♦ ISBN 0-89213-285-X ♦ 6.5" x 9.5" ♦ Hardbound ♦ 1068 pgs.
♦ 29 full-color plates

Standard edition, including translation and elaborate purports:

$12.95 ♦ ISBN 0-89213-123-3 ♦ 5.5" x 8.5" ♦ Hardbound ♦ 924 pgs.
♦ 14 full-color plates

BHAGAVAD-GITA

THE SONG DIVINE

A New, Easy-to-Understand Edition of India's Timeless Masterpiece of Spiritual Wisdom

By Carl E. Woodham

The *Bhagavad-gita*, India's greatest spiritual treatise, contains far too much drama to remain the exclusive property of philosophers and religionists. Woodham presents the timeless wisdom of the *Gita* in contemporary English poetry, bringing to life its ancient yet perennially applicable message. It recounts in metered stanzas the historic conversation between Krishna, the Supreme Mystic, and the mighty warrior Arjuna as they survey the battlefield preparations for the greatest world war of all time. This reader-friendly edition will attract the minds and hearts of not only spiritualists and philosophers, but of dramatists, musicians, children, poetry-lovers, and all who seek inspiration in their daily lives.

$15.00 ♦ £9.99 ♦ ISBN 1-887089-26-8 ♦ 5" x 7"♦ Hardcover ♦ 112 pgs.

INTERACTIVE CD

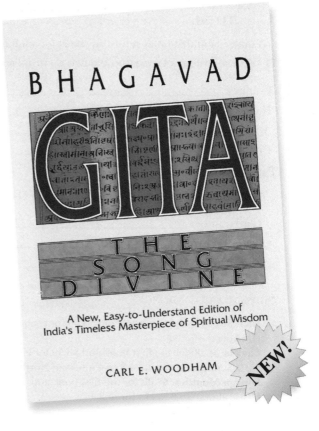

Interactive Multi-media CD-Rom version, over 30 hours of Audio, 275 full-color illustrations, video clips, and nearly 1000 pages of text.
$19.95
ISBN 91-7149-415-4.

BOOK ORDER FORM

◆ Telephone orders: Call 1-888-TORCHLT (1-888-867-2458)
   (Please have your credit card ready.)
◆ Fax orders: 559-337-2354
◆ Postal Orders: Torchlight Publishing, P O Box 52, Badger, CA 93603, USA

🔥 **World Wide Web: www.torchlight.com**

PLEASE SEND THE FOLLOWING:	QUANTITY	AMOUNT
☐**Bhagavad-gita As It Is**		
Deluxe (1,068 pages)—$24.95	x_____	= $_____
Standard (924 pages)—$12.95	x_____	= $_____
☐**Bhagavad-gita**—The Song Divine—$15.00	x_____	= $_____
☐**Bhagavad-gita Interactive CD**—$19.95	x_____	= $_____
☐**Art Treasures** of the Mahabharata—$24.95	x_____	= $_____
☐**Mystical Stories** from the Mahabharata—$17.95	x_____	= $_____
☐**Ramayana**—$27.95	x_____	= $_____
☐**Mahabharata, unabridged**—$39.95	x_____	= $_____
☐**Mahabharata, condensed**—$19.95	x_____	= $_____
Shipping/handling (see below) · · · · · · · · · ·		$_____
Sales tax 7.25% (California only) · · · · · · · · · · ·		$_____
TOTAL · · · · · · · · · ·		$_____

(I understand that I may return any book for a full refund—no questions asked.)

☐ PLEASE SEND ME YOUR CATALOG AND INFO ON OTHER BOOKS BY TORCHLIGHT PUBLISHING

Comany _____

Name _____

Address _____

City _____ State _____ Zip _____

PAYMENT:

☐ Check/money order enclosed ☐ VISA ☐ MasterCard ☐ American Express

Card number _____

Name on card _____ Exp. date _____

Signature _____

SHIPPING AND HANDLING:

USA: $4.00 for the first book and $3.00 for each additional book. Air mail per book (USA only)—$7.00.
Canada: $6.00 for the first book and $3.50 for each additional book. (NOTE: Surface shipping may take 3 to 4 weeks in North America.)
Foreign countries: $8.00 for the first book and $5.00 for each additional book. Please allow 6 to 8 weeks for delivery.